100 THINGS
DOLPHINS FANS
SHOULD KNOW & DO
BEFORE THEY DIE

Armando Salguero

TRIUMPH
BOOKS

Library of Congress Cataloging-in-Publication Data

Names: Salguero, Armando, author.
Title: 100 things Dolphins fans should know & do before they die / Armando Salguero.
Other titles: One hundred things Dolphins fans should know & do before they die
Description: Chicago, Illinois: Triumph Books, [2020] | Summary: "This book is about the Miami Dolphins football team"—Provided by publisher.
Identifiers: LCCN 2020018403 (print) | LCCN 2020018404 (ebook) | ISBN 9781629377223 (paperback) | ISBN 9781641255110 (epub)
Subjects: LCSH: Miami Dolphins (Football team)—Miscellanea.
Classification: LCC GV956.M47 S25 2020 (print) | LCC GV956.M47 (ebook) | DDC 796.332/6409759381—dc23
LC record available at https://lccn.loc.gov/2020018403
LC ebook record available at https://lccn.loc.gov/2020018404

This book is available in quantity at special discounts for your group or organization. For further information, contact:
Triumph Books LLC
814 North Franklin Street
Chicago, Illinois 60610
(312) 337-0747
www.triumphbooks.com

Printed in U.S.A.
ISBN: 978-1-62937-722-3
Design by Patricia Frey

To Jesus Christ, my Lord. My Savior.

Contents

Foreword

In April of 1997, I received a draft day phone call from Jimmy Johnson that would change my life forever. In that moment I realized so many of my dreams were within reach, but something else soon became very apparent: the only thing this Pittsburgh kid knew about the Miami Dolphins was Dan Marino. And while No. 13 is a great place to start, I spent the next 15 years of my professional career and nearly every day afterward learning more and more about one of the National Football League's most storied franchises, one with a history that is rich, unique, and when you get right down to it, perfect.

My first training camp in Miami was an eye-opening experience, to say the least. From Jimmy's borderline inhumane practices, to being manhandled by Richmond Webb, to seeing a living legend hurl passes by my ear that looked, sounded, and felt like they were shot out of a cannon, I thought I had landed in a Hollywood movie about professional football, and the stars were everywhere.

But something else was evident. Tradition meant something here. It was valued. It was celebrated. And it was plentiful. My rookie year marked the 25th anniversary of the Dolphins' perfect 17–0 season in 1972. I learned that this was the only undefeated, untied, championship team in league history and I saw the pride that came along with that. Heck, I *felt* the pride. As the year went on, I had the honor of meeting the great Don Shula, and before you knew it, Hall of Famers like Larry Csonka, Bob Griese, and Larry Little were around all of the time.

Of course, this commitment to history didn't stop in 1997. I soon found out how meaningful our alumni base was to then-team owner Wayne Huizenga. Men like team presidents Eddie Jones and Bryan Wiedmeier carried out his marching orders of preserving our treasured past. From Paul Warfield to "The Marks Brothers," from Jim Langer to Dwight Stephenson, from Nick Buoniconti to the Killer Bees and John Offerdahl, we saw these guys nearly as often as we saw our current teammates. You understood the responsibilities of putting on that aqua and orange. Those responsibilities extended from the playing field to the meeting rooms to the community. It was a special fraternity, and I was honored to be a part of it.

What I didn't realize then but certainly understand now was how our generation of players were making some history of our own. Guys I was humbled to play alongside—like Zach Thomas, Tim Bowens, Sam Madison, Patrick Surtain, Trace Armstrong, Derrick Rodgers, Brock Marion, Shawn Wooden, and so many others— made the new logo that was unveiled in '97 matter. I tried to do my part as well.

Those were special times, but one thing you learn in the NFL is that the only constant is change. And as the years went by, the names did indeed change. O.J. McDuffie handed the baton to Chris Chambers and Randy McMichael. Tim Bowens gave his to Keith Traylor. Zach gave it to Channing Crowder, and Dan gave it to Jay Fiedler. And so it went on. Unfortunately, player changes came with regime changes, and I played for more coaches than I care to count. We were making history all right—just not always the kind you want to be remembered for.

Through it all, the media was on hand to document what transpired. One constant among this group was—and continues to be—Armando Salguero. In fact, for the past 30 seasons, Armando has seen, heard, talked about, and most certainly written about every move the Dolphins have made. As crazy as this may sound, I would often read Armando's work to find out things about my own team that even I didn't know!

When you learn that legendary journalist, the late Edwin Pope, mentored Armando, you begin to gain a greater understanding of his commitment to his craft, as well as his historical perspective, particularly in covering our beloved Miami Dolphins. Edwin passed a lot along to Armando, including his seat as a selector for the Pro Football Hall of Fame, so I must thank both of these gentlemen for what I have heard was as prepared and passionate of a presentation as any that had come before when my name was brought up for discussion in front of the Hall of Fame's prestigious Selection Committee on the eve of Super Bowl LI. It is this same preparation and passion that makes Armando the perfect person to write this book.

And if I know anything about our fanbase, you are the perfect group to read this book because you embrace our history every bit as much as the organization does. Our incredible DolFans are fiercely loyal, perfectly impassioned, and beautifully diverse—just as our South Florida community is. For these reasons and so many more, this book was written for you. The stories will bring back fond memories, stir up some unsettled feelings, and undoubtedly provide insight you just didn't have before. Each chapter transports you back to exactly where you were when you lived each piece of Dolphins history the first time.

In perusing this incredible collection Armando has assembled for Dolphins fans, two things jump out at me. The first is that this would have been a valuable handbook to receive as a rookie in 1997 who didn't know what he didn't know. It took me an entire career to learn (or live) what you now have at your disposal.

The second is a bit more personal. I feel pretty strongly, and hopefully you will agree, that Armando should have stopped at 99 things. That number is just a little more special, so please forgive me if I remove a few pages.

—*Jason Taylor*
Miami Dolphins edge rusher (1997–2007, 2009, 2011)
Pro Football Hall of Famer (inducted in 2017)

1 The Perfect Season

On that first day the players gathered in the locker room before training camp, the 1972 Miami Dolphins didn't feel like a perfect team. "All the black guys were on one side of the room, and all the white guys were on the other side," recalled Marv Fleming, a tight end who had won titles on Vince Lombardi's Green Bay Packers squads of the 1960s. "I stood up in the middle and said, 'You guys don't mind if I dress right here on the Mason-Dixon Line do you?'"

Laughter ensued. "The next day the offensive line dressed on one side together and the defensive line on the other side together," Fleming said. "There were white guys and black guys on the offensive line, and there were white guys and black guys on the defensive line. They dressed together as units."

Indeed, a team that would soon make NFL history and American sports history was bonding. Many of the players lived in the same apartment complex and carpooled to practice. Linebacker Nick Buoniconti said players and their wives or girlfriends hung out at Mike's Lounge on Le Jeune Road in Miami. "It wasn't just like five couples either," Buoniconti said. "It was like 35 couples."

Jim Mandich, who shared time with Fleming at tight end on that '72 team, described that Perfect Season team as "a very special group of people." "It was an innocent time, much less complicated," Mandich said. "We didn't have agents. We didn't have cell phones. We talked to each other. We didn't sit in the locker room calling our agents or texting."

Pretty soon the team that came together off the field was cohesive on the field. Pretty soon the team that looked like a bunch of individuals weeks before embarked on the Perfect Season. "That's what we are

1

always going to be known for," coach Don Shula said proudly. "It is something you are proud to be associated with because no one had done it before, and no one has done it since. What else is there?"

The Perfect Season began on September 17, 1972 in Kansas City, where the Dolphins and Chiefs had played the NFL's longest game the previous December. And while that 20–10 Dolphins opening victory seemed otherwise routine, it said something important about the '72 Dolphins. "It showed how much better we were than the previous season," offensive coach Monte Clark said. "That was a fight against the Chiefs on Christmas Eve in 1971. There were times they seemed to be the better team. But by the following September, our young team was maturing. We weren't the new kids on the block anymore. We were now showing people the block belonged to us."

The Dolphins' No-Name Defense dominated that day. The Chiefs scored their only touchdown of the game with nine seconds to play. It was an afterthought score in a thorough Miami victory.

The third game of the season was at Minnesota, and that would prove one of the season's benchmark victories. The Vikings were a veteran team led by veteran quarterback Fran Tarkenton. They were at home. And their defense, which featured the Purple People Eaters, was aggressive and intimidating. The Vikings took a 7–0 lead on their first series in that one. But the Miami defense recovered, sacking Tarkenton five times. However, the Dolphins still trailed 14–9 in the final two minutes, and the offense hadn't scored. Suddenly, the ball-control Dolphins had to throw at a time everyone in the stadium knew it. And, well, they did with success. "One of the unspoken abilities our team had in 1972 was being able to answer in adverse situations," Mandich said. "We lost our quarterback and responded. We handled the weekly pressure of being undefeated. We traveled in the playoffs despite having the best record in the NFL. And that day we came from behind and beat a very good Minnesota team at their place. It was a notable win in my estimation."

All of the Dolphins' games in 1972 had their own storyline that explained why this team could make a successful assault on perfection. The victory against the New York Jets the next week showed the versatility of the 53 Defense—one in which linebacker Bob Matheson, who wore No. 53, sometimes rushed the passer and sometimes dropped into coverage, confusing quarterbacks.

The next week against the San Diego Chargers, the Dolphins lost quarterback Bob Griese to a fractured ankle. And that game showed Miami's depth at the most important position as Earl Morrall famously took over and authored an MVP season.

In Week Six against the Buffalo Bills, with Griese on crutches, the Dolphins played their closest game of the season. That game's highlight? Manny Fernandez, the small but quick nose tackle, swept past a block and actually took a handoff from the Buffalo quarterback for a turnover that set up a score. The Dolphins won 24–23. The rematch at Buffalo on November 15 was a sign the Dolphins were getting better. The Bills keyed on stopping the inside running of fullback Larry Csonka. So the Dolphins instead featured Mercury Morris, who rushed for 106 yards on only 11 carries. "Some people forget I averaged 5.1 yards per carry for my career," Morris said. "Look up how many NFL running backs averaged over five yards a carry over their careers."

Well, it's just Barry Sanders, Gale Sayers, Jim Brown, Jamaal Charles—and Morris. That's it.

The perfect Dolphins enjoyed other notable milestones: the offense led the league in points, and the defense allowed the NFL's fewest points. Miami had not one but two running backs rush for more than 1,000 yards, led the league in rushing as a team, and broke a 36-year-old record for most rushing yards. And Shula became the first NFL coach with 100 wins in his first decade after a 52–0 beating of the New England Patriots. "Lost in the narrative that we won every game, which believe me, is a worthy narrative," Mandich said before his death in 2011, "is the fact we dominated in a number of ways and in a number of statistical categories. It wasn't an accident that team won every game."

The Perfect Season Dolphins won the AFC East by a whopping seven games—in a 14-game schedule. They wrapped up the division title by Week 10. And about that time is when Shula's ability to motivate paid dividends. "As we kept winning and playing better, he kept asking for more. He became more demanding," Fernandez said of Shula.

"We thought he was a pain in the ass," Buoniconti said. "Years later we understood what he was doing and why he did it. But at the time, some of us couldn't stand the guy some days."

The Dolphins finished their undefeated regular season with an easy, 16–0 win against the Baltimore Colts, the same team who had released Morrall in the spring of '72. The Colts didn't score in two games against the Dolphins that year, and Morrall was at quarterback in both Miami wins. "Nah, that wasn't about revenge for me personally," the affable Morrall said years later. "That was all about doing the job against another opponent. It didn't occur to me that I was beating my old team, but I did smile a lot on my way home."

The Dolphins trailed 14–13 with 8:11 to play in their playoff game against the Cleveland Browns on Christmas Eve of 1972. Morrall led an 80-yard touchdown drive, and Jim Kiick scored the winning touchdown. Miami won 20–14. "I remember being really happy the moment I scored that touchdown," Kiick said. "But afterward the feeling was mostly of relief. It would have been embarrassing being one and done in the playoffs after going 14–0 in the regular season."

The Dolphins had to travel for the AFC Championship Game against the Pittsburgh Steelers. And the Steelers led 7–0 after their first series. That Steelers game featured the Larry Seiple fake punt on fourth and 5 and the decision to bench Morrall in the second half in favor of a now healthy Griese. "We'd talked about having Griese ready if we needed him, and I made the decision that the team needed a spark," Shula said. "Good thing it worked, or I would have been killed in the papers for replacing an All-Pro quarterback with a guy who had been out for months."

Super Bowl VII was the Perfect Season's crowning achievement. Everyone knows that now. But in the days before the game, Shula was sweating. He had lost a Super Bowl in a huge upset. He had lost the previous Super Bowl as the underdog. "When you're 0–2 in the Super Bowl, a lot of people say unkind things about you," Shula said. "They say, 'He can't win the big one.'"

But Shula's team completely dominated the Washington Redskins and held a 14–0 lead in the fourth quarter of Super Bowl VII. Then kicker Garo Yepremian tried to pass in order to salvage a botched field-goal attempt. The pass was intercepted by Mike Bass and returned for a touchdown. "We lose this game," Buoniconti told Yepremian on the sideline, "I'm going to kill you."

Yepremian was spared as the Dolphins finished off the Redskins 14–7 and completed their undefeated, untied season. And the Perfect Season remains unique because no other team has won the Super Bowl to complete an undefeated and untied season. "For someone to go undefeated again is asking the impossible," former Colts coach Ted Marchibroda said. "The competition is too close and too keen. It won't happen again. Those guys will be toasting for a long time."

2 Don Shula

There was that day in training camp in the late 1970s or early 1980s when the Dolphins were already on the field early in the morning. And this rookie—a late-round pick—overslept. Upon waking up, he realized he was missing the start of practice. So the kid made his way across the parking lot that divided the rooms where players bunked during camp to the locker room where they put on their gear. He crouched behind one car and then another as he went so as to not be seen by anyone on the practice field. And now in full practice pads and helmet, the rookie trekked back across the parking lot, again hiding behind cars as he went, then behind dorm rooms, and then the back fence that bordered field. After first hiding behind a tree, this player picked the right moment—when seemingly no one was looking—and jumped over the fence. And soon he melted into a big group of players, who were waiting for their next practice repetition, seemingly unnoticed by anyone. Except as the next set of drills was about to begin, Don Shula called the rookie over.

And Shula cut that rookie right there on the spot for being late. And not only did the Miami Dolphins legendary coach cut the player on the field, he banished him from that field.

And when the rookie started to dejectedly walk off, Shula stopped him. The coach told him to go back to the dorm to gather his belongings the same way he had come: over the back fence, behind the tree, around the dorms, across the parking lot while hopping behind one car and then another. "And he did it," Dolphins defensive end Kim Bokamper recalled. "Not only did Shula see the whole thing while he was running practice, but he had the respect to get that guy to follow his orders even after he'd been cut. Only Don Shula."

Shula, who died in May of 2020 at the age of 90, goes down in the annals of NFL history for a couple of main things: being the coach who won more games than anyone else and the only coach whose team finished a season undefeated. But Don Shula is so much more than that. He's a husband, a father, and an example to both his players and children. He demanded excellence from both. "His wrath lasted seconds, but it was brutal," Sharon Shula, the second of the coach's three daughters, said. "It only took one time, and you got the message. But the rewards: his smile, a wink, a hug, were oh-so-worth-it. And those rewards are what I sought every single day."

Shula was a man of great focus. And during his career, that focus was almost always exclusively on football. That was obvious following one mid-1980s victory in the Orange Bowl after which a team executive invited actor Don Johnson into the Dolphins' locker room. The executive introduced the actor to Shula as "Don Johnson from *Miami Vice.*" Shula shook Johnson's hand and congratulated him on the "great job" Miami Vice—the police squad—was doing for the community. "I didn't know it was a TV show," Shula said through a chuckle years later. "I didn't spend my Friday nights watching *Miami Vice.* I was focused on winning football games pretty much morning, noon, and night."

Born on January 4, 1930, in Grand River, Ohio, to Hungarian immigrants, Shula was a child of the Depression. From his parents Dan and Mary, he learned to value integrity and fair play and work ethic. He went to church every Sunday and, when his job as a coach prevented that, Shula attended mass on Saturdays or went to church to pray during the week. "We had a big family, and you had to abide by certain rules to keep things in order," Shula said. "I learned those rules and carried them over through my career because things like integrity never go out of style."

Shula is a man who had a vision for his players and he had a great perspective on his career and life. He easily discerned the greater meaning of things. He lamented, for example, never being able to get a Super Bowl win for quarterback Dan Marino. He called that one of his "greatest disappointments." He also understood and talked about what winning Super Bowl VII meant on so many levels. "I heard him say after Super Bowl VII that if we'd lost, the only thing we'd be remembered for was failing to go undefeated, and the only thing he'd be remembered for was choking in the big game because he'd already lost two previous Super Bowls," Garo Yepremian said in 1998. "Luckily, that's not how that team or Coach Shula will be remembered."

Instead, Shula goes down as the coach who brought a Vince Lombardi Trophy to Miami—twice. He goes down as a winner. He goes down as the man who first made the Dolphins relevant. "The guy's a legend," center Jim Langer said before his death in 2019. "Some accomplish things but then get sort of forgotten. But Don Shula's story from the start is so impressive that it will be a long time before anyone forgets what he stood for and what he accomplished."

3 Dan Marino

Super Bowl LIII had taken over downtown Atlanta in early 2019, and hundreds of thousands of people from around the world were milling around, mingling with members of Aerosmith, Bruno Mars, or the hundreds of athletes being herded to and fro. Because security at Super Bowls in the 21st century is very tight, everyone, including the celebrities, wore laminated credentials around their necks to identify them and certify they belong. Dan Marino wasn't wearing any credential as he zigzagged the World Congress Center to fulfill a dozen radio row and television responsibilities. "You see that badge you and everybody else is wearing?" Marino joked to a visitor. "I don't have to wear one of those. I don't need one of those for people to know who I am."

Dan Marino needs no identification badge—and no introduction, really. That's the way it is more than 20 years after he played his last NFL game because Marino is simply one of the greatest quarterbacks ever to play and one of the most recognizable faces to ever emerge from the sport. He's the greatest sport hero South

Florida ever saw. He's the greatest passer western Pennsylvania ever produced, and that includes Joe Montana and Joe Namath. "He's the best pure passer that's ever played the game." Don Shula has said repeatedly. "And anyone remotely familiar with pro football would have a hard time arguing the point."

When Patrick Peterson, one of the NFL's most decorated cornerbacks with eight Pro Bowl selections to his name, crossed paths with Marino during a national radio appearance, he asked Marino for an autograph. And he referred to the quarterback he grew up watching as a resident of Pompano Beach, Florida, as "Mr. Marino."

That is respect bordering on reverence. And it is shared by players and coaches from yesterday and today. It is shared by Hall of Famers. It is shared by teammates and opponents. "I played against 15 Hall of Fame quarterbacks during my career," Pro Football Hall of Fame defensive back Rod Woodson says. "[Marino] could throw the ball better than anybody."

The quarterback greats—many of whom broke Marino records—were at times in awe of Marino and appreciate his game to this day. "If I was starting a team today and wanted a quarterback, a young Marino is the quarterback I'd pick," Brett Favre told NFL Films.

After Archie Manning retired from football in 1984, his middle son, Peyton, was searching for a quarterback to follow and emulate. He picked Marino. And when Manning reached the NFL in 1998, he made sure whenever his Indianapolis Colts played the Miami Dolphins, he got off the bench to watch the Miami offense. "Because that was Dan Marino out there," Manning said.

We all know Marino was great. We know about the records, including most touchdown passes and most yards, he set before he retired after the 1999 season. But what made him so good? What made Marino, well, Marino?

It began at 3261 Parkview Avenue in the Oakland neighborhood of Pittsburgh, a 10-minute walk to the 50-yard line at the old Pitt Stadium where Marino played collegiately. It was there that Dan

Marino Sr. taught his only son lessons that would endure a lifetime. Dad was Marino's Little League baseball coach, and to show that there was no favoritism, he would let all the other kids pick their uniform numbers before his son could. "The number nobody ever wanted was 13," Marino said. "So after a while I just decided I might as well make that my number."

But more important than driving Marino to his number, Dan Sr. helped teach his son how to drive a football down the field. It was Dan Sr. who helped Marino birth that amazing release. Say the words "quick release" to any Dolphins fan, and it's immediately understood you're talking about Marino. "Dan Marino Sr. not only taught his son the finer points of football, but also the finer points of life," Pitt chancellor Mark Nordenberg said in a statement in 2008 when Dan Sr. died. "Dan Jr. readily credited his father with teaching him the throwing motion that led to a Hall of Fame career—along with the more lasting lessons of hard work, discipline, and integrity."

Up and out, up and out, up and out. That was the lesson and key to Marino's quick release. "It's uncanny and it isn't something you can teach everyone," Shula said. "He just has the ball up here, and—boom—the ball is out. It's like an explosion and it happens in the blink of an eye."

When Marino arrived at Pitt as a freshman, coach Jackie Sherrill approached the youngster with sage advice: "It was probably the first practice my freshman year, and I'm throwing the ball, and Coach Sherrill comes over and says, 'Don't ever let anyone change the way you throw a football,'" Marino said.

Marino has never claimed to be intellectually brilliant nor book smart. But even as a young man, he showed wisdom. While other superstars of the day tripped up with drugs or run-ins with the law, Marino, who admittedly liked to drink, bought a limousine and paid a driver so he'd never drive under the influence. And when he arrived in Miami in the spring of 1983, he took to the Dolphins playbook like he was a monk memorizing scripture. "It didn't take long for him to know the offense forwards and backward," Shula said.

Once the studying was complete, Marino was free to be himself on the field. And part of who he was included an air of invincibility. "He was a cocky guy," teammate Mark Duper said. "But it wasn't the kind of cocky and confident that makes you dislike a guy. It was the kind that makes you believe in a guy."

Said Marino: "It's cocky, but if you know me, that comes across when I'm kidding around. But I'm never going to be seriously bragging about myself. I just always felt—even when I was young—that I could throw the football as well as anybody. I knew I could do it. That was just in me. I had a God-given gift, and my job was to develop it the best I could."

When the Dolphins inserted Marino into the lineup, they were soon labeled a finesse offense, but the quarterback at the helm of the finesse attack was "one tough SOB," as Lyle Alzado called him in 1984. "He's the toughest guy on the block. That's usually the second thing he told you about himself," Nat Moore told NFL Films. "And he's never intimidated by anything."

Marino showed the toughness time and again during his career. He played hurt. He played with pain. For goodness sake, he played virtually on one leg the final six years of his career after that right Achilles injury. But the toughness was most obvious in the face of withering pressure from defensive linemen and linebackers. Bruce Smith played against him twice a year. Mark Gastineau, Howie Long, and the Pittsburgh Steelers defense all faced Marino. And in the face of all that orneriness, Marino wanted to keep passing. "When they blitz you, you know you're going to have a chance to make plays down the field," Marino said. "You know you're going to get hit, but you're also going to make big plays. That's a fair trade for me."

There was also the Marino very few people knew. The man off the field is often described as "just a regular guy" by former teammates.

And that guy has a heart. He beat Steve DeBerg in the quarterback challenge in Hawaii in 1990. Marino drilled a 45-yard line drive on the money to score the winning points on his final throw. DeBerg had been leading the competition to that point and was counting on earning the money from the contest. The difference between first and second place was $17,000. DeBerg joked with Marino about how he'd expected to spend that money. "The next day he wrote me out a personal check for $17,000," DeBerg recalled in 1993.

On multiple other occasions, Marino wrote out other checks—six figure checks—to former teammates who were down on their luck and in need. Those were "loans," but he never asked for nor got his money back.

During the early '90s whenever the Dolphins traveled to road games, Shula had his team conduct a walk-through practice at the stadium where the game would be played the next day. Those informal practices were open to the media. And soon they became sessions that had to be attended because watching Marino throw the football to Duper and Mark Clayton was like watching the Murderers' Row of the New York Yankees swat home runs at batting practice.

Invariably, during those sessions Marino would throw a pass 40 yards or so by flipping it underhanded behind his back as he spun in place. He would do this time and again with pinpoint accuracy. "Tomorrow," Marino said sheepishly after one of those walk-throughs, "I'll throw it the regular way."

4 You Are a Dolphins Fan

This is about you. And you know who you are…

You were there in those early years when all the expansion Miami Dolphins could deliver was a promise. You were there in the 1970s when the abstract idea of perfection in sports became tangible and expressed in numbers: 17–0.

You were there in the 1980s when Don Shula's discipline kept you grounded, and Dan Marino's passing made your heart soar. You sat in the old Orange Bowl and watched a team that renewed your faith on Sunday. You sat in the stadium in north Miami-Dade that took on more names than Prince and kept believing better days were coming.

You are a resident of South Florida, though like practically everyone else down here, you come from somewhere else. And you're a resident of London—or someplace else in the United Kingdom. Or someplace else in Europe. And when the Dolphins play at Wembley Stadium, you fill the stands.

You love Zach Thomas. And you think his memory should forever be enshrined in the Hall of Fame. You hate Nick Saban and think he's headed somewhere else in eternity. You aren't too cozy with the Parcells era. But, of course, you were saying "In Tuna we trust" after the 2008 division title win. You really thought Ryan Tannehill was going to develop in 2014. And 2015. And 2016. And 2017. And 2018.

You were at Miami International Airport the winter of 1973 when the Super Bowl champion Dolphins arrived from California after beating the Washington Redskins in Super Bowl VII. You were at Miami International Airport the winter of 1983 when the Super

Bowl runner-up Dolphins arrived from California after losing to Washington in Super Bowl XVII.

When Marino became the NFL's all-time career passing yardage leader in 1995, the game was stopped, and the ball was handed to the quarterback. And he spent the next minute or so pointing to you up at the stands, thanking you. He didn't say anything then, but you knew he appreciated you. That was confirmed when Marino spoke to you directly at his Hall of Fame speech. "Last January when I was elected to the Hall of Fame, I challenged all Dolphins fans to overrun Canton, Ohio," Marino said near the top of his induction speech. "And you know what? We've taken it over! Thank you. Thank you, all of you."

Jason Taylor also showed you love during his "mountaintop moment" at the Hall of Fame: "To the great city of Miami and our amazing, passionate Dolphins fans," Taylor said, "you guys joined me on a long ride filled with ups and downs. But your support never wavered. I thank you for that. In my opinion, the greatest fans in the NFL—Miami Dolphins fans."

You knew Ted Ginn and "his family" wouldn't work out. But, be honest, you pined for Brady Quinn because you thought he'd be the answer. And he didn't turn out to be anyone's answer.

When Marino pitched those nice gloves, you bought them. When Marino wore those hideous, lightning-striped Zubaz pants, you rushed out to buy them, too. It was a brotherhood of ugliness. But it was a brotherhood.

The turnstiles said 26,776 of you paid to get into the Orange Bowl for that first game in 1966, and you saw Joe Auer return that opening kickoff in franchise history 95 yards for a touchdown. And over the next 50 years of his life in South Florida, Auer was amazed how many more than 26,776 told him you were there that night. Those were great days in the Orange Bowl, weren't they?

You saw the Dolphins beat the Chicago Bears. You helped the Dolphins beat the Philadelphia Eagles by making the place a din. You didn't care that you were soaked after the Dolphins beat the New York Jets in the mud. You didn't care that you were sunburned all those years when 1:00 PM starts were a Dolphins weather advantage.

You are Pitbull and love the 305. You are Johnny Depp and love the 954. And both of you love the Dolphins. You are Vince Neil, and the Dolphins kickstart your heart. You are Darius Rucker, and the Dolphins make you cry.

You ran for president because you are Marco Rubio. You are also the guy who delivers pizzas and the woman who heads a *Fortune 500* company.

Perhaps distance or time or money have prevented you from ever visiting the team's house. But you invite the team to your house every time it's on television.

There have been tough times. You've seen those. You cringe every time Drew Brees throws a pass and breaks another Marino record because, well, you know why. But even in the tough times, you've made your mark.

You made your voice heard in 2009 when new owner Stephen Ross tried to shelve the franchise's old fight song. He unwisely tried to replace it with an unlistenable T-Pain remix, and you complained so loudly that the team was forced to play the old song going to the fourth quarter. Ross won't be the owner one day. But you will endure. And the fight song will remain.

You've tried to get the team to return to its roots. You asked for more running and defense during Marino's prime. You asked for more passing and offense when he was declining. The requests were counterintuitive—when you really think about it. But you were absolutely right to ask because John Elway won two Super Bowls when the Denver Broncos finally started playing great defense and running the ball. And letting Jimmy Johnson handcuff Marino at the end was just wrong, and you knew that.

Lately you've been asking—demanding actually—that the team go back to its original uniform. You love that look from 1966. You love the old logo. You don't understand why the Dolphins bring it out of mothballs only a couple of times a year. It's dumbfounding, and you know it.

You expect this season to bring a turnaround. Or a championship. Or the magical high draft pick that will make everything right again. You keep hoping, praying, believing. Because you're a Miami Dolphins fan. And there is no quit in you.

5 The Beginning

The story of the Miami Dolphins really begins in Lebanon's Bekaa Valley. That's where Joseph Arabi lived before immigrating to America in 1900 at the age of 11. When the boy arrived, he immediately faced challenges with English, and that manifested when the immigration officer couldn't understand the boy's name and changed it from Arabi to Robbie.

Joseph Robbie ended up in Sisseton, South Dakota, a small town bordering the Sioux Indian reservation. He worked in a hotel, a restaurant, and a pool hall. In 1910 he was running a local restaurant when he hired a young woman named Jennie Ready as a pastry cook. They were married four years later. The Robbies started a family, and Joe Jr., the second of five children, was born on July 7, 1916. Fifty year later, Joe Robbie watched from the old Orange Bowl's press box as his expansion Miami Dolphins played their first American Football League game.

Lebanon was also the home to a poor couple who immigrated to America at the start of the last century and eventually moved to Michigan where they had 10 children. Amos Muzyad Yaqoob Kairouz was born on January 6, 1912, in Deerfield, Michigan, to

Charles Yaqoob Kairouz and his wife, Margaret Taouk. Charles later gave the boy the Christian name Amos Jacobs. But the world remembers him by his stage name: Danny Thomas.

Thomas and Robbie became friends through their work in the St. Jude Children's Research Hospital and in 1965 became business partners. "You can't show me any Lebanese boy raised in Toledo, Ohio, who didn't want to own a Miami ballclub," Thomas said in 1965.

Robbie, a debate champion in high school and a Bronze Star winner during World War II, ran for governor of South Dakota in 1950 as a Democrat. He lost to the Republican candidate named Sigore Anderson. In the GOP primary, Anderson had defeated another war hero named Joe Foss, a man who would later figure prominently in Robbie's football fortunes.

Robbie caught the attention of the Harry Truman administration in the 1950s and he was asked to move to Minneapolis to organize a regional headquarters of the Office of Price Stabilization. He opened a law office there and became a supporter of Hubert H. Humphrey Jr., a Democratic U.S. senator from Minnesota. Robbie served as Humphrey's campaign manager in the presidential primaries of 1960. After Humphrey became Lyndon Johnson's vice president, Robbie was his representative on the 1965 inaugural committee.

Around that same time Vic Potamkin, who made his fortune through a network of car dealerships, hired Robbie to approach Foss, then the commissioner of the American Football League. Potamkin wanted a franchise in his hometown of Philadelphia. Foss said Miami was better. Potamkin didn't want Miami, but Robbie did. An AFL franchise in 1965 cost approximately $7.5 million— funds Robbie did not have. So Robbie mortgaged his home, pooled his assets, and came up with approximately $100,000. Then he approached Thomas, who loved the idea of owning a team. An expansion committee met in New Jersey, and with Commissioner Foss' endorsement, the league awarded a Miami franchise to Robbie and Thomas. That happened on August 16, 1965. It was the date the Miami Dolphins became a reality.

Although Thomas was the primary financial backer, he was willing to take only 20 percent of the team because his lawyers wanted him to be protected from liability if the Dolphins or AFL folded. The Dolphins needed a general partner to accept total liability for the partnership's debts in return for operating control. "They wanted to know if I would be the general partner, and I said yes," Robbie told the *Miami Herald.* "And the tax lawyer looked at me somewhat astonished that I would answer so quickly, and said, 'Why?'

"And I said, 'Because if I'm going to handle the money, I'm not going to go broke.'"

Robbie and Thomas sold other limited partnerships to make payments on the franchise fee, but operating capital was often in short supply. During the first year, Robbie borrowed money from banks. Once in the fall of 1966, Robbie couldn't meet the team's payroll. He went searching for a loan. Miami bankers weren't interested. He had to go to a Chicago banker who listened to Robbie's pitch and asked one question: "What would you do if you were me?" Robbie was asked by the banker.

"If I were you," Robbie responded, "I'd throw me out of here."

He got the loan.

There were financial crises and disputes between Robbie and other partners. During the late '60s, three different partnerships formed to keep the team afloat. Thomas cashed out in 1967. When the Dolphins won back-to-back Super Bowls in 1973 and 1974, Robbie had championship rings made for Thomas.

Robbie died in January of 1990 at age 73. Thomas died in February of 1991 at age 79. But even after Robbie was gone, the words of former Dolphins public relations man Charlie Callahan echoed in truth. "No Joe Robbie," he said, "no Miami Dolphins."

6 The Fledgling Season

That sudden electric moment of that fledgling Miami Dolphins season is part of team lore now. It's forever memorialized on black-and-white film taken that September evening in 1966. Joe Auer cradled the opening kickoff in team history and returned it 95 yards for a touchdown.

It was the signal that something amazing had been born in South Florida. And it's how that first Dolphins season began. It's the first paragraph to the team's nearly six decades of history. There were maybe 26,776 fans in the old Orange Bowl's stands that night, or at least that was the official count. "I can't tell you how many thousands of people came up to me during my life to tell me they were there to see that play," Auer said years later before passing away in 2019. "It was many more than actually attended the game, I know that."

The 1966 season came with noteworthy milestones. Miami's first victory—a 25–7 rout of the Denver Broncos—happened on October 16. The first road win came one week later on October 23 in a 20–13 decision against the Houston Oilers.

But the expansion franchise's first year was about much more than milestones. It was about wonderful memories. For example, after Auer gave the Dolphins their first ever lead 15 seconds into their existence, majority stockholder and well-known comedian Danny Thomas felt compelled to celebrate with his player. With his signature cigar in his mouth, Thomas ran the length of the Miami sideline and embraced Auer as the player was still trying to catch his breath. "The cigar nearly burned my ear," Auer said.

The Dolphins lost that first game to the Oakland Raiders 23–17. But they trailed only 17–14 with 2:12 to play. And the deficit was a source of frustration rather than fulfillment for the fledgling franchise because kicker Gene Mingo missed kicks of 17 and 19 yards, which would have given Miami the lead. "They were sensational," Thomas told the *Miami Herald* on that long ago night. "I wandered through both sides of the stadium during the game, and hundreds of people yelled, 'Danny, you've got a great ballclub!'"

The ballclub began signing their 21 draftees the day after the bowl games were played in January of '66. Personnel executive Joe Thomas was in New Orleans for the Sugar Bowl, and his mission was to land No. 3 pick Larry Gagner. He signed with the National Football League's Pittsburgh Steelers instead. "I'm more than satisfied with our draft progress," managing partner Joe Robbie told the *Herald*. "Any time you can draft most of the players you want in this ridiculous financial war with the National League, especially for a new team such as ours, you've accomplished a great deal."

Among the players in that first Dolphins draft class, receiver Howard Twilley, the team's 12th-round pick out of Tulsa, got a reported $23,000 in bonus and salary. The Dolphins stocked their first roster with veterans chosen from existing American Football League teams. Each of those teams was permitted to exclude 23 players from being drafted by the expansion franchise, but the Dolphins could pick two players from the list of unprotected players. Then the original clubs could exempt one more player, and Miami could then select two more players from any one team. Among the players the Dolphins selected in their expansion draft was Norm Evans, who started 14 games for Houston in 1965 and went on to start 135 regular-season games and three Super Bowls for the Dolphins.

The Dolphins hired George Wilson to be their first head coach on January 29, 1966. He'd coached the Detroit Lions and compiled a 57–46–6 record, including the NFL championship in 1957. "We got the most experienced and best man available," Robbie said.

Robbie looked for experience first. He found it in Wilson and then again in Don Shula, who came from the Baltimore Colts. Decades later other Dolphins owners hired six consecutive head coaches with zero years of NFL head coaching experience.

At his press conference, Wilson said he'd hire six assistant coaches, which gave the Dolphins the third most assistants in professional football. He even promised to hire a linebacker coach, which most teams at the time didn't do. "Linebackers get lost in the shuffle," Wilson said. "We won't do that in Miami."

Wilson and Robbie also said they'd soon go hunting for a training camp site. "We don't know where it will be except we know it will be within 80 miles of Miami," Robbie said.

The Dolphins opened their first training camp on July 5 in St. Petersburg, about 265 miles from Miami. The team's dormitory was next to SeaWorld. "We couldn't sleep," Evans famously told reporters. "The seals kept barking all night."

Eighty-three players reported for that first day of training camp. The next morning there were 82 because Paul Skeans, a rookie linebacker from Miami, left camp. He decided he'd rather accept a job offer as a teacher. The Dolphins eventually deemed the field at their St. Petersburg training camp to be unsuitable and hastily moved to the St. Andrews School in Boca Raton, Florida, that August. "Someday we'll look back," Wilson said as his team prepared to leave St. Pete, "and remember this place fondly. We'll be celebrating championships and remember our very humble beginnings."

7 Hiring Don Shula

It can be argued the biggest game in the history of the Miami Dolphins may have been one in which the Dolphins never participated. That fateful game was Super Bowl III, which was played in Miami's venerable (even then) Orange Bowl in January of 1969. In that game a New York Jets quarterback with a playboy reputation summoned all of his future Pro Football Hall of Fame talent to match his incredible confidence. And thus Joe Namath, who guaranteed the New York Jets would beat the heavily favored Baltimore Colts days before the game was played, delivered on his word in New York's startling 16–7 win. Namath famously left the Orange Bowl field wagging an index finger above his head—a sign the Jets were No. 1 in the football world.

The Colts head coach left that same field with his reputation and standing with his team in tatters. Don Shula was that 39-year-old Baltimore coach. He was the NFL's winningest active coach and a three-time Coach of the Year during his seven seasons in Baltimore. He was a prodigy who began to lead older men to the brink of championships at the age of 33. But that loss to the Jets wounded Shula, and the relationship between Shula and starting quarterback Johnny Unitas soured. "I wouldn't walk across the street to piss down Don Shula's throat if he was on fire," Unitas was quoted as saying in *Johnny U: The Life and Times of John Unitas.*

Having never forgiven Shula for the upset loss to the Jets, Colts owner Carroll Rosenbloom similarly stopped supporting his coach. "My relationship with the owner was never quite the same after that game," Shula said. "Every time he felt bad, he picked up the phone and passed that feeling onto me."

As a direct result of that Super Bowl loss, Rosenbloom ultimately let Shula leave to an otherwise unsuccessful expansion franchise: the Dolphins. Shula's hiring in Miami was made possible by the perfect alignment of timing and circumstances. While Shula had fallen out of favor in Baltimore for not winning that Super Bowl, Dolphins coach George Wilson had fallen out of favor in Miami for not winning much at all.

Wilson was the first coach of the Dolphins when they took the field as an expansion club in 1966. And it was understandable Wilson and the fledgling Dolphins managed only three wins in 14 games that first year. And it was acceptable they were 4–10 in 1967 and 5–8–1 in '68. But when the club regressed to 3–10–1 in 1969, owner Joe Robbie had enough. So he started looking around for a replacement. He asked *Miami Herald* sportswriters Edwin Pope and Bill Braucher for suggestions. "We both suggested Shula," Pope said before his death in 2017, "because everyone knew he and Rosenbloom were feuding. But it was Braucher who played the biggest role in the whole thing."

Officially, the hiring of Shula in Miami is considered a trade between the Dolphins and Colts. The Colts got Miami's first-round pick in 1971, and the Dolphins got a proven head coach. But the truth is that "trade" was actually the compensation then-NFL commissioner Pete Rozelle exacted from the Dolphins for tampering with Baltimore's coach. And this is how the tampering happened:

Braucher, the Dolphins beat man for the *Herald* from 1966 to 1974, had attended John Carroll University as had Shula. The two knew each other through Braucher's younger brother, who was at the school at the same time as the future coach. Shula was still under contract to the Colts at the time. So Robbie asked Braucher to contact Shula and ask if he'd be interested in leaving Baltimore and moving to Miami.

A deal between Robbie and Shula was completed within a couple of weeks. The *Herald*, not surprisingly, broke the story. "It really began with that Super Bowl game," Shula told the *Herald* years later. "I might still be in Baltimore eating crab cakes instead of down here eating stone crabs."

8 The 1970s

There was a lot of change and even turmoil around the world when the 1970s dawned. National Guardsmen shot four students protesting the Vietnam War on the campus of Kent State. The Beatles released their 12th and final album. Apollo 13 suffered an explosion in space, turning a failed moon mission into one of NASA's finest hours. And in South Florida, a professional football dynasty was born.

The year began with Don Shula's hiring on February 18 after he spent seven years coaching in Baltimore. Owner Joe Robbie hired Shula, and the coach hired an outstanding staff that included Bill Arnsparger, Howard Schnellenberger, and Monte Clark. The Miami Dolphins had already traded for future Hall of Fame wide receiver Paul Warfield a couple of weeks earlier and would add such dynasty cornerstones as Jake Scott, Curtis Johnson, Tim Foley, Jim Mandich, and Mike Kolen in the draft. Add a maturing Bob Griese about to start his fourth season, along with Nick Buoniconti, Larry Csonka, Dick Anderson, Larry Seiple, Mercury Morris, Bill Stanfill, Bob Heinz, and Jim Kiick—all of whom had arrived in previous drafts—and you had the nucleus of greatness about to bloom.

But it didn't get off to a roaring start with the start of training camp. "When I got down here, the players were on strike," Shula said. "So I had all these elaborate plans and timetables for how to get them ready and I got down here and didn't have anyone to coach.

Finally, when the strike was settled, we had to go into hurry-up mode to get everything done as if we'd never missed a day. I worked them morning, noon,.and night, and they complained about it, but then we won. And at the end of the year when people asked how we did it, they told everyone we worked harder than other people. We wanted it more than other teams. They said all the things you want them to say."

Shula didn't originally plan to hold those famous (and infamous) three-a-day practices with an added walk-through for good measure. He was going to work the team as he had the Colts, but that strike actually played a part in getting Miami's young team to bond amid the adversity of training camp. It also didn't hurt that Shula, who had an imposing granite jaw, youthful passion, and a character that accepted nothing but excellence, shook things up. The fact he was also vice president of the team, giving him powers many other coaches simply didn't enjoy, played a role, too. "The difference in having played for George Wilson, who was a good individual, and Don Shula was fear," Anderson told the *Miami Herald*. "With Shula you were going to get it done, and you knew if you didn't, you were gone."

Fear was one asset Shula employed. But at his core he was simply a good coach who hired other good coaches. And that staff got more out of the players. Many players, who underperformed or struggled under Wilson, flourished under Shula.

Csonka was one of those. "I know there were questions about Zonk after the 1969 season," Buoniconti said. "We all remember him as what he developed into. But before Shula arrived, he simply wasn't that guy yet. When Shula came in, he and Carl Taseff taught Csonka how to run with the football. They taught Csonka to lead with his forearm rather than his head. It was as if they reengineered Csonka to where he became the Hall of Fame player we know today."

Shula told his players they had been "a party team." And now the party was over. Armed with all his new talent and a team fully conditioned in South Florida's heat and humidity, the Dolphins went to Boston for their grand 1970s unveiling. And they lost 27–14 to the Boston Patriots. "Yeah," Shula recalled decades later, "a real downer. But an NFL season is not one game. We went back to work, and the hard work paid off."

The Dolphins, who had never won more than two consecutive games, authored a four-game win streak. But that was followed by two consecutive shutout losses to the Cleveland Browns and Baltimore Colts and another loss at the Philadelphia Eagles. At the halfway point in the season, the Dolphins were merely 4–4. The team was headed toward a mediocre season, and Shula understood he needed a course correction. "I remember coming back on the plane after losing three in a row, and there were questions whether I should stick with Bob Griese as the quarterback," Shula said. "I made up my mind on the plane that I was going to stick with him. Now after three losses in a row and you get beat 35–0 [by the Colts], you do a lot of soul searching. The thing is: I've always been a guy that had a lot of confidence and a lot of faith. I believed if we stuck with our hard work, we'd get back on track. I wasn't about to show doubt from a leadership position."

The Dolphins won six consecutive games to finish the regular season. That was a milestone for a team that two years later would win 17 in a row. And there were other notable accomplishments in 1970. The Dolphins had never beaten the Oakland Raiders or the New York Jets. But the 1970 Dolphins beat those two teams in consecutive weeks that October. And Shula's team actually swept the Jets.

Despite the questions about him during the losing skid, Griese eventually emerged as the quarterback. The defenders that would eventually grow into the No-Name Defense allowed the fewest points of any defense in the AFC. The Dolphins' 1970 season ended in the postseason with a 21–14 loss to the Raiders, but even that setback was a setup for future success. "We got a handle on what it would take to be a great team," Buoniconti said. "We matured to the point we would not be happy just to get to the postseason again. We wanted to do damage the next time we got there. And we did. That lesson was learned in 1970."

9 Larry Csonka

The timeless portrait a generation of Miami Dolphins fans have set in their minds when they think of Larry Csonka is of a bullying, bleeding brute plowing headfirst through the defense.

That imaginary snapshot in time from Miami's glory years always includes Csonka finishing off his downhill run by crashing into some sad defender who pays a steep physical price for merely grabbing Csonka by the jersey or around his legs. It was toughness personified. "When Larry Csonka goes on a safari, the lions roll up *their* windows," Dolphins offensive line coach Monte Clark joked.

The estimates on the number of concussions Csonka suffered during his football career range from four to six. One in 1968 caused him to spend two days in the hospital. He broke his nose about a dozen times. "I saw defenders going for his head and facemask because they knew if they grabbed him there, they had a chance to bring him down easier because they weren't tackling him by grabbing his torso," Hall of Fame center Jim Langer said. "That's why his uniform so often had blood on it because he was bleeding from his nose or lips when guys would try to punch him during a tackle. It was their desperation technique. But come to think of it, a lot of that blood wasn't all his. A lot was theirs."

Csonka played at 6'3" and 237 pounds, which would make him an enormous running back even in today's NFL. So he was a veritable giant back in his heyday. He was so big that he was a defensive lineman while playing in high school and a middle linebacker early in his career at Syracuse University. Eventually everyone figured out what a mismatch the tough-running fullback could be, and Csonka broke many of the Syracuse rushing records that had been set by Ernie Davis, Jim Brown, and Floyd Little. He was Miami's first-round draft pick in 1968 and by the time his NFL career ended 11 years later he'd carried the ball 1,891 times for 8,081 yards and 64 touchdowns.

But those were just the accomplishments, the career highlights. That isn't what made Csonka interesting. After his playing days were over, Csonka became something of a renaissance man. He did speaking engagements. He hosted fishing and hunting television shows. He was an analyst on *American Gladiators* in the 1990s. He did a couple of beer commercials. "I always admired *The American Sportsman*," Csonka told the *Miami Herald* in 2006. "Curt Gowdy was my hero. He hunted and fished and got paid for it, and I thought, *There is a lesson to be learned here.*"

Csonka visited Alaska briefly in 1969 when he took part in a USO tour for the troops serving in Vietnam. The plane carrying Csonka stopped in Anchorage to refuel. Csonka got the lay of the land during the stopover and was sold. Clocks don't matter as much in Alaska as they do most everywhere else, especially the NFL. The sun takes 22 hours in the summer before it sets. Curfews are not a thing. Regimens are not common. "Shula would go crazy here," Csonka said.

Csonka remembers some of Don Shula's early 1970s practices in the South Florida heat and humidity. Players were drenched in sweat. They pushed each other to exhaustion. And Shula demanded his fullback's full attention: "Are you here? Are you here?"

"He was afraid you were just gliding through the motions, and I was," Csonka told the *Herald*. "He knew my mind wasn't there.

Your body is there, but your mind's not. Mine wasn't. Mine was in Alaska somewhere fishing."

The man, who tormented linebackers and abused defensive backs with roundhouse blows during his NFL days, has spent his latter years surviving false starts by real bears and living off beans and crackers while stranded in snowstorms. He was also once fished out of the Bering Sea's building-sized waves by a Coast Guard rescue helicopter after a boat he was on wasn't quite as hardy as it needed to be. But the Pro Football Hall of Famer, the man famous for being the most violent player on the any football field, has found serenity in the wilderness. "You'll live longer out here," he told the *Herald*. "It's just so tranquil that I think it gets in your DNA. People were doing this for centuries, and now they're sitting around in their houses looking at TV sets."

10 The Longest Game

"After a while we were thinking we were going to play until somebody won or somebody died, whichever happened first," Larry Csonka said years after the Miami Dolphins and Kansas City Chiefs played for what seemed like an interminable 82 minutes and 40 seconds in an AFC divisional playoff game on Christmas Day of 1971.

This game wears the crown as the NFL's longest game because it was and remains the league's longest uninterrupted game ever played. It was a nationally televised saga that came replete with joy and tears after the fact and plentiful storylines even before kickoff. It was the Chiefs' last game at Municipal Stadium before they moved the following season to Arrowhead Stadium, where they still play today. It was Kansas City's first home playoff game and Miami's first playoff win. "This game is sometimes overshadowed by the Super Bowl wins and the Perfect Season, but 1971 was a very important season," coach Don Shula said years later. "We started to gain confidence. Players started to play to their maximum potential. And this game was the first time that rise became apparent."

The Dolphins won their division for the first time in 1971. The expansion franchise was growing into a contender. And the Chiefs were looking for their third Super Bowl in six years. They were established and well-versed in success. The Chiefs had never lost to the Dolphins in six previous games. And with 11 Pro Bowl players and seven future Hall of Famers on the roster, the Chiefs didn't believe their first loss was on the horizon. "They were the elite in the old AFL, now the AFC," quarterback Bob Griese told NFL Films in 2011. "When we went into Kansas City, we just wanted to play well. We just wanted to be respectable."

The Chiefs' experience and accomplishments were impressive. And it seemed to overshadow the fact the teams were much more evenly matched at most positions than anyone considered before the game.

The Chiefs had Len Dawson at quarterback. The Dolphins had Griese.

The Chiefs had Otis Taylor at wide receiver. The Dolphins had Paul Warfield.

The Chiefs had Willie Lanier at linebacker. The Dolphins had Nick Buoniconti.

Even the kickers seemed to somehow parallel each other. Both were foreign imports. Kansas City's Jan Stenerud was from Norway, and Miami's Garo Yepremian was from Cypress.

Ultimately, this nearly evenly-matched game would boast a combined 15 Hall of Famers. Maybe that's the reason Shula didn't feel his team was inferior when he confidently told his young players it's "our day" in a huddle right before kickoff.

With fans wearing Santa Claus outfits in and around the stadium, the Chiefs seemed to be celebrating in the first quarter when they took a 10–0 lead on a Stenerud field goal and a screen pass for an Ed Podolak touchdown. The Chiefs' defense, meanwhile, used its great size (with Curley Culp, Buck Buchanan, Bobby Bell, and Lanier) to thwart Miami's physical running attack. "We had a great running game with Csonka, Kiick, and Mercury Morris but were bashing our heads against the wall early," Shula said. "So it was time to do something else to move the football."

The Dolphins wisely decided to get the football to Warfield, who was a Pro Bowl player at the time and a future Hall of Famer. The problem with that strategy, though, seemed to be Warfield was covered most of the day by cornerback Emmitt Thomas, who was also a Pro Bowl player at the time and future Pro Football Hall of Famer. Although Thomas was bigger, stronger, and faster, Warfield got the better part of the epic matchup, catching seven passes for 140 yards. But it was Marv Fleming, who caught a 16-yard pass and drew a pass interference penalty to set up Miami's first touchdown. And it was Fleming, a blocking tight end, who caught a five-yard touchdown pass with 1:36 left in regulation to tie the game.

Despite the grand amount of talent in this game, it featured multiple mistakes. Stenerud missed three field goals, including one with 35 seconds remaining in regulation and another in overtime. Both Griese and Dawson threw two interceptions. And the Chiefs lost two fumbles, the first of which led to a Yepremian field goal that tied the game at halftime.

This game was tied at halftime, tied at the end of three quarters, tied at the end of four quarters, and tied after one overtime period.

As the game bled into the second overtime period, the players traded heroic performances. Buoniconti recorded 20 tackles; Lanier had 22. Podolak contributed a whopping 350 all-purpose yards. "I got tired of seeing him that day," Buoniconti said of Podolak. "I was so frustrated I tackled him one time in overtime and drove his helmet into the mud as I was getting up. But give the guy credit. He just kept coming."

The Dolphins did as well. Although their running game was mostly ineffective, it was a running play—*roll right trip left*—that helped Csonka break free on a 29-yard run to set up the winning field goal. Yepremian booted the deciding 37-yard kick. Confident it would sail through, he turned toward the Dolphins sideline to celebrate as the ball was still in flight. "I was just hoping I'd get that chance," he said in the locker room afterward.

This classic game is properly highlighted for being the NFL's longest game, but its historical meaning is deeper than that. It signaled the sunset of Hank Stram's Kansas City dynasty and the sunrise of the NFL's soon-to-be-recognized new dynasty: the Miami Dolphins.

11 The Champagne Toast

The story about neighbors Nick Buoniconti and Dick Anderson sharing one champagne toast one time as a singular impromptu celebration to the legacy of the 1972 Miami Dolphins remaining the NFL's only undefeated team started getting twisted in the late 1990s. By the mid-2000s when the New England Patriots arrived at Super Bowl whatever-it-was with an 18–0 record, the stories of annual meetings, at which those old-time Dolphins ungraciously celebrated someone else's failure, were rampant. In media depictions and descriptions, an understandable celebration of an achievement was turned ugly and boorish. The men of the Perfect Season became just as often recognized as the NFL's grumpy old men. Ridiculous. And unfair.

And here's a call to push back against that narrative. No matter the time or place, Dolphins fans themselves should enjoy a champagne toast every time the last unbeaten NFL team goes down in defeat each season. As the men of the Perfect Season age and, yes, die off, the champagne toast tradition should live on with their fans—as surely as the 17–0 record continues to be unmatched. That's not the Dolphins telling you this. That's not the men of that 1972 team making the suggestion. That's just tradition that exclusively belongs to the Miami Dolphins.

The men who coached and played during that fabled Perfect Season began to push back on the narrative of being grumpy and unsportsmanlike sometime around the time the criticism of them spiked. "We have been portrayed that way, and that's not right," said Don Shula, the coach of the undefeated '72 Dolphins. "One time I was at Nick Buoniconti's charity golf tournament up at Jack Nicklaus' golf course. It was a day after one of those years where the last undefeated team got beat, and Jack Nicklaus brought out a bottle of champagne. He had Nick and I get up, and he toasted us with the champagne. That happened. But that was Jack Nicklaus doing that on his own. There have never been any get-togethers. There's never been any big celebration or sitting around hoping and praying that last undefeated team gets beat. If one of them finishes undefeated, I'd be the first guy to pick up the phone and congratulate that team's coach on the accomplishment…And I'm sure our players would do the same thing. They'd call some of the players they know or would happen to have a relationship with and congratulate them. But until that happens, I don't see anything wrong with being proud of our record. We've been accused of being, I guess, too proud of it. But I don't think [Joe] DiMaggio ever apologized for his 56-game hitting streak."

This perch the Dolphins occupy atop the NFL pile is lonely and precarious. But they've been accused of being filled with paranoia and anger that some team will match or beat their feat. But the '72

Dolphins are not atop their plateau kicking dirt on the teams trying to climb to their heights. "It's nice to create a myth," Anderson said. "We set the record. No one else has it. So why would we be grumpy?"

That's not to suggest the Dolphins of that magic yesteryear don't protect their turf. They were football players. They got paid to take and protect turf. Running back Mercury Morris often talks about the '72 team residing in "Perfectville." He talks about Perfectville having "a population of one." "If another team were to ever go undefeated like we did, I would still know we did it first," he said. "No one can take that away from us. A lot of people have climbed Mount Everest. Only one guy did it first."

12 What Made Don Shula Great

Don Shula is the winningest coach of all time and was inducted into the Pro Football Hall of Fame in 1997. Shortly before his induction, he broke down what his duties as head coach entailed. "What coaching is all about is taking players and analyzing their ability. Put them in a position where they can excel within the framework of the team winning," Shula said. "I hope people will say I did that in my 33 years as a head coach."

People say that. There's no denying it. But the reasons for Shula's greatness include a few other notable factors: integrity, longevity, and versatility. Of all those, Shula values integrity most. His career and his work mirrored who he was at his core, and that was someone who believed in doing things right. That included working hard and never giving up.

He believed in fair play, which is the reason he was disgusted by the New England Patriots' snowplow incident. He believed in playing by the rules, which is a reason he showed a distaste for the Patriots and Bill Belichick after the Spygate and Deflategate incidents. Before one notable game against the Oakland Raiders, Larry Csonka came across the Raiders gameplan in a locker room the Dolphins were using at Oakland's stadium. He handed it to offensive line coach Monte Clark to give to Shula. The Raiders beat the Dolphins, and Csonka asked Clark why the gameplan he handed over hadn't helped. Clark told Csonka that Shula ordered him to throw the gameplan in the garbage before he even looked at it. "Shula would never cheat," Csonka said.

"You have to have the courage of your convictions to be a successful football coach and really to be a successful person in life," Shula said. "I was instilled with certain convictions and I applied those throughout my life and my career."

And that career certainly had longevity. George Halas, who started coaching in 1920, was active when Shula became head coach of the Baltimore Colts in 1963. And Belichick, the best coach in the game today, was an active head coach when Shula retired after the 1995 season. Shula began coaching when John F. Kennedy was president. And he was still coaching when Bill Clinton was president. "The key to coaching as long as I coached—33 years—is winning early and often," Shula said. "You do that, you have a chance to stay around."

He stayed around for so long because he was versatile. Shula was never so wrapped in his own schemes and football philosophies that he forced players to mold themselves and their games to him. Instead he adapted his schemes and philosophies to his players. When he had great runners in Csonka, Jim Kiick, Mercury Morris, and Andra Franklin, the Dolphins ran the football. When he had great passers such as Johnny Unitas and Dan Marino, Shula's teams threw the football. Defensive coach Bill Arnsparger in the early '70s told Shula that Miami's personnel seemed better suited to the newfangled defenses being used in the college ranks. So despite Shula liking the 4-3 front his Colts teams employed, the Dolphins employed the 3-4. And when personnel suited both schemes, the Dolphins used both.

The coach also molded himself to different personalities. Morris was often at odds with the coach. So were Jake Scott, Nick Buoniconti, and sometimes Mark Clayton. But the coach often made it work with players with whom he had differences. "He wasn't my friend when I was playing. That's for sure," Buoniconti said. "We butted heads. But after I retired, I realized he had the best interest of the team at heart. And we became friends."

Yes, Shula had great players on his teams. He had three Hall of Fame quarterbacks in Unitas, Marino, and Bob Griese, and his rosters with both the Colts and Dolphins were peppered with Hall of Famers and Pro Bowlers. But his ability to both manage those varied personalities and maximize their talents was a Shula trait that served him over three decades on the sidelines.

Shula obviously authored a great career, and his 347 career wins remains the unsurpassed standard for success by an NFL coach. His teams had a winning record 27 out of his 33 seasons. In 20 of those seasons, Shula's teams won more than 10 games, including 11 times in years with a 14-game schedule. He led the Colts to a winning season his first year in 1963 and led the Dolphins to a winning season in his final year in 1995.

People say the Shula coaching tree wasn't exceptional because Arnsparger lacked success with the New York Giants. Clark didn't win any titles with the San Francisco 49ers or Detroit Lions either. However, Howard Schnellenberger was Shula's offensive coordinator in the 1970s with the Dolphins. He won a national title with the University of Miami and built a dynasty there. Shula had Don McCafferty on his Baltimore staff as an offensive assistant. McCafferty took over when Shula went to the Dolphins, and McCafferty's Colts won Super Bowl V. Shula also had a defensive backs coach and defensive coordinator under him in Baltimore who did pretty well once he became a head coach in 1968. His name was Chuck Noll. And he led the Pittsburgh Steelers to four Super Bowl titles in the 1970s. So the Shula coaching tree was quite sturdy and prosperous, thank you very much.

Shula won as a head coach in four different decades with multiple different approaches and under rules that changed the game over time. "When we lost he'd give us hell on Monday, but on Tuesday that game was history," Griese told ESPN. "When we won he'd say, 'You've got to come back and do it again the next week.' Even when we won them all, he said, 'That was great, but now we're going to come back next season and do it again.'"

13 The 1983 NFL Draft

As the first round of the 1983 NFL Draft unfolded before his disbelieving eyes, Don Shula demanded to know: "What the hell's going on? Why's he dropping?"

The Miami Dolphins were the Super Bowl runner-up but had finished the previous two seasons with their starting quarterback David Woodley benched during putrid postseason performances. So this good team at the bottom of the draft was interested in finding a good quarterback when that Tuesday (yeah, the NFL draft was in the middle of the week) dawned.

But after John Elway and Todd Blackledge were gone, the Buffalo Bills picked Jim Kelly from the University of Miami down the road, Tony Eason was gone, and even Division II quarterback Ken O'Brien was picked by the New York Jets—surprising everyone in the Dolphins draft room—Shula was seriously wondering why

Dan Marino has dropped in the first round like a boulder in water. The Dolphins had rated Marino the draft's second best quarterback behind Elway. Dolphins personnel boss Chuck Connor was from Pittsburgh and went to high school with Pitt coach Foge Fazio's wife. He vouched for Marino. "We wanted to get a quarterback and we would have taken Ken O'Brien," Connor said. "But he's gone. And Don said, 'I don't want a [bleeping] quarterback. I want Marino.' Let's just say we had him rated very highly, very high."

Marino's draft fall caused the Dolphins to momentarily second-guess themselves. What did other teams passing on Marino know that they didn't? Why did the hometown Pittsburgh Steelers, who rarely made draft mistakes the past decade, pick defensive tackle Gabe Rivera instead of Marino? Shula got on the phone with Fazio and asked the Pitt coach for the truth: "What's wrong with Marino?" Shula said.

Fazio was used to such calls. He had a similar one with Jets head coach and close friend Joe Walton about a week earlier and had endorsed Marino in every way possible. But the Jets passed anyway. That moment when New York selected O'Brien with the 24th overall selection was the tipping point for Marino. His home in Pittsburgh was packed with family and friends, and they'd been watching the draft on cable. And when O'Brien was selected even as Jets fans at NFL draft headquarters were chanting Marino's name, the pick floored Marino. "Very disappointing," Marino recalled in 1994. "I felt sick at that point, if you want to know the truth."

Five quarterbacks had been picked. Marino, who was expected to go much earlier, not only wasn't the first quarterback picked, he also wasn't even the first University of Pittsburgh player picked. Pitt teammates Jimbo Covert and Tim Lewis both went earlier in the first round.

Fazio, the Pitt coach, later coached in the NFL. In 1990 when he was a Jets assistant coach, Fazio said Shula asked if Marino was involved with drugs. Dorothy Shula, the coach's first wife, also told

Miami Herald sports editor Edwin Pope in the 1980s that Marino's drug rumors were discussed in that conversation and added the quarterback got drug treatment in Miami in the '80s. (Pope never wrote the story for lack of more on-the-record confirmation.)

For the record, however, Fazio said during his draft call with Shula that Marino was clean. "I even told him he'd been tested—just like many of our players had been—and he'd passed," Fazio said. "Did Dan go out and drink and date and that sort of stuff? Of course he did. He was a typical college kid in that respect."

That's when the Dolphins went back to the film of Marino's senior season one more time. His touchdown production had fallen from 37 as a junior to 17 as a senior, and he threw a cringe-worthy 23 interceptions as a senior. "You have to look at football realistically," Marino told Miami reporters about that senior year. "Sometimes things don't go the way you want them to go. That's what last year was like. Overall, I think I learned from the experiences I went through."

Shula ultimately ordered the Dolphins to go with Marino but still had to sweat the Cincinnati Bengals picking at No. 25 and Oakland Raiders at No. 26. If Marino went to either team, the Dolphins intended to select defensive lineman Mike Charles in the first round. But Cincinnati selected center Dave Rimington, and Al Davis picked Don Mosebar. Within 10 minutes of that happening, Dan Marino was a Miami Dolphin. "He certainly has good credentials," a jubilant Shula told reporters. "He didn't have the best senior year, but when you look at him and evaluate him throughout his career, you have to be pretty impressed. When you can get a guy the caliber of Marino as late as the 27th pick, you've got to be able to make that move. He'll come in here and compete. He's a drop-back passer who has thrown a lot of balls. He should make it interesting. The decision on Marino is you've got a guy who could possibly come into this league and do a fine job as a quarterback. We wanted to have that opportunity."

It was a bittersweet day for Marino. He was upset he fell so far. He was either upset or didn't care—depending on when you ask— that the hometown Steelers passed on him. "I was upset. I was mad. I was disappointed," Marino said. "Then I said to myself, *You know what, I'm going to get in the best shape of my life and go down there and prove something.* It really was a blessing when I look back on it. I didn't think that on draft day in 1983, that's for sure. But I had an opportunity to be drafted by a very good football team that went to the Super Bowl the year before and had good veteran players. I got an opportunity to play for Don Shula, and he showed great confidence in me early in my career. I think those are all reasons I was able to play at such a high level so early in my career."

14 Paul Warfield: The Greatest Receiver in Franchise History

The 1972 Miami Dolphins had the best running game in the NFL and two 1,000-yard rushers in their backfield. This was unapologetically a running team, and coach Don Shula took pride in the fact that everyone *knew* the Dolphins were going to run the football but still couldn't stop them. But in any game during that perfect Super Bowl season and the one that followed in 1973, when quarterbacks Bob Griese or Earl Morrall went to the line of scrimmage and saw a major strategic blunder by the defense, they yelled, "40" to the left and again "40" to the right. And everyone on the offense knew what came next: a pass to the best receiver in franchise history. Paul Warfield.

That audible was a signal that the defense had deployed single coverage against Warfield. And although it didn't happen often, it was almost always a mistake. "Nobody could cover Paul Warfield man-to-man," former teammate Mercury Morris said. "It just wasn't fair."

Warfield was a proven NFL star in 1970 when the Cleveland Browns traded him to the Dolphins in exchange for a first-round draft pick. The Browns used the pick to draft quarterback Mike Phipps. The Dolphins used Warfield to help them win a couple of Super Bowls. "He was just a special player, and having him helped make our offense special," Shula said. "We didn't throw it a lot back then because running the football was working so well. But when we needed to throw it or wanted to throw it, we knew we could be successful because of Paul."

Warfield's work in Miami is well chronicled. He was a Pro Bowl player the five seasons he was with the team from 1970 to 1974. In an era when throwing the football was Miami's second thought, Warfield averaged only 31 catches per season and never caught more than 43 passes in a season. But he maximized his opportunities. He caught 33 touchdown passes in those five seasons, including 11 in 1971 and again in 1973. He was voted to the 1970s All-Decade Team. And he did it all while being the consummate deep threat receiver, averaging a whopping 21.5 yards per catch.

But those were simply the statistics and factoids. Those weren't what made Warfield special and eventually got him elected into the Pro Football Hall of Fame on the first ballot.

Shula once called Warfield "poetry in motion," and he was exactly that. He was 6' tall and lanky at 188 pounds, but he was chiseled and strong. He walked with a cool effortless glide and ran like a blur, having covered the 100 meters in 9.7 seconds while still in high school.

And yet Warfield was more than that as well. Yes, he was a gifted athlete. But he was also a technician who studied his craft to maximize those gifts. "I would draw my patterns on a board," Warfield said. "I'd transfer that to my mind. And then when I got on the field, I'd run the pattern the way I had drawn it and transferred it. I cut at precise angles. I didn't draw patterns rounded off and I didn't run patterns rounded off. It was precise. I came from the Browns, and they were greatly advanced in pass pattern running. The organization had cutting edge ideas about how to throw the football vertically down the field. I both adopted those ideas and adapted them to my skills."

So he had skills and worked hard, but a lot of great players had that over the NFL's 100 seasons. But Warfield also ran laser precise patterns, and his attention to his assignment was similarly razor sharp. "When the football was coming to me, that's really all I saw," Warfield said. "I blocked out everything else. I didn't think about anything else in that instance. I knew where I was on the field, but I was not aware of the environment around me. I was not aware of the fans. I was not aware of sounds. I was focused solely on the football and catching it. After the catch then I came back to awareness of defenders and started reacting to avoid them and get away from them."

Warfield's escapes from defenders became so routine that it became a source of amusement for his teammates. "We'd watch film, and Paul would catch a pass and no one else was in the picture," Morris said. "And it wasn't that the defender forgot to cover Paul. It was that Paul had left him back there somewhere. The defensive back was covering the spot where Paul had been but wasn't there anymore."

In 1974 the Dolphins drafted receiver Nat Moore, and Shula immediately wanted the rookie to learn the art of playing the position from Warfield. "One that will always stick out for me was the opportunity I had to room with Paul Warfield on the road my rookie year," Moore said. "That changed my life. Here's a guy that not only taught me to be a professional on the field, but also off the field. He taught me how to run routes, how to dissect defenses. We only played together one year, but it changed everything for me. Even today we still talk once or twice a year."

Moore was one of the great receivers in Dolphins history. Mark Clayton and Mark Duper were also outstanding. But Warfield was the greatest. He played during a time when defenders could grab and hold all the way down the field and deliver kill shots to the head with impunity. And yet he ran across the middle. He got open deep. "As great as Duper and Clayton were, they're not in the Hall, should be in the Hall, and you'll never get me to stop saying that, but they're not Paul," Moore said. "Could you imagine if Dan Marino was playing with a guy like Paul Warfield?

15 Bob Griese

Not long after Bob Griese became the NFL's first quarterback to wear eyeglasses during a season—and Griese did this in multiple seasons during the latter part of his career—the Pro Football Hall of Fame asked for and received a game-worn pair to put on display.

Griese was the starting quarterback of a two-time Super Bowl champion. He was a first-round draft pick in 1967. He called his own plays throughout his career, which means he was the architect of all those dominating first possession drives the Miami Dolphins were known for during their championship years. And yet it was the glasses that became a focus. "I've always had a weak eye and a strong one," Griese told *Sports Illustrated* in October 1977. "Last season I started to notice some double vision and dizziness…I figured, well, I'd go to contacts. For me, though, contacts weren't the answer because of the prisms. I just had to put on glasses."

Miami ophthalmologist David Sime, who pioneered intraocular lens transplants for cataracts patients and was the grandfather of Carolina Panthers running back Christian McCaffrey, designed and fitted Griese with his corrective lenses. When the Dolphins opened the season 3–0 for the first time since the Perfect Season, much credit was given to Griese's improved accuracy and passing prowess. The glasses were a thing.

After one game when Griese struggled amid a driving rainstorm, which left droplets on his lenses and distorted his view, people wondered if Griese would play well in bad weather later in the season. Asked on the long-running *Don Shula Show* what his answer to such inclement weather would be going forward, Griese, who was not known for his sense of humor, pulled out a pair of large round glasses with miniature battery-powered windshield wipers. "This is my answer," Griese said, as the wipers flapped.

It was fitting that throughout his career, Griese was considered a thinking man's quarterback. Because with those glasses tucked behind his face mask, he was a portrait of a classic thinking man.

Although Miami's running attack was the focus of the Dolphins' offense during the Super Bowl years, Griese threw well enough to win the AFC passing title in 1971, Miami's first Super Bowl season. And with a revamped roster that no longer boasted Larry Csonka, Jim Kiick, or Paul Warfield, Griese won the passing title again in 1977 while wearing his glasses.

So lenses or not, Griese was quite polished when he wanted to pass the football. That was clear on Thanksgiving Day in 1977 when the Dolphins traveled to St. Louis and clobbered the Cardinals 55–14. Griese threw six touchdown passes. "I said, 'Bob, want to go for the record of seven?' And he said, 'No, let the backup get some work,'" Shula said years later. "He got as much of a thrill seeing Csonka, Morris, or Kiick run for a touchdown as throwing a bomb to Warfield."

Griese retired after the 1980 season. His 192 touchdown passes surpassed the totals of seven quarterbacks—Otto Graham, Sid Luckman, Sammy Baugh, Joe Namath, Roger Staubach, Bart Starr, and Norm Van Brocklin—already in the Hall of Fame at the time.

But Griese was bypassed by Hall of Fame selectors four times in the mid-to-late 1980s. "If I was thinking of the Hall, I'd have been out there throwing instead of running. I was calling the plays, so I could have," Griese told the *Miami Herald*. "If I intended to be selfish, I could have aired it out."

Instead Griese and his son, Brian, turned the Hall of Fame snubs into a running family joke that, of course, had to include the glasses. Every year when the Grieses got news that Bob had failed to make it into the Hall, Brian would joke with his dad that the glasses would be as close to being in the Hall of Fame as he'd ever get.

Bob Griese was finally inducted in 1990, and that August day was a dream come true. The Griese family contingent included Bob's mother, Ida; relatives from Fort Wayne, Indiana; and his three football-playing sons. Bob Griese, 45 at the time, said his only regret was that he didn't make the Hall of Fame before his wife, Judi, died of cancer in 1988. "I know she has a very good seat today," he said.

Judi and Ida were the people most disturbed when Bob Griese did not get into the Hall of Fame on his first four tries. "Judi and Bob just had that communication," Ida Griese told the *Miami Herald* in 1990. "I can still remember him coming out of the locker room after a loss, and they're walking away hand-in-hand, not needing to say a word."

Bob Griese was the center of attention on that 1990 day and he joked with Brian, who spent one of his 11 years in the NFL with the Dolphins, that he had finally joined his glasses in the Hall of Fame. "In your face, Brian," he said.

He then put on his gag glasses, the ones with the wipers, that he had worn on the *Don Shula Show* many years before. Everyone chuckled. It was quite the spectacle.

16 Earl Morrall to the Rescue

Bob Griese sat on the Orange Bowl turf, clutching his right ankle in pain, and there was a hush over the crowd of 80,010 because everyone feared the hopes for the remainder of this 1972 season had been dashed. As the quarterback who helped the Miami Dolphins reach the Super Bowl the season before was wheeled off the field on a stretcher with a broken ankle, the backup quarterback reached the huddle to continue the drive, win the game, and continue Miami's season.

Earl Morrall, the NFL's oldest player on this October 1972 day, was about to rescue the Perfect Season. "There wouldn't have been any 17–0, and there wouldn't have been any Super Bowl if it weren't for Earl Morrall," Griese told the *Miami Herald* a quarter-century later. "He just is a tremendous person who came in here and helped our team when it needed help."

Morrall was no stranger to the big stage and big moments when he replaced Griese. In 1968 the Don Shula-coached Baltimore Colts signed Morrall to back up Johnny Unitas, who had led the Colts to an 11–1–2 record the previous season. When Unitas, the NFL's best quarterback, couldn't overcome a right elbow injury, Morrall authored an MVP season that included an NFL-leading 26 touchdown passes.

The Colts won 15 games that year and were considered the league's best team. Except consideration isn't how champions are decided in sports. Championship games are. And Baltimore was upset by the New York Jets in the Super Bowl. Joe Namath had famously guaranteed a Jets victory, but he didn't just make the bold prediction. He made some disparaging statements about his upcoming opponents. Speaking of Morrall the week of the game, Namath said there were "five quarterbacks in the AFL who are better," including himself, of course.

Years later, Morrall sometimes referred to what Namath did before that Super Bowl as "showboating." But he respected what his opponent did in the game. "He played one whale of a game. You have to give him that," Morrall said during the 30th year anniversary of Super Bowl III. "It shouldn't have happened, but it did. You look back, you remember, and you go through the what ifs. Then you snap out of it and keep living. "

Morrall's problem is he threw more interceptions than touchdowns in two of the next three seasons in Baltimore, and in one of those years, 1969, he completed only 46.5 percent of his passes. By 1972 everyone mostly remembered Morrall for his struggles and how he looked like a 13-year journeyman. The Colts released Morrall in the offseason.

But Shula, who had been with Dolphins since 1970, remembered Morrall as the backup who got the Colts to the Super Bowl. So on April 25, 1972, Morrall was claimed off waivers by Shula for just $100—plus a hefty salary. "I knew what Earl could do from our time in Baltimore," Shula said. "He was an intelligent quarterback who won a lot of ballgames for me. I wanted to pick him up as an insurance policy. I had to talk [then-owner] Joe Robbie into doing it because Earl was making $90,000. I wanted to claim him off waivers, and Robbie said, 'Paying $90,000 for a backup—are you out of your mind?'"

Robbie reluctantly agreed to pay. But Dolphins players didn't foresee the move paying off. "He was older than some of our coaches," defensive lineman Manny Fernandez said.

"We lockered next to each other. Our equipment manager Danny Dowe got a rocking chair and put it in front of Earl's locker because he was so much older than the rest of us," Griese told the *Herald*. "We all had folding chairs, but Earl had a rocking chair. And if he wasn't the first guy off the field, by the time he got to his locker, there was always someone else sitting in that chair—me, Zonk, Mercury, or one of the defensive guys. But Earl didn't care—he just laughed and pulled out a folding chair for himself. That's the kind of person he was—always a team guy."

After Griese's injury it was time for the team guy to become *the* guy. "The first time Morrall came out after going in for Griese, I told him: 'Old man, get those cataracts in motion, turn up your hearing aid, and let's go,'" defensive end Bill Stanfill said.

Morrall completed eight of 10 passes, including touchdown strikes to Howard Twilley and Paul Warfield, in a 24–10 victory against the San Diego Chargers. Maybe the season wasn't lost after all. In a November 19 game against the Jets, Morrall rallied the Dolphins twice. He helped his team overcome New York leads of 10 points in the second quarter and three points early in the fourth to win 28–24. Morrall scored a touchdown on a 31-yard run. "Shades of Little League," he said afterward. "It has been—I don't know how long—since I made a run like that. Believe me. I was giving myself a pep talk all the way."

The Dolphins won all 11 starts Morrall made in 1972, including two in the playoffs. "He was just a great influence on our football team," Shula said. "They all realized that Griese was our starting quarterback and the quarterback of the future. But they all knew Earl was capable of being a great backup, and he proved that to everybody."

Despite his regular-season heroics, Morrall was replaced in the second half of the AFC Championship Game. Then Shula decided to start a healthy Griese in Super Bowl VII. "I called him in, sat him down, and told him what I was going to do, that this is how I think we have the best chance to win," Shula said. "He said, 'I don't agree with you, but I'll be ready if and when you need me.'"

Being the unselfish person he always was, he is remembered as having stepped aside with grace, which was absolutely correct. But some folks forget he was also an intense competitor. "I didn't like it," Morrall said years later of the benching. "But it wasn't about me. I was an individual on a team. And although I was an unhappy individual for a little bit, other things took precedence. The good of the team and getting myself ready in case I was needed again was more important."

Morrall remained with the Dolphins the next four seasons before announcing his retirement on May 2, 1977. Sporting his trademark flattop buzz cut, Morrall also served as quarterback coach at the University of Miami from 1979 to 1983, tutoring the likes of Jim Kelly, Bernie Kosar, and Vinny Testaverde and was mayor of Davie, Florida, for one year. Morrall died in April of 2014 at age 79.

17 The No-Name Defense

The story goes that before Super Bowl VI was played, a reporter asked Dallas Cowboys coach Tom Landry what he thought of the Miami Dolphins defense his team would soon see in the NFL's biggest game. "They have a good defense," Landry answered politely. "I don't know any of the names of the people playing on the defense, but they play good defense."

That's how, depending on what account you believe, the famed Dolphins' No-Name Defense was born in the early 1970s. But, of course, a unit as complex and fabled as the No-Names couldn't have just one story about its genesis, right? "I think it began when somebody wrote about analyzing the defense and what made it tick, but they looked around, and there were no big names on the defense," middle linebacker Nick Buoniconti said. "They said, 'It's really a no-name defense.' And that was how it started."

Believe whichever competing story you wish, but about this there can be no disagreement: the No-Name Defense of the glory years was elite. The unit did not have a Pro Football Hall of Famer to its name until Buoniconti was inducted in 2001. It played in years when the men behind the facemasks didn't have social media accounts or marketing strategies. But as a group, this band was as dominant and feared as any defense of the time. And that was a time during which Dallas' Doomsday Defense and the Pittsburgh Steelers' Steel Curtain were a thing.

Miami's No-Name Defense was No. 1 in the NFL in 1972 and allowed the league's fewest points. The unit allowed the NFL's fewest points again in 1973. And in Miami's back-to-back Super Bowl victories, the No-Names gave up one touchdown. Six points. That's it. "The thing that really made our defense go was how prepared and well-versed all the players were," defensive coordinator Bill Arnsparger reminisced years later. "They studied their opponents and knew their assignments. In 1972, the year we were undefeated, that defense made only 13 mental mistakes in 17 games. Think about that: 13 mental mistakes the whole season. I've known players who made 13 mental mistakes during warm-ups in practice."

To the laymen observing them, the No-Names were a conservative defense. They played mostly zone. They weren't exceedingly big. They weren't extraordinarily fast. But a deeper dive into the unit revealed Arnsparger employed some brilliant strategy and cutting edge stuff. The No-Names often asked linebackers Mike Kolen and Doug Swift and even Buoniconti to match up in man while the secondary played zone.

The No-Names were considered a 4-3 defense, but they were often a 3-4 defense. Imagine that, the No-Names were a multiple defense 40 years before teams such as Bill Belichick's New England Patriots popularized having multiple defenses. Arnsparger employed what he called the 53 Defense within Miami's scheme. The 53 Defense was really a 3-4 defense with three defensive linemen and four linebackers. The genesis of the 53 Defense is muddy now because some people say Arnsparger simply liked running the 3-4 alignment, and part of that was using linebacker Bob Matheson as an edge rusher. "We called it the 53 Defense because that was Matheson's number," Buoniconti said. "It had nothing to do with the alignment."

Others say the 53 Defense came about when the Dolphins were a lineman short one week, and Matheson was something of a hybrid because he was bigger than the other linebackers but smaller than the defensive linemen. Arnsparger, seeing those traits, inserted Matheson.

And it worked because suddenly the Dolphins had a player on the field who might rush like a lineman or cover like a linebacker. "We had a lot of success with that defense," Don Shula said. "We didn't use it on every down, but we substituted him in plenty depending on the situation."

The Dolphins used Bob Heinz at defensive tackle in the four-man line alignment. Heinz was actually the starter and made 32 starts during Miami's three Super Bowl seasons. But when the situation demanded, the Dolphins replaced Heinz with Matheson. It was the advent of situation substitution. "The whole idea was to keep the offense guessing," Dick Anderson said. "They wouldn't know who was rushing or where they were coming from. That caused them to make mistakes against our defense, which rarely made mistakes."

One reason the Dolphins could have such great success using the 53 Defense was because nose tackle Manny Fernandez, all 6'2" of him and an alleged 249 pounds (often much less on gameday), dominated the middle of the line. "We couldn't run our defense without an effective nose tackle," Arnsparger said. "And Manny Fernandez was strong and disruptive and he could control the center and make plays laterally along the line of scrimmage."

The Dolphins put pressure on the passer with Bill Stanfill and Vern Den Herder at defensive end. Sacks were not an official NFL statistic during those years, but tape study has revealed Stanfill had 18½ sacks in 1972. Free safety Jake Scott and strong safety Anderson were arguably the best safety tandem in the league. Scott was the MVP of Super Bowl VII, and Anderson was a three-time Pro Bowl selection, the NFL's interception leader and Defensive Player of the Year in 1973, and was picked to the 1970s All-Decade Team.

But the undisputed leader of that defense was Buoniconti at the middle linebacker spot. He was only 5'11" and not exceedingly strong. But he was older than all the other players on the unit and respected for his great instincts and leadership. "He wouldn't stand for anything but best effort," Shula said of Buoniconti. "He wouldn't tolerate mistakes by his teammates and he never made many mistakes himself."

Together all these men had, well, no names. And with the notable exception of Fernandez, they all mostly liked the nickname. "At first, I personally resented it, but after a while, I warmed to it," Buoniconti said. "We all did. We actually felt pretty good about it. Honestly, the idea that we were all lumped into a heap of names, and no one name was above any other was good because it bonded us. It was good for us."

Perhaps the nickname fit because of the kind of guys Shula and Arnsparger brought together. Or perhaps it was a sign of a much simpler era. "I had a bunch of sacks in 1972, but that was just a different time," Stanfill said after his career ended in 1976. "I could still walk down the street in Miami Lakes or Miami Springs, and nobody would recognize me. We didn't have guys marketing themselves. We didn't have publicity agents. We were 11 talented individuals who worked together as one. We really were no names. I'm perfectly fine with that."

18 Super Bowl VII

The Miami Dolphins had completed the NFL's first unbeaten and untied season hours before. Then running back Mercury Morris, perhaps South Florida's coolest cat in the early 1970s, decided to improve the celebration that began in the Miami locker room after the game to heights befitting perfection. So Morris and some teammates headed out to a nightclub in Los Angeles, where Super Bowl VII had been played. And there Morris was introduced to Frank Sinatra. "Frank says, 'Kid, you made a lot of money for me,'" Morris recalled years later. "'What fool bets against a team that has won every game? Thanks, kid!'"

Hard to believe, isn't it? With 16 victories in 16 games, the Dolphins entered Super Bowl VII as two or three-point underdogs, depending on what bookie you used. The team that plowed through the AFC East, winning it by seven games, and beat the future Steelers dynasty in Pittsburgh in the AFC Championship Game was punctuated by question marks rather than extolled with exclamation points before that fateful Super Bowl against the Washington Redskins. Winless in two Super Bowls, could Don Shula finally win one? Out most of the season, could Bob Griese show no rust? And the most prominent question of them all: would the unbeaten Dolphins choke? "Everybody had questions," offensive line coach Monte Clark remembered. "Personally, I was confident we had answers."

The answers began rolling in pretty quickly. The Dolphins were generally loose before the game. On the 40-minute bus ride from the team hotel to the Los Angeles Memorial Coliseum, Manny Fernandez took a nap. The Dolphins then took a 7–0 lead on a 28-yard pass from Griese to wide receiver Howard Twilley with one second remaining in the first quarter. "That was a play Bob and I talked about and fought about and practiced time and time and time again," Twilley said. "I knew they would double cover Paul Warfield, so I would have single coverage. He called a post pattern where I usually faked inside on a three-step fake and then went to the corner."

But Twilley improvised against 5'9" (in his cleats) cornerback Pat Fischer. "This time I made the inside fake a five-step fake, and on about the third step, Pat broke on the move," Twilley said. "It took longer to develop, but we had the timing down."

Fischer spun 180 degrees as Twilley leaped for Griese's pass at the 5-yard line. Fischer caught up with him at the four, but Twilley dragged him over the goal line, falling just inside the pylon. NFL official Tom Kelleher signaled a touchdown for the Dolphins on a very close call, and Twilley patted Kelleher on the back as he headed off the field. "Thanks, neighbor," joked Twilley, who lived a couple of houses over from Kelleher's Miami home.

Garo's Gaffe

During those final two minutes of Super Bowl VII, Garo Yepremian was a villain among his teammates. "If Garo wasn't such a likeable guy," Howard Twilley said, "we would have killed him."

"I had a sick feeling in my stomach," Dick Anderson recalled. "But no one would say anything to Garo."

Actually, Manny Fernandez gave voice to what so many other teammates were thinking. "Garo kept walking down the line, looking for someone to stand next to," Fernandez told the *Miami Herald*. "He finally stopped next to me. I thought, *I'm not going to be the one to make him feel good.* So I threatened him...Ten minutes later we were laughing about it. But at the time, it was catastrophic."

Yepremian turned the blunder into something of a cottage industry. He joked about it. He embraced the moment. And years later he estimated he collected close to $400,000 in speaking engagement and television commercial fees because of it. "It had been a boring game," Yepremian said. "I had to do something to liven it up."

Kelleher didn't appreciate Twilley's humor. The longtime NFL official wanted to give no sense of favoritism whatsoever. "You don't thank me for something I didn't do," Kelleher growled. "You scored a touchdown, and I called it."

With less than two minutes left in the first half, Miami linebacker Nick Buoniconti intercepted a pass from Billy Kilmer and returned it to the Washington 27. A few plays later, Jim Kiick scored from one yard out for a 14–0 lead.

The Dolphins were dominant against Washington. Larry Csonka rushed for 112 yards. Jake Scott had a couple of interceptions and was named the game's MVP. Manny Fernandez, the nose tackle, made 17 tackles. "He easily could have been the MVP that day," Dick Anderson said of Fernandez.

And then *it* happened. Washington's only touchdown came with 2:07 left in the game when a misplayed field-goal attempt and fumble by Garo Yepremian turned into a 49-yard score by the Redskins' Mike Bass, who picked the ball out of the air as the Dolphins sideline watched in horror. Yepremian was a two-time All-Pro and set the NFL record by converting 20 consecutive field goals in addition to leading the NFL in field goal accuracy three times and being voted to the NFL's 1970s All-Decade Team. But that attempted pass he tried was simply an NFL blooper on the league's biggest stage. "I figured if I threw the ball downfield, it would be a positive play," Yepremian said. "But the ball slipped out of my hands, and disaster ensued."

The Redskins had one last chance. But Kilmer, who had a reputation as a pressure-proof quarterback, overthrew receivers on first and second down before running back Larry Brown lost four yards on a swing pass. That made it fourth down. The Dolphins' perfect 17–0 season was about to end on a perfect note. Kilmer dropped back, looked up, and saw linemen Bill Stanfill and Vern Den Herder in his face. Kilmer was sacked for a nine-yard loss with 33 seconds remaining to seal the victory.

Dolphins fans had already swamped the field when the clock officially expired, and players carried Shula off on their shoulders. "After the game I remember thinking one thing," Anderson said years later. "*We did it!*"

19 Super Bowl VI and Its Aftermath

Super Bowl VI promised something of an even matchup in the days leading up to the January 1972 championship game. The Miami Dolphins and Dallas Cowboys were both expansion teams; one was from the AFL, and the other was born years before to the NFL. Both teams and—to a large degree—both coaches came to the game with reputations as being unable to win the big game. The Cowboys had fallen to the Green Bay Packers time and again during the playoffs in the 1960s, and the Dolphins had fallen to, well, everyone until Don Shula stopped the bleeding in 1970.

Both teams had young, dynamic scrambling quarterbacks in Bob Griese and Roger Staubach. Both teams had defenses so proficient they had earned nicknames: the Dolphins' No-Name Defense and the Cowboys' Doomsday Defense. "There was no human alive in January of 1971 who could convince me the Super Bowl we were about to play was going to be anything but a classic decided in the final quarter and probably in the final minutes," Dolphins guard Bob Kuechenberg said years later. "But there we were in the fourth quarter, and we were down two touchdowns and then three touchdowns. They thoroughly kicked our butts. The feeling of hopelessness was secondary only to the sheer embarrassment of it."

The Dolphins were held to 185 yards, and only a 31-yard Garo Yepremian field goal four seconds before halftime averted a shutout.

To this day Miami is one of only two teams not score a touchdown in the Super Bowl. The Los Angeles Rams in February 2019 were the other.

The Cowboys' offense, meanwhile, brought their multiple sets and rushed for a then Super Bowl-record 252 yards. The Dallas gameplan was designed to attack Dolphins middle linebacker Nick Buoniconti, who Landry said he respected for his "great recognition and great lateral movement."

Landry designed plays to take advantage of Buoniconti's strengths by using them against him with misdirection plays. A concussion suffered in the third quarter (there was no concussion protocol in 1972) was the final insult Miami's outstanding middle linebacker remembered from that game. "I don't know what happened in the second half of that game," Buoniconti told the *Miami Herald* in 1984. "I was knocked out and never even saw the game films. You'd have to ask a doctor how I was able to keep playing. I don't really understand it. You lose all semblance of what's going on, but you stay on your feet and react on instinct."

Super Bowl VI felt devastating. It made Miami players feel as if all their dreams had been nuked, and then they walked around like lost zombies in some dystopian, apocalyptic wasteland. "I was crushed," Buoniconti said. "I was a nine-year veteran and didn't know if we would ever get back again. We were a young club that went very far awfully fast. With all respect to us as a team, we weren't ready to win that game. We were too young."

And yet...the Perfect Season blossomed like an ash-caked flower out of that 24–3 loss to the Cowboys. Miami's Super Bowl VII's glory was born in Super Bowl VI's humiliation. Five months after that loss, the Dolphins gathered to begin preparation for their 1972 season. On that day Shula opened the first team meeting by turning on the projector and showing the team Super Bowl VI's film. Running back Mercury Morris, who was still steaming from not carrying the ball at all in Super Bowl VI, says he recalls word for word that first team meeting of '72. "He made us watch the film of that game," Morris said. "And then he turned the projector off and said, 'Now, you see how sick and sorry you feel. Just think how sick and sorry you'll be if you don't come back and redeem yourselves for last year.'"

Morris even pronounced "sorry" the way Shula did in his Ohio accent "*Surry*."

The agenda for the Perfect Season was set in that moment. And, surprisingly, the agenda wasn't to be perfect. "Our agenda wasn't to go undefeated," running back Jim Kiick said. "Our agenda was to redeem ourselves for getting our asses kicked in Super Bowl VI."

Throughout the 1972–73 season, as the Dolphins piled one win atop another, questions began about being undefeated. But players and coaches weren't concerned about that hardly at all. "Believe it or not, there was no pressure on us to go undefeated because nobody on our team really talked about it," safety Dick Anderson said. "The only pressure on us was the fact we got thumped by Dallas the year before in the Super Bowl and embarrassed. Even though we got to that Super Bowl, the only thing we heard the whole offseason was, 'What happened to you bums? You lost the Super Bowl.' The intensity that season was to win enough games in the regular season to get to the playoffs and erase that memory."

The feeling was, from all accounts, universal among Dolphins players. "We talked about it all the time," Kuechenberg said. "We didn't exactly tell outsiders that we were motivated by revenge because it wasn't the kind of revenge that we wanted to play Dallas again. It was about wanting to play in the Super Bowl again. That was our driving force. I'd say it worked out pretty well."

20 Super Bowl VIII

The Perfect Season had been amazing, and champagne toasts of the offseason celebrating the achievement were worthy of the feat, but Don Shula gave his players a cold and instant sense of sobriety on the very first day the Miami Dolphins gathered to begin training camp in the summer of 1973. "It was important when that team came to training camp that I let them all know, even though we had won the Super Bowl and were the defending champions, I wasn't going to assume anything," Shula said. "We were going to work as hard as we did the year before—and harder."

Welcome to the Dolphins' attempt to win back-to-back Super Bowls. Welcome to the pursuit for Super Bowl VIII.

Shula explained to his players winning it all in 1973–74 was actually going to be *harder* than going undefeated. "I just felt we were going to be a target," Shula said. "Everybody was going to be aiming for us. It was going to be tougher to stay on top than it was to get to the top"

And that's how the Dolphins kicked off the new year. It was to be a chase for another championship and it was a race the Dolphins felt confident they could run. "We had gained such great confidence in that Perfect Season," Shula said. "And back then with players not leaving in free agency like they do know, we had pretty much the same team from the year before. So we felt back-to-back titles was something our football team should do."

That all sounds inspiring now. But it felt pretty empty when Miami traveled to Oakland the second game of the season and lost 12–7 to the Raiders to mark their first defeat in 19 games. "I don't have a great recollection of that loss," former offensive line coach Monte Clark said years later, "because we all went to great lengths to put that one away in whatever dark place it belonged and move on. I do remember we didn't look back after that."

Indeed, the Dolphins rolled, winning 13 of the next 14 games, including a convincing 27–10 revenge victory against the Raiders in the AFC Championship Game. The 17-point victory margin in that championship game didn't truly indicate the thorough beating Miami gave Oakland that day. "Nobody treats us like they did and gets away with it," Raiders linebacker Phil Villapiano said. "But they did."

Two weeks later the Dolphins found themselves back where they expected to be all along: at Super Bowl VIII and on the verge of another championship. But, amazingly, the team that had won 31 of its previous 33 games was picked to lose against the Minnesota Vikings by *Sports Illustrated*. That was shocking even to the Dolphins. "Some people actually felt we were a better football team that year than the previous year," Shula said.

During the week leading to the game, Minnesota coach Bud Grant seemed troubled by, well, everything. He described his team's practice facility in disparaging terms. He bemoaned the lack of blocking sleds and maintained the Dolphins were supplied a set. Grant also was upset when he found a bird's nest in the shower of the facility. "Men, consider yourself honored," defensive lineman Jim Marshall said of the finding. "It is the first time we have ever showered in an aviary."

Grant was fined $1,500 for his public complaints. Then Sunday came, and the week got much worse for Grant. Miami scored on its first two possessions on drives of 62 and 56 yards. Larry Csonka scored the first touchdown on a five-yard run with a little more than nine minutes remaining in the first quarter. Eight minutes later Jim Kiick scored on a one-yard plunge to give the Dolphins a 14–0 lead. With the duo pacing Miami, quarterback Bob Griese attempted just seven passes. Garo Yepremian added a 28-yard field goal with nine

Kuechenberg's Toughness

The amazing thing is Bob Kuechenberg played Super Bowl VIII and every playoff game that postseason with a steel rod in his arm because he had broken it in a December 9 game against the Baltimore Colts. On the flight back from Baltimore, Kuechenberg asked the team doctor, "How are you going to fix my arm?"

The doc seemed confused. They were going to set it in a cast and let it heal like, "a normal broken arm," he told the lineman.

"No, I didn't mean how are you going to do that?" Kuechenberg said. "I mean, how are you going to get me to be able to play in the game next week?"

The doctor informed Kuechenberg he was out with a broken arm. Kuechenberg informed the doctor that wasn't happening. So that week bone marrow was drilled out of the arm, and a 10-inch alloy rod was shoved in. Kuechenberg lived with a five-inch scar from his wrist to the middle of his forearm where the break occurred and another five-inch scar up to his elbow. "We were headed to the playoff," Kuechenberg said, "I wasn't going to miss that. And I definitely wasn't going to miss the Super Bowl. It's the Super Bowl for God's sake!"

minutes remaining in the first half. The Vikings trailed 17–0 and they had not crossed their own 40-yard line yet.

Csonka, who was named the game's MVP after rushing for 145 yards, got his second touchdown in the third quarter on a two-yard run to give the Dolphins a 24–0 lead. The work the Miami running game did that day was a testament to the offensive line's dominance of The Purple People Eaters. Miami's line dominated the Vikings up front, and nowhere was the dominance demonstrated more clearly than the job left guard Bob Kuechenberg did against Alan Page, who was one of the star defensive linemen of his time and was eventually inducted to the Pro Football Hall of Fame. But in that game, the Dolphins ran the football 53 times, and Page was an afterthought with only two solo tackles.

Minnesota averted the shutout with a four-yard run by quarterback Fran Tarkenton one minute and 35 seconds into the final quarter of Super Bowl VIII. By then the Dolphins had made their point. "The way I see it," Vikings linebacker Wally Hilgenberg said, "the only way to stop Miami is to kick them out of the league."

Afterward, Shula and defensive coordinator Bill Arnsparger put their arms over each other's shoulders and walked off the field at Rice Stadium. The both knew Arnsparger, the architect of the No-Name Defense, had already accepted a head coaching job with the New York Giants. Arnsparger was fighting back tears of joy. A picture of that moment hangs in the Pro Football Hall of Fame.

21 48 Touchdown Passes

The onslaught began surprisingly on the road. Against a two-time Super Bowl team. Still uncelebrated as an NFL star that first regular-season weekend in September of 1984, Dan Marino took a team mostly known for its coach and defense and proceeded to set America's favorite sport ablaze.

He threw a 26-yard touchdown pass to Mark Duper the second time the Miami Dolphins had the football against the favored Washington Redskins. And then he threw another touchdown in the second quarter. And three more in the third quarter. Marino tossed five touchdowns in a surprisingly easy 35–17 whipping of the defending NFC champions. "It was like we didn't see what hit us," Redskins coach Joe Gibbs said. "Nobody could have been ready for that."

The NFL was not ready for what would happen next. Because what happened next was like Babe Ruth hitting 60 home runs in 1927. It was Wilt Chamberlain scoring 100 points in a game. It was

Wayne Gretzky scoring 92 goals. Dan Marino threw 48 touchdown passes in 1984.

He passed for 5,084 yards in a league where great quarterbacks aimed for 3,500 yards. "He did things in 1984 that other quarterbacks had never done before," Don Shula said. "And he was able to do that because he could do things other quarterbacks just couldn't do. It was special."

Y.A. Tittle had thrown 36 touchdown passes in 1963, and over the next 21 seasons, only four quarterbacks had reached the 30-touchdown plateau. No one had ever climbed to 40. But by early November, Marino had Tittle in his sights.

It was no coincidence Marino, who wore No. 13 at the University of Pittsburgh and with the Dolphins, started wearing No. 14 during some practices. The official explanation was the Dolphins had run out of No. 13 jerseys because they'd been stolen out of their training facility locker room. No one mentioned Tittle wore No. 14, and Marino was about to pass his touchdown record like a Corvette (Marino's favorite) speeding past a jogger. Marino tied Tittle's record during a nationally telecast *Monday Night Football* game in November and sped past 40 touchdowns the second week of December. Other quarterbacks watched in amazement. "He was *waaay* ahead of anything anybody else was doing at the time," John Elway told ABC. "We were all chasing Danny because of the success he was having. And it wasn't much of a race, to be honest."

Marino actually didn't get really hot until late in the season. He threw 16 touchdown passes in three December games. Those 16 touchdowns that month were more than 40 quarterbacks, who started multiple games that year, threw *the entire season*. "He's the best pure passer that probably ever played, and that year he was unstoppable," said future teammate Bernie Kosar. "He changed the standard for what a great year by a quarterback was measured by."

Marino rewrote the single-season records for completions with 362, attempts with 564, passing yards (by becoming the first ever to surpass 5,000), and touchdowns (by becoming the first to surpass 40). Those single-season yardage and touchdown records have been matched and broken multiple times since 1984. Drew Brees, Tom Brady, Peyton Manning, Brett Favre, and others rocketed past Marino's record in latter years. But a 5,000-yard and 40-touchdown season is something Marino did first. He was Neil Armstrong taking that first, giant leap for quarterbacks.

Marino was named to the Pro Bowl in 1984. He was All-Pro. He was Offensive Player of the Year and NFL MVP. The MVP award is overlooked, but consider that Eric Dickerson also rushed for 2,105 yards and scored 14 touchdowns that season, showing the value of what Marino accomplished. "He's in his second year and he's broken many of the great passing records in the NFL," Shula said in 1984. "That covers a lot of quarterbacks, a lot of great quarterbacks. And Marino has just passed everybody this year and sort of tipped his wings flying by."

The 48-touchdown mark was broken by Manning twice. He set the current record of 55 touchdown passes in 2013. But Manning is the first to put Marino's historic mark in perspective. "Forty-eight touchdowns today is a great season," Manning told the NFL Network. "Forty-eight touchdowns in that era, in that time, was remarkable."

Manning threw 49 touchdowns to set a new mark in 2004—the season *after* the NFL's illegal contact rules were changed to prohibit defenders from touching receivers after a five-yard release from the line of scrimmage. The rule wasn't a consideration in 1984. There also weren't rules prohibiting defenders from hitting the quarterback too high or too low. Nor were there helmet-to-helmet rules to give defensive backs pause and receivers greater confidence of not being hit.

So how many yards could a 23-year-old Marino throw for today? "Probably like 6,000 or so," Marino said with a smile. "Everyone knows it's a lot easier to play the position now because of the rules.

People are throwing it more now. They're throwing touchdown passes by just flipping the ball to a receiver on a sweep. They got bubble screens that we didn't do too much of. That's popular now, and it's not exactly a tough throw to make. We had screens but not bubble screens along the line of scrimmage. I understand the rules changes. I'm not against those because the quarterback is the most important guy in the franchise probably. So you got to protect him. I got no problem with them. But it did change things. Things are totally different now."

Marino threw short and threw long in 1984. Eighteen of his touchdowns traveled 20 yards or more. Both Duper and Mark Clayton averaged more than 18 yards per reception that season. That stunning 1984 season caused a ripple effect across the league. Suddenly, other teams felt they had to throw more. And the quarterback's work also caused a seismic shift in Miami. "I was a ball control, time of possession coach," Shula said. "That's how we won games, how we won Super Bowls. But then everyone realized how Dan and his great ability could put points up on the board. Then people began to see how important that was, and things changed."

The Winningest Coach of All Time Is Crowned

The measure of respect Miami Dolphins players have for what Don Shula accomplished on that special November day in 1993 showed in how they changed their plans. Several of them wanted to shower their coach with Gatorade after his record 325th overall victory, and then sanity prevailed. The players decided that because Shula had just become the NFL's all-time winningest coach, surpassing Chicago Bears legend George Halas, that he was now the king of coaches. And that merited royal treatment. "We looked at the Gatorade and said, 'You know, we need to do a classy thing, and that isn't it,'" guard Keith Sims said. "So we put him on our shoulders instead."

Players lifted their coach and carried him around for a bit. And during that celebratory ride, Shula found himself in the same place his historical accomplishment had already put him: above everyone else. "I never envisioned this," he said. "I've never made any long-range plans, just tried to take them as they come. I've been so fortunate to have such a family and such owners as Carroll Rosenbloom and two generations of Robbies."

Shula finished his career with 347 victories, including playoff games. That's the most of any coach. He won 328 games in the regular season. That's the most of any coach. But this record-breaker against the Philadelphia Eagles showed some of what made Shula great. Indeed, the entire '93 season, in which the Dolphins only managed a 9–7 record, showed some of what made Shula great. Consider that a month before, the Dolphins lost quarterback Dan Marino for the season with a torn right Achilles tendon. That put backup Scott Mitchell in the lineup for the first time in his career.

The Dolphins were prospering with Mitchell and won all three of his previous starts. But in the first series of the second half, Mitchell separated his throwing shoulder on a scramble. It was a Grade 2 separation, meaning he'd miss the next four starts and not really be right the rest of the season. That represented both a long-term and short-term problem for Shula. In the short term, the coach had to insert either raw third-stringer Doug Pederson (yeah, the Eagles coach now) or veteran Steve DeBerg. Pederson had been with the team since the start of the season but had never taken an NFL snap. DeBerg was 39 years old, but he joined the team only four days earlier.

With his team trailing 14–13, Shula picked Pederson. And it was, shall we say, challenging. The Dolphins shuttled plays into the huddle with a messenger player because Pederson was not fully familiar with the team's hand signals. And Pederson, who had fumbled the snap on an extra point in the first half, fumbled one of his first snaps from center at the Philadelphia goal line. He later admitted he had never practiced short-yardage and goal-line situations with Miami.

Eagles errors helped the Dolphins take a tenuous 16–14 lead on a field goal, and then in the fourth quarter, Pederson led a drive for another field goal by completing two 11-yard passes for first downs. "I didn't want to think that I was in there not to lose the game, although some people may say that," Pederson said. "I was thinking about getting first downs and moving the team. I wanted to be in a position to help the team win because for me this victory is as special as it is for Coach Shula. This is his 325th, but for me, I'll think of it as my first."

Despite the heroics and the celebration, everyone understood the season could be slipping away. Most teams see their season crash if they lose their starting quarterback. The Dolphins were now without their starter or backup and were about to turn the reins over to the oldest player in the league who had been retired days before. But Shula was not moved. "We did it with Earl Morrall after Bob Griese went down in the 17–0 season of 1972," he said.

To some extent he did it even before that with running back Tom Matte at quarterback with the old Baltimore Colts when both Johnny Unitas and Morrall went down. And that is a wonderful Shula trait: amid his great constancy, he also embraced change. Shula won Super Bowls running the ball with Larry Csonka and Mercury Morris. He went to a Super Bowl throwing the football with Marino. The man adapts.

The historic victory improved Shula's record with Miami to 28–8 in regular-season games started by a reserve quarterback.

The next week Shula inserted DeBerg and beat the New England Patriots. And then the Dolphins beat the defending Super Bowl champion Dallas Cowboys on Thanksgiving. Those victories were Shula's 326th and 327th. They improved his record in Miami with yet another reserve quarterback to 30–8. "We just have to try to keep things together and somehow hang in there," Shula repeated over and over.

Critics would point out the '93 Dolphins collapsed at the end. They had a 9–2 record at one point and finished out of the playoffs at 9–7. But that happened after DeBerg also got hurt, cornerback Troy Vincent went on injured reserve, Louis Oliver went on injured reserve, and starting center Jeff Uhlenhake went on injured reserve.

23 The Greatest Offensive Line There Ever Was

Castoffs. Misfits. Discards no one else wanted. That was the general description that fit the offensive linemen Miami Dolphins line coach Monte Clark had to work with in the early 1970s.

The right tackle had come to the Dolphins in an expansion draft so unpopular and unpredictable that four players the Dolphins picked had retired immediately. The right guard was never drafted out of tiny Bethune-Cookman and was traded by the San Diego Chargers. The center was never drafted out of tiny South Dakota State and had been cut by the Cleveland Browns. The left guard signed as a free agent after playing for the mighty Chicago Owls of the prestigious Continental Football League. (Note the sarcasm.) The left tackle was never drafted and was cut twice by the San Francisco 49ers. "Larry Little was traded to Miami for a little-known defensive back," said Norm Evans when he reflected on the group years after the fact. "Jim Langer was picked up off waivers, Bob Kuechenberg was picked up off waivers, Wayne Moore was primarily a basketball player in college, and here we were a bunch of guys, and Monte Clark had to mold us into one unit."

Clark had one message for these disparate retreads. "I would tell them: you're going to be the best in the business," Clark said. "There were some days—maybe after practice in the early years—when I didn't necessarily believe what I was telling them. But by the time the championship seasons came around, they were exactly what I expected. They were the NFL's best offensive line. No question."

The best offensive line of the day was a grand union of men who were intimate with rejection. But also intimate with perseverance, work ethic, and professional excellence. Despite being discarded by the Houston Oilers in the 1966 expansion draft, Evans turned that dismissal into 135 starts in 10 seasons with the Dolphins. He was selected to the Pro Bowl in 1972 and 1974. "The only reason Norm Evans didn't make the Pro Bowl in 1973 is because I made the Pro Bowl in 1973," Dolphins left tackle Wayne Moore said before his death in 1989. "Nobody wanted to put two Miami Dolphins offensive tackles in the Pro Bowl at the same time so only one of us got in, but we both had good years in '73, and there's no reason we both shouldn't have been there."

Evans was a clean-cut man who trusted Clark and worshipped Jesus Christ. But he had a nasty side. "Football is a game of intimidation," Evans said. "And often what happens is you try establish that intimidation. The Miami Dolphins used to intimidate the opponent's defense. Everyone knew we were going to run the football and when we got out there it was, 'Look out 'cause here we come.' And it was intimidating for the defense that they knew what we were going to try to do, and they couldn't stop it."

Miami's offensive line boasted two Pro Bowl tackles and three Hall of Fame caliber interior linemen. Right guard Larry Little was voted to the Pro Bowl five times, including four consecutive times from 1971 to 1974. Interestingly, he wasn't voted to the Pro Bowl in 1975 but was voted All-NFL just as he had been the previous four seasons. That was quite a feat for a man who had only two college scholarship offers—to Bethune-Cookman and St. Augustine College in North Carolina—after coming out of Miami's segregated Booker T. Washington High School.

Despite being a fine player at Bethune-Cookman, he was not drafted. "Before the draft I got a call from Houston and the Rams telling me they were going to draft me," Little said. "My dorm room was right next to the telephone. And I wouldn't let anyone use that phone all day long because I was expecting that phone call. It was a call I never got."

Little did get calls from three teams over the next two days. All were interested in signing him as a free agent, but one, the Baltimore Colts, were offering no signing bonus. Another, the Dolphins, were offering $500 while the Chargers offered $750. "San Diego was giving me $750," Little said, "so I went with San Diego."

Little was the finest pulling guard of his day and arguably the best in NFL history. The film of Mercury Morris grabbing the back of the burly guard's jersey and basically guiding him into defenders, whom Little buried, is iconic. Little was inducted into the Pro Football Hall of Fame in 1993. He joined center Jim Langer, who had been selected in 1987 along with running back Larry Csonka. "It's a tribute that one of pro football's greatest centers can enter the Hall during his first year of eligibility," Don Shula said when he presented Langer. "He got it done within the rules. He had very few holding calls and was the solid cornerstone of the great Dolphin teams of the '70s. He was our leader."

Langer was a leader but also another undrafted player. Despite that inauspicious entrance into the league, Langer was selected to the Pro Bowl six times. If Csonka, Morris, Jim Kiick, and Paul Warfield were Miami's thoroughbreds, then Langer was the workhorse. He played every down of the Perfect Season. He played 141 consecutive games over a 10-year span. "You don't get to this podium by your-self," Langer said during his Hall of Fame induction speech. "I've been very, very fortunate throughout my career. And I will cherish this moment the rest of my life."

That leaves left guard Bob Kuechenberg. He fit the mold of a Dolphins lineman because he came to Miami after a desert experience with other pro teams, including a short stint with the Philadelphia Eagles. Kuechenberg did things no one thought he could in Miami, including starting in four Super Bowls. "Kooch was the toughest son-of-a-gun I ever coached," Clark said.

True to that form, Kuechenberg played Super Bowl VIII with a fractured arm and still was dominant against Minnesota Vikings defensive lineman Alan Page. Csonka was voted MVP of that Super Bowl after he rushed for a then-record 145 yards. "The reason I performed so well was that I was going through the line virtually unmolested," Csonka said. "It was nice to get the MVP trophy, but let's put it where really rests: it rests on the shoulders of No. 1, Bob Kuechenberg, in that game and then the rest of the offensive linemen."

Nick Buoniconti: The Lawyerly Linebacker

NAB. Those outlined letters stenciled on everyone's helmet was the solemn and heartfelt way the Miami Dolphins paid tribute to Nicholas Anthony Buoniconti in 2019. It was a simple way to celebrate the full life of a complex man. It was a small decal celebrating a giant.

That's what Buoniconti was during his 78 years until his death in July of 2019. He touched both college and professional football as one of its most decorated players. And when his playing days were complete, he had an amazing second act in television, business, and as the president of a *Fortune 500* company. So, yes, the 5'11" son of a Massachusetts baker, who had to work out and eat extensively to maintain his weight of 220 pounds, was a larger-than-life figure. Not that people immediately recognized Buoniconti this way. "Size was always something people seemed to notice first when I played," Buoniconti said after his career ended in 1976. "It was at first something I resented because they didn't know me. They didn't know what was inside of me. They didn't know my heart. But later in life, when I was doing other things, other work, nobody mentioned my size, and I almost started wishing they would. Because when I started working as an attorney and on the television show and even in the corporate world, I knew people thought I didn't measure up at first, but they were never transparent enough to say so."

Doubting Nick Buoniconti was never a smart move. Not in football. Not in business. Not in 1985 when his youngest son, Marc, suffered a spinal cord injury that left him clinging to life and eventually paralyzed. Buoniconti answered that tragedy with boldness and tenacity. When he first saw Marc after the football accident that left him immobile, Nick urged his son to cling to life and then promised he'd do everything in his power to help him walk again. "My father made a promise to me that caused a revolution in paralysis research," Marc Buoniconti said after his father passed.

Nick Buoniconti helped found The Miami Project to Cure Paralysis, and that led to hundreds of millions of dollars going to research so that people anchored to wheelchairs or unable to move could regain their motion. That was a long, painful, emotional fight that Nick, Marc, and the entire Buoniconti family waged. It was a battle they never really won, but also one in which they never surrendered. Because Nick Buoniconti wasn't good at quitting.

Nick Buoniconti played middle linebacker and guard at Notre Dame. "As a two-way player, he was an excellent player but never received the notoriety as a linebacker," said college teammate Ed Hoerster. "Coaches failed to recognize or accept his real strengths. One of the coaches said Nick would 'go through a wall, but he would leave a small hole.' Nick carried this as motivation the rest of his career. While undersized both as a pro and college player, he had the largest heart and greatest motivation."

The Boston Patriots of the old AFL drafted Buoniconti in 1962. He was their pick in the 13th round. And that apparent afterthought gave the Patriots a perennial star who would earn a spot on their All-Decade Team and eventually a place in the club's Hall of Fame. "Those were wonderful years for me," Buoniconti said. "I was playing in the town I grew up. I was doing well, and then things changed. And I hated it at first."

In 1969 the Patriots traded Buoniconti to the Dolphins for John Bramlett, Kim Hammond, and a fifth-round pick. Buoniconti, who had earned his law degree while playing in Boston, said he considered retiring. Instead he negotiated his own contract, which he would later do for many others he represented as an agent. Don Shula was hired as the Dolphins coach in 1970, and let's just say he wasn't immediately impressed when he saw Buoniconti up close. "When I first saw him, I couldn't believe a guy that small was able to accomplish as much as he could accomplish as a player," Shula said in *The Many Lives of Nick Buoniconti*, an HBO documentary on the linebacker. "I said, 'This is the guy? I've got to work with him?'"

Shula was astonished that Buoniconti was not very strong. So he ordered him to lift more weights, something not all players did in the late 1960s. Buoniconti was so embarrassed that he would lift in private rather than with teammates. But he worked out every day to make sure he eventually met Shula's standards. Eventually, Buoniconti earned Shula's respect not only as the leader of the budding No-Name Defense, but also as the entire team's leader. And when that respect spread across the entire locker room, Buoniconti became something of the team spokesman and representative. "If you remember back in those days, we were having two-a-days, even three-a-days," said Nat Moore, who joined the Dolphins in 1974. "There was no water. Maybe you could punch a hole in a bag and steal some ice from a guy who was injured. But when it just got really too tough and we were losing our legs, Nick was the guy who could go in and talk with Coach. Nick was the strong-willed, strong-minded guy that could go in and sit down and horse trade with Coach and get us in the right situation, so that come Sunday, we were ready to perform."

Buoniconti didn't ask to be the guy always negotiating with Shula. He knew some in the coaching staff and the press saw him as something of a clubhouse lawyer. "That was a derogatory term then," Buoniconti said. "I ignored it because I was helping the players be better, and that made the team better."

Bouniconti played until 1976 and by the time he left the field the final time he had become a two-time Super Bowl champion, a two-time Pro Bowl player, a six-time All-Star in the AFL, and written a resume worthy of being in the Pro Football Hall of Fame, which inducted him in 2001. "I kissed the ground in the Orange Bowl after that last game," Buoniconti said. "I was blessed."

And then it can be argued, Buoniconti embarked on the most impressive part of his life. He served as a sports agent for a time and then became the president of the United States Tobacco Company. Then he joined the set of HBO's *Inside the NFL* and remained a fixture there until 2001. All this happened after a full and impressive football career. Call it greatness followed by brilliance. "I am thankful to have had Nick in my life," Shula said the day Buoniconti died. "I will miss him."

25 The WFL Demolishes a Dynasty

As his life was being changed forever, Larry Csonka called Howard Cosell at around 10:30 AM on Sunday, March 31 in 1974. The two men and their wives had shared dinners and become friends in the years while Csonka was the face of back-to-back Miami Dolphins Super Bowl wins, and Cosell was the most articulate voice on ABC's *Monday Night Football.* And now the star athlete wanted to share what he thought was a pretty big scoop with the star journalist. "We may have the biggest story in the history of sports," Csonka announced to Cosell.

Yeah, the man who ran the football with all the finesse of a sledgehammer wasn't big on understatement. Csonka told Cosell he and Dolphins teammates Jim Kiick and Paul Warfield were about to sign contracts with the Toronto Northmen of the World Football League. The package deal would be worth $3.5 million and signal the breakup of professional football's most dominant dynasty. That spring was an amazing time in sports. Hank Aaron was only days from tying Babe Ruth's career home run mark. Muhammad Ali's "Rumble in the Jungle" bout against Joe Frazier was being planned. But Csonka rightly saw the defection of three Miami stars as huge news.

And it certainly was a shocker when the Cosell show aired that afternoon with Csonka, Kiick, and Warfield sitting side by side by side, announcing their departure to Cosell as ABC beamed the news on national television. "It was like watching a funeral," Dorothy Shula, coach Don Shula's first wife, told the *Miami Herald* days later.

Dolphins' owner Joe Robbie was equal parts livid and frustrated. In a hastily-called press conference that evening, he said Ed Keating, the agent for the players, first informed him of the trio's WFL intentions the night before. Robbie said he was told the only way the players would return to Miami was if the Dolphins matched the WFL offer immediately. "I asked Mr. Keating to conduct negotiations with us in good faith," Robbie said. "I told him at the outset of our conversation that our offers would be substantial."

Robbie said he and Coach Shula wanted to meet with the players and negotiate in person, but that request was denied, and they were instead instructed to deposit $3 million in an escrow account for the players. Robbie said the Dolphins wouldn't agree to such "a complex" deal over the phone. So the deal with the WFL was closed. Csonka, Kiick, and Warfield would play for Miami in '74 but leave in 1975. It was a coup for the WFL but a disaster for the Dolphins because the three players were woven into the fabric of Miami's success.

Csonka had rushed for a Super Bowl-record 145 yards against the Minnesota Vikings in Super Bowl VIII and been named the game's MVP in Miami's 24–7 victory. Warfield's last regular-season game of the 1973 season was a four-touchdown performance against the Detroit Lions. And, oh yeah, he was not only selected to the Pro Bowl, but also named All-NFL. And Kiick, who Shula referred to as "Old Reliable," was the insurance policy in the Miami backfield. If the Dolphins needed to give either Csonka or Mercury Morris a respite, there was Kiick. If the Dolphins needed a key third-down conversion, there was Kiick catching passes out of the backfield.

The WFL effectively ravaged the Miami offense, taking one of the NFL's best receivers, most versatile running backs, and, of course, most physical and productive fullbacks, who no less an authority than Shula called the "heart" of the Dolphins offense. "He was blood and guts and dirt all over him," Shula said. "Some called our offense in those years businesslike or conservative or boring. I called it brutally effective, and Csonka had a lot to do with the brutally part."

The reaction among the rest of the team's players was expected to be mixed. But it really wasn't. "So what?" Linebacker Doug Swift said. "The defense won all the games for us anyway, remember?"

He was kidding. Other players were much more serious in making the case NFL owners had been underpaying players for years because there was no competition for their services. And the WFL would change that. "You can only play this game for so long," Pro Bowl safety Dick Anderson said at the time. "If you took the kind of beating Larry Csonka takes every game, you'd understand why he's doing this. I do not feel they are being disloyal to the Dolphins or the National Football League. I knew they were talking to the Toronto people, but I didn't think they'd sign. All I can do is wish them luck."

"I'm just sorry I'm not going up there with them," future Hall of Fame guard Larry Little said.

Few remember the trio were not the only Dolphins who considered leaving the dynasty they helped build. Jake Scott talked to the WFL Hawaii franchise. Manny Fernandez talked to Portland. Jim Mandich talked to Birmingham. Nick Buoniconti told reporters he was negotiating with two different WFL teams, though he declined to identify them.

"We were in a situation where we were making $50,000 per year, which was a good salary in the NFL back then," Csonka told NFL Films. "But we were offered an opportunity to make $3.5 million over two-and-a-half years. That's why I left the Miami Dolphins."

Csonka's portion of the deal was for $1.4 million. He estimated years later he collected $1 million of that.

Neither the looming departures nor the WFL flirtations by other players diminished Shula's expectations for the 1974 season. "One of the hallmarks of excellence is the Triple Crown," Shula said before that fateful season. "What we want to dedicate ourselves to this year is winning a third consecutive Super Bowl and becoming the NFL's first Triple Crown winner."

None of the three players ever again played up to the reputations they had authored in Miami. The Northmen moved to Memphis, became the Southmen, and Csonka carried the ball 99 times for 421 yards and one touchdown for Memphis in 1975. The entire league folded midway through its second season. And the Dolphins? Well, that early 1970s dynasty passed into history.

26 Mercury Morris and Jim Kiick

Whenever it didn't go exactly right, Don Shula recalled that he'd spend a couple of minutes every morning after a Miami Dolphins game nursing one of his halfback's egos.

If Mercury Morris got more playing time than Jim Kiick, Kiick would be in the coach's office asking why and wanting more work for himself. If Kiick had the edge in workload that game, Morris would be in the coach's office, reminding Shula about his impressive five-yard-per-carry average. "Every Monday morning it was like that," Shula recalled with fondness. "I almost knew to carve out time for it because I knew one or the other was coming in."

The scene Shula recounted includes no bitterness or envy but rather competitiveness and desire. It was part of what made Morris and Kiick work so well. It was also part of what made them so close. The relationship between Kiick and Morris developed into a special relationship during those wonderful days of the Dolphins dynasty in the early 1970s.

Morris and Kiick once shared one position on the Super Bowl Dolphins. Both played the halfback position to Larry Csonka's fullback. And while Csonka was so battering ram effective that he bulldozed his way into the Hall of Fame, the other two combined to be just as productive.

Morris and Kiick combined for 1,521 yards and 17 rushing touchdowns during 1972's Perfect Season. The next year they combined for 1,211 yards and 10 rushing touchdowns. And while Morris did most of the damage on the ground, Kiick was a dangerous receiver out of the backfield. "Jim and I shared that spot and we made it work," Morris said. "It was such a perfect fit."

Kiick agreed. "He and I together were the best running *back* in football," Kiick said, putting emphasis on running back as a singular word. "We were the perfect combination. What he could do, I couldn't. What I could do, he couldn't. Together we could do it all."

Their careers went in different directions after 1974. Kiick went to the World League, and when that folded, he finished with the Denver Broncos and then the Washington Redskins. Morris stayed with the Dolphins until he was traded to the San Diego Chargers before the 1976 season. But that didn't stop them from keeping in contact. And the years haven't stopped them from strengthening their friendship. "I love this guy, honestly," Morris said. "Plus we're kind of like opposites, and opposites attract."

Said Kiick: "Yeah, some people like to talk a lot, and some people don't. Guess which one of us is which."

Once the consummate 1970s stud with the bushy dark hair and beard and the mysterious and mischievous demeanor, Kiick passed away in June of 2020 at the age of 73. He died following a battle with Alzheimer's disease, and his death occurred the month after Shula passed away.

Morris, who was John Shaft cool before *Shaft* hit movie screens, is a picture of fitness for a man of any age—let alone one in his 70s. Hugging him is like wrapping arms around a muscle. "I used to go the gym and warm up for 15 minutes and work out for 50 minutes,"

Morris said. "Now I go and warm up for 50 minutes and work out for 15."

After Shula's story of those Monday morning meetings was broached, Kiick had a different take. "I don't think it was like that at all," Kiick said. "That's just a story. We were like brothers. We were both competitors and wanted to win. It didn't matter how."

27 The Marks Brothers

In the summer of 2005, as he was enjoying the highest honor of his NFL career—induction into the Pro Football Hall of Fame—Dan Marino spoke of his father and mother, his hometown, the "greatest coach ever, Don Shula," and his teammates. And although he apologized for not being able to name all the teammates that he shared huddles and sidelines with, he started that list with a pair. "Two guys," Marino said, holding up two fingers. "Mark Duper and Mark Clayton."

"In 1984 we set a standard for throwing that football that teams are still trying to match today," Marino said. "And the one thing I remember most about Duper and Clayton: their competitive spirit and their attitude that they were the best. Every time they would come back to the huddle, they would always insist they were open and that they always wanted the ball."

Marino appreciated that. Respected that. Loved that, actually. Because he felt the same way about himself. "They constantly reminded me that they were making me a star," Marino said.

It's without argument that Marino was one of the premier pure passers ever to step on an NFL field. Perhaps he was the best ever. But it's also without argument that the portrait of Marino's greatness is incomplete without its most exciting plays, its grandest moments, its amazing throws. And for a decade, most of those plays, moments, and throws landed in the hands of Duper and Clayton, the Marks Brothers. They were the broadest and most exciting strokes of that portrait. "They couldn't have done the things they did without Dan Marino," Shula said. "And Dan probably couldn't have done the things he did without the Marks Brothers."

The Miami Dolphins record books, indeed the NFL record book, speaks to the heights the Marks Brothers reached with Marino. "We all made each other," Marino said. "Knowing you had those two guys outside to throw the ball to and knowing they would beat the coverage and go get it, that was special."

During Marino's 48-touchdown season, Clayton had 1,389 yards and 18 touchdowns, and Duper had 1,306 yards and eight touchdowns. "You want to know the reason one of them didn't put up numbers that would make you think he's the greatest receiver of all time?" Bob Kuechenberg asked rhetorically. "Because we had another monster on the other side who also went for over 1,000 yards and a bunch of touchdowns. Those two were just unstoppable that year, and it wasn't because they surprised people. They were just that good."

"The things these guys today can do because the rules are relaxed, we were doing 30 years ago when the rules didn't make it easy for us," Clayton said. "We felt like we were the best. We put on a show."

As part of that show, Duper was the speedster, the track guy. He supposedly ran a 4.25 time in the 40-yard dash before the Dolphins drafted him in 1982. So he was the deep threat. "I was coaching the Lions when Duper kind of burst on the scene and saw how teams around the league tried to cover him man-to-man early on," Monte Clark said. "That was a mistake. I knew that was a mistake right away."

Clayton was fast but not quite as fast as Duper. It didn't matter because Clayton combined amazing quickness, good speed, great leaping ability, and precise route running to become a five-time Pro Bowl player. "He was a zone killer," Clark said. "He understood where the open areas in zones were going to be and he could sit down there whenever he wanted. And every once in a while, he'd run a post or slant across the deep middle of the field and kill you."

The combination was simply unstoppable for a time. And they knew it. "Those guys were going to beat you," Marino said. "Pick your coverage: man-to-man, zone, off, they were going to find a way to win."

Neither the 5'9" Clayton nor the 5'9' Duper were prototypical receivers by today's standards, but Clayton made up for his apparent lack of height with a 40-inch vertical leaping ability. "When he got up in the air, he was like a 6'4" receiver," Shula said. Duper made up for his average height with great strength, particularly in his lower body, which he could use to separate from a defender in tight quarters.

Record Breakers

Most career touchdowns in a Dolphins career: Clayton is first with 82. Duper is third with 59.

Most touchdowns in a season: Clayton is first with 18 in 1984, which set the NFL record at the time. Clayton also had a 14-touchdown season in 1988, which is fifth in team history.

Most consecutive games scoring a touchdown: Paul Warfield, Ricky Williams, and Clayton each had six.

Most career receptions: Clayton is first with 550. Duper is second with 511.

Most career receiving yards: Duper is first with 8,869. Clayton is second with 8,643.

Duper was in his second year when Marino and Clayton joined the Dolphins after the 1983 draft. All contributed that year. By the next season, they blossomed, and Shula, who had won Super Bowls (plural) running the football, decided it would be best to throw now. "We wanted to throw the ball," Duper said. "We didn't like running the ball."

Despite their obvious chemistry and kinship, there were moments tempers flared among the trio of Marino and the Marks Brothers. "He's out there yelling and pointing at us after a play, and the truth is he ain't saying nothing to us. He's cursing at himself," Clayton half-jokingly said in the locker room. "But it looks like on television that he's yelling at us, so everyone thinks we messed up. We didn't mess up nothing. He messed up."

Within earshot at his locker stall, Marino sheepishly nodded his head in agreement.

There were other times, however, that Marino was upset with the duo. "I was an emotional player," he conceded. "So there were times I yelled at them because something was their fault."

On that day Marino was inducted into the Hall of Fame, he decided he wanted to throw one more pass while still in the limelight. "I'm going deep," he said before sending Clayton out of his chair and down an aisle. He then threw the football from the stage into Clayton's hands about 40 yards away.

He could have just as easily thrown it to Duper. "You probably can't say one without the other," Duper said. "When you say Mark Duper, you gotta say Mark Clayton. When you say Mark Clayton, you gotta say Mark Duper."

28 Sea of Hands

After he helped kill the Miami Dolphins dynasty, Clarence Davis threw a party. That December evening back in 1974 still lives in the memory of the former Oakland Raiders running back. Earlier that afternoon Davis caught an eight-yard pass from Ken Stabler with 26 seconds to play to help his team beat the Dolphins 28–26 in an AFC divisional playoff game. The catch through heavy traffic would forever be known as the Sea of Hands play.

That play on December 22, 1974, ended Miami's chance at an unprecedented third consecutive Super Bowl title. That game marked the bitter farewell for Larry Csonka, Jim Kiick, and Paul Warfield. That loss inaugurated a nine-year playoff victory drought in Miami. "There might have been a few tears in my eyes after that one," Don Shula said a quarter-century after the fact. "All the disappointment of getting knocked out of doing something that had never been done—winning three consecutive Super Bowls—was hard to take. It took a great play to beat us. It was just one of the great plays in the history of the National Football League."

Davis years later didn't remember the play as a dynasty killer. He remembered it for what came afterward. "It was just another game for us, and the fact we beat Miami led to a nice celebration," Davis said. "All I was really thinking at the time was we won the game, we would be playing the next week, and we had a chance to make more money in the playoffs."

Davis suffered a stroke in 1995 and was still fighting its effects years later. He spoke slowly, deliberately. He said he no longer moved like a running back in his prime. A daily trip to the mailbox wasn't a bad workout now, but it still delivered a flashback to that play. "I'm still receiving a lot of fame from that catch," Davis said.

"A receiver loves fan mail, you know? I guess that catch was the highlight of my career—that and winning the Super Bowl."

The years have turned the classic Oakland victory into the stuff of lore. The legend goes that Shula yelled at the walls in the halftime locker room because he thought Al Davis planted listening devices in there. In truth Shula does not discount the possibility Davis planted the devices, but he maintains he did not speak to the walls.

Miami defensive players spent part of the second half angrily questioning defensive coordinator Vince Costello's strategy of rushing Stabler with only three defensive linemen. One Dolphins player supposedly barked at Costello, "Lou Costello could do a better job for us today than you're doing."

Manny Fernandez recalled Costello was fired on the plane ride back to Miami, but Shula said he didn't fire Costello. The assistant, who left Miami and eventually became the defensive coordinator for the Kansas City Chiefs, simply "pursued another opportunity," the coach said.

"Vince was a nice guy, and I liked him personally," Fernandez says. "But it was terrible coaching. Let's just say there were a lot of opinions being given on the sideline that day. Overall, it wasn't a pretty sight."

The ax also fell on defensive back Henry Stuckey after that game. Shula was livid that a brain-locked Stuckey failed to tag a fallen Cliff Branch on a pass play. Branch got up and turned a short, routine catch into a 72-yard, fourth-quarter touchdown. Stuckey never played for the Dolphins again.

Following the game, one Miami player sarcastically suggested running back Benny Malone scored too soon when he gave Miami a 26–21 lead with 2:08 left to play. Newspapers ran with the idea the next day, and today the sentiment persists in the minds of some participants. "He scored too fast if there is such a thing," said Nat Moore, who opened the fateful game with an 89-yard kickoff return touchdown.

Despite the subplots the moment that stood out was Davis' game-winning catch. "It was a traumatic experience," Vern Den Herder said. "I'd been in the league four years, and it was the first time in my career the season ended before we went to the Super Bowl. I felt I had a sack on that play. It was the first time all day I wasn't double-teamed so I got some pressure on Stabler. As I lunged for his ankles and he and I both went down, I felt it was a sack. But I looked up and saw the ball being caught. That was the ballgame. I went from a feeling of victory to disbelief in a matter of two seconds."

Davis uses the word "cool" to describe the play. And it indeed still puts a chill over the men who covered him. Linebackers Larry Ball and Mike Kolen were bracketing Davis when Stabler threw the desperation pass into a tight window as he was being tackled. Kolen was in front, and Ball was behind Davis. "There was a little crack between Kolen and I," Ball said. "I was sure one of us would knock the ball down, but it went through that little crack right between us. It was just a sick feeling. It was an awful feeling that hung with you well past the time we got on the plane to come home. You carry it with you for several days or a couple of weeks."

After football, Ball enjoyed a fruitful 30-year career in the Miami-Dade public school system as a guidance counselor, department head, and football coach. But when strangers of a certain age speak to Ball, they often ask more about the Sea of Hands moment. "People mention it sometimes, and it comes up whenever Miami and Oakland are playing," he said. "Sometimes, it comes up during the playoffs. But it's not on my mind all the time, and I don't talk about it a lot. When you start talking about it again, it makes it that much worse."

29 *Monday Night Football vs. the '85 Bears*

The greatest regular-season victory in Miami Dolphins history happened on December 2, 1985. The Dolphins defeated the previously unbeaten Chicago Bears 38–24 in what was a spectacle of palpitation-inducing moments that put the sublime talents of Miami's legends on an enormous national stage. The game was perhaps Dan Marino's finest hour because the quarterback, who never won a Super Bowl, threw three touchdown passes and preserved the franchise's sole claim to a Perfect Season. And that's where this drama has to start nearly a dozen years before that night.

In January of 1973, the Dolphins defeated the Washington Redskins in Super Bowl VII to complete the NFL's only Perfect Season. And until that Monday night, no team had threatened that distinction as ferociously as the '85 Bears. Chicago entered the game leading the NFL in points scored and fewest allowed. Their average margin of victory was 19 points per game. The defense had given up no points in nine quarters, no touchdowns in 13 quarters, and just three touchdowns in the seven games prior to this one. The Bears were a physical, unyielding, thoroughly talented team that savaged opponents and their schedule.

And, oh yes, they came to the Orange Bowl with a 12–0 record and publicly stated their designs on going undefeated and actually surpassing the 17–0 Dolphins' achievements by going 19–0. "They're the best team in football," Marino said before the game. "And they think they might be up there up among the greatest teams ever."

The idea that the Dolphins, a Super Bowl team the season before, and Marino, who had thrown 48 touchdown passes the season before, might challenge the Bears and uphold Miami's distinction electrified South Florida. And so three hours before the game even began, the energy in the Orange Bowl was already palpable. Dozens of members of the '72 Dolphins soon arrived, and they were on the sideline and field motivating and imploring the current team to safeguard their accomplishment. "In the locker room before the game," Don Shula said, "I told our players, 'The important thing is what happens here and now, but there's a lot of Dolphin history on the line, things that are important to the coaching staff and to the organization.' I would never ask them to win one for the Gipper, but I wanted them to know what was at stake."

The previous season the Dolphins had roared out to a 11–0 start, seemingly on course for a Perfect Season themselves. And this says how much those '72 guys felt protective of their undefeated mark: on that sideline before the Bears game, Larry Csonka said, "That wasn't so bad. But when I was a little kid, I didn't want to share my favorite toy even with my own brother."

Against that backdrop the Orange Bowl was packed an hour before kickoff. The Dolphins sold 75,594 tickets for the game, and 75,594 people were in the venerable stadium's old bleacher seats that night. Not one ticket went unused, according to the NFL. This game had the feel of a heavyweight fight between two champions. It was the most watched ever on *Monday Night Football* and remains so to this day. ABC estimated more than 70 million people watched all or part of the contest. Nearly one-third of U.S. homes with a television tuned in.

And then the fireworks began. The first time the Dolphins had the football, they scored on a 33-yard pass from Marino to Nat Moore. That drive immediately displayed Shula's genius and Marino's gifts. The Dolphins designed multiple rollouts for Marino. This combined with quick passes, utilizing Marino's quick release and taking advantage of Chicago's blitzes, seemingly confused the

Bears. Sometimes the quarterback took a short drop, throwing to receivers slanting across the middle before the Bears could get to him. Other times he escaped the rush by rolling out while pocket protection floated with him. "Anytime you let Marino get outside," said Bears middle linebacker Mike Singletary, "I don't care who his receivers are. They're going to have time to get open. And that's what happened."

That's not all that happened. Before the game Chicago defensive coordinator Buddy Ryan put William "Refrigerator" Perry on the nose in his 46 Defense, hoping to foul up the Miami blocking scheme. Because Dan Hampton ordinarily played on the nose and the Dolphins ordinarily double-teamed the nose man, Ryan expected the Dolphins to double-team Perry and leave Hampton one-on-one against guard Roy Foster. But the Dolphins put the responsibility of blocking the nose tackle solely on center Dwight Stephenson. And despite playing with basically one arm because he had a sprained shoulder, Stephenson dominated Perry and allowed Miami's other linemen to double Hampton. "Stephenson taught Perry some lessons," Bears coach Mike Ditka said.

"He dogged me," lamented Perry, who was so thoroughly dominated he was benched.

That matchup gave the Dolphins a chance to feature the moving pocket. And while Dolphins fans today mostly remember Marino as an immobile pocket passer fighting the ravages of countless leg injuries, Marino circa 1985 could move and evade rushers adeptly. It was, well, beautiful. The Dolphins pressed their advantage by utilizing wide receivers Mark Duper, Mark Clayton, and Moore, who shared all 14 of Marino's completions. The Bears couldn't match up and often found themselves covering Moore with linebacker Wilber Marshall. (Yeah, more Shula genius.)

In converting four third-and-long plays during the first half, Marino threw for 130 yards. When he needed 18 yards, he received time afforded by the moving pocket and connected with Duper for 30. When he needed 19, he hit Moore for 22. When he needed 13, he then found Duper for 52. When he needed seven, he hit Clayton for 26.

Miami's offense had five possessions in the first half and scored all five times. The Dolphins led 31–10 at halftime. "We played a perfect or near-perfect first half," Shula said, "as good as I've been associated with."

It's easy to forget that while the Miami offense was on fire, the defense also had fine moments, especially in the second half. The unit was ranked 26th in the NFL before the game but collected six sacks and four turnovers. Steve Fuller was constantly hounded and eventually hobbled off on a damaged ankle. After having missed three games because of a sore shoulder, Jim McMahon took over at quarterback. There was anxiety in the crowd when McMahon came in because he was an inspirational leader for the Bears, and the Chicago sideline seemed lifted by the quarterback switch. But McMahon completed just 3-of-6 passes for 42 yards with two sacks and didn't get the Bears on the board at all.

As time ticked off the Orange Bowl's worn scoreboard, players from the '72 team and the '85 team mingled on the Miami sideline. "That was something," Shula said. "Seeing Kooch [Bob Kuechenberg] worried and having Zonk hitting you on the shoulder."

In the Bears locker room, Walter Payton was frantically searching for the fur coat he'd brought to wear—yeah, in Miami. Before he left he said, "We'll go 15–1."

The prediction was indicative of the '85 Bears. Confident. Brash. Even arrogant. But no one suggested what happened that night was a fluke. It was instead a comeuppance for a team that thought itself unbeatable. "We could play them a thousand times and not beat them," Ditka said. "Their field position was excellent; ours was lousy. They executed; we didn't. We had no chance."

Years later, when he was voted into the Pro Football Hall of Fame on the first ballot, the owner of nearly a dozen significant passing records was asked what was his career's greatest achievement. "Had to be," Marino said, "beating the Bears on Monday night."

30 Visit the Orange Bowl

The Orange Bowl's west end, the closed end of a horshoe stadium the Miami Dolphins once called home, was literally shaking on its foundation, and Ron Jaworski was rattled. This October 1981 game between the Philadelphia Eagles and Dolphins was tied at 10 in its final five minutes, and the shirtsleeve crowd has just figured out that it was in the head of the quarterback who won the NFC Championship Game a season ago.

So Jaworski went to the line of scrimmage, and the noise multiplied. Jaworski backed away and waved his team back to the huddle. And when the Philadelphia offense eventually lined up again, the crowd lit up again, sending echoes throughout the stadium and into the surrounding Little Havana neighborhood. Five times Jaworski and the Eagles lined up but refused to run a play because it was too darn noisy. And then the officials became involved. They conferred with Eagles head coach Dick Vermeil, who seemed sympathetic, and Don Shula, who seemed much less so. "He finally said, 'Run the play, Ron, or we'll never get out of here,'" Jaworski recalled years later.

Jaworski snapped the ball amid the bedlam and promptly threw an interception to Lyle Blackwood. The Dolphins took possession, drove all of nine yards, and kicked a game-winning field goal. "It's the night our fans found out they could be part of the game," Shula said. "After that fan noise became more prevalent around the NFL. After that our place was one of the loudest in the league."

The Dolphins' place was the Orange Bowl. It was a dump. The bathrooms featured tubs into which dozens of men, casually standing side by side, relieved themselves en masse. The concessions featured hot dogs and hamburgers and not much else. The press box rocked when the crowd roared. Many seats came with obstructed views. Every seat for a long time was an uncomfortable steel bleacher. There were zero luxury suites. It was awesome!

This run-down, archaic place always felt old. It often felt dirty. But it also felt bathed in history. Joe Auer returned the first kickoff in franchise history for a touchdown here. Shula won his first home game as the new coach here. Dolphins seasons came and went in 1972, 1973, and 1974, and the team didn't lose a game here.

Fans waving white hankies was born here. Flipper jumping out of his tank was a touchdown celebration here. A.J. Duhe plodding in the rain and mud, sending the Dolphins to the Super Bowl, was a gorgeous day here. Dan Marino to Mark Duper became a thing here. Marino to Mark Clayton, too. That TV shot of the palm trees swaying in the open east end with Biscayne Bay in the distance was how people spent December and January here. The Dolphins defeated the previously undefeated Chicago Bears here. Black people and white people and Hispanic people sat together and cheered for people wearing aqua and orange here. The Dolphins won three AFC Championship Games here. They were an expansion franchise in 1966 and stayed for 21 years, but when the Dolphins moved, they had forged a 110–38–3 record (.738 winning percentage) here. Marino threw his 48th and final touchdown pass of his transcendent 1984 regular season here.

Five Super Bowls were played here, and multiple college football national titles were decided here. Roberto Duran, Alexis Arguello, and Aaron Pryor all fought for titles here—on the same night.

And the Miami Hurricanes won two of their national titles and enjoyed a 58-game home win streak here. But this stadium on any given Sunday was a cornucopia of confetti and balloons and police sirens and beer salesmen. It smelled of grilled meats on the stadium grounds and Cuban food from the surrounding neighborhood. The Orange Bowl spanned decades and filled memories.

We don't remember many of the losses any more—except one for sure. That came in May 2008 when the demolition team showed up to pound the venerable stadium into rubble. It took only 11 days to pulverize a structure that survived countless hurricanes and 71 years.

The Dolphins now play at Hard Rock Stadium. Marlins Park, the little attended home field for the Miami Marlins, now sits on the historic Orange Bowl site. Marlins Park is a nice, modern stadium that lacks history or nuance. But the east plaza features those bold orange letters that once proudly spelled out Miami Orange Bowl across the top deck of the old stadium, an acknowledging bow to great, great memories.

31 WoodStrock

Even in the early 1980s, the idea of letting two men share the most important position on the team—the quarterback position—was considered football apostasy. But that is exactly what Don Shula did with David Woodley and Don Strock. And, darn it, he had good reasons for using that South Florida timeshare. "Both of them contributed heavily to our success in very different ways," Shula said in 1982. "If they were similar in abilities, you could put it up for grabs and let the best man play. But their talents are so different that we might be better off just trying to utilize the talents of two people similar to what you do at a lot of other positions."

Yeah, go ahead…argue with the winningest NFL coach of all time. Besides, Shula had one more reason for using Woodley as the starter and then often letting Strock, the backup, relieve late in games if the Miami Dolphins needed a lift: "Woodley obviously has to work on his drop-back passing and reading coverages," Shula said. "Strock obviously has to work on evading the pass rush."

The early 1980s was a time of transition in Miami. The Anglo population was decreasing while Hispanics—most of them exiles from Cuba's communism—became the majority. The southern tip of Miami Beach started to experience a revitalization that would soon boom into, well, South Beach. And the Dolphins were between Hall of Fame quarterbacks.

Bob Griese, who helped the team to three Super Bowls, retired after a 1980 season, in which he'd lost his starting job. Dan Marino was still three seasons in the future. So 1981 and '82 was a time for a little improvisation. Hence the deployment of WoodStrock. "It caused some problems for the defenses because they had to prepare for two different styles of offense," Strock said years later while he served as head coach at Florida International University. "David and I understood what Shula was going to do, and the combination was successful. When you have success, it's hard to beef about it."

Woodley was a public figure who loved his privacy. "He was very introverted," teammate Joe Rose said. Strock was and remains more gregarious and embracing of his status in the community. "Look, you're talking about a guy who came in as a rookie and made Griese comfortable about being his backup," offensive line coach John Sandusky said of Strock. "You ever try to be friendly with Bob Griese? Not easy. And when Marino came along, a guy he instantly felt close to was Strock. That's a gift."

Neither player was really expected to start when they were drafted. Strock was selected in the fifth round of the '73 draft and

Woodley in the eighth round of 1980. But in 1980 both got the chance, and Woodley won the job. "David was a special individual and an exciting guy to coach," Shula said. "What I enjoyed about coaching David was when you have an athlete like that playing quarterback, you could design special things for him. We won a lot of games with David at quarterback."

That's true. The 1981 Dolphins won the AFC East with an 11–4–1 record before losing that classic overtime playoff game to the San Diego Chargers. Strock made five relief appearances in 1981 and added another relief appearance against the Chargers. In fact, Strock actually had the Dolphins ahead in the fourth quarter of that loss to San Diego. That game has become an "I was there" moment in team history. "There were at least 250,000 people at that game," Strock joked, "even though the Orange Bowl only held 75,000."

The '82 Dolphins finished second in the AFC during a strike-shortened season; beat the New England Patriots, Chargers, and the New York Jets in the playoffs; and then bowed to the Washington Redskins in Super Bowl XVII. "We were that close to saying we were the best in the world," Woodley told the *Miami Herald* in 1987. "We didn't win, but it's not too bad a memory to have."

The 1983 draft signaled the virtual end of WoodStrock. The Dolphins picked Dan Marino in the first round, and although Woodley opened the season as the starter and Strock as the backup, Marino was a freight train coming, and everyone needed to clear the tracks. Marino started the sixth game of the '83 season against the Buffalo Bills, and the Dolphins were 9–2 in his 11 regular-season starts. One of the NFL's finest backups behind Griese, Strock returned to that role behind Marino. Woodley was traded to the Pittsburgh Steelers after the season. "I know he went from one to three in a matter of a couple weeks," Strock told the *Miami Herald* in 2003. "That kind of demotion is pretty hard. Shula gave him an opportunity by trading him to Pittsburgh to continue his career.

After that I don't know what happened, but we all know how things ended up with No. 13."

Woodley was scheduled to be the Steelers' highest-paid player in 1986, but he called coach Chuck Noll days before training camp and said he was quitting—at age 27. He required a liver transplant in 1992 and died in 2003 of complications from kidney and liver failure. He was 44.

Strock still lives in South Florida and regularly attends Dolphins functions. He spoke to the *Herald* in 2004 when the Dolphins were juggling Jay Fiedler and A.J. Feeley at quarterback, and his take struck an ironic chord. "If you look around the league, you don't see anybody else doing it, do you?" he said. "I don't know how this is going to work out. I question it."

32 The End of the Shula Era

One day removed from a thorough beating at the hands of the Buffalo Bills and fresh out of a meeting with Wayne Huizenga, in which the Miami Dolphins owner told Don Shula changes must be made, Shula still envisioned the possibility of ending his career as a champion. Shula had just completed an unfulfilling 1995 season. "It was the toughest season I've ever had to deal with," Shula said.

And now he was at a crossroads because what he saw ahead and what he wanted to see were two different views of the future. Shula wanted to believe that with the right moves and by adding the right players that he might salvage a franchise that had been pretty good but was 22 years removed from Super Bowl. Shula hoped he still could get Dan Marino a diamond encrusted championship ring in 1996. With one year remaining on his contract, Shula dreamed he could make one more attempt at a season that ended with him riding the shoulders of his players off the field after winning one more Super Bowl. It obviously never happened.

Four days later Shula was out. A 33-year coaching career was snuffed out in the span of six days. So how did Shula so quickly go from dreaming of winning one more Super Bowl to retiring? Go back to Saturday, December 30 in Orchard Park, New York. The Dolphins, the sixth seed and a wild-card team, played the Buffalo Bills that day. And it was a disaster. The Bills took a 27–0 lead into the fourth quarter. They rushed for 341 yards, which was the second most rushing yards in NFL playoff history. Afterward, players openly talked of teammates quitting and coaches not knowing what to do. "We had a couple of guys out there giving everything they've got, flying around, playing hard," cornerback Troy Vincent said. "But we got guys who never showed up…Maybe some guys wanted to go home and start playing golf. They can do that now. I felt like some of my teammates let me down today."

Said defensive end Jeff Cross: "What they did strategically should have given us problems for about a quarter."

The enduring snapshot of this game is of Buffalo running back Thurman Thomas running for yet another first down as he went out of bounds along the Miami sideline, but having no way to slow down—because Miami defenders obviously didn't slow him down all day—he plowed into defensive coordinator Tom Olivadotti and knocked him over. "That was the best thing to happen to me all day," Olivadotti said after the game.

That moment put Olivadotti in the unenviable position as Miami's fall guy in both a literal and figurative sense. Because the next afternoon—a Sunday—when Huizenga met with Shula, the owner asked the coach to blow up his coaching staff, particularly on the defensive side and most particularly to fire Olivadotti. The Dolphins had lost 12 consecutive late-season games that were either in the playoffs or had playoff implications to the Bills. There was no progress being made. And Huizenga believed significant change was the only way to make it. The request was not a palatable one for Shula. With only one more year remaining on his contract, it would be nearly impossible for even the winningest coach in NFL history to hire top-notch assistants for what was essentially a one-year stay. But Shula did not rule out the attempt.

Huizenga wouldn't ask Shula to resign. He had too much respect for the coach to do that. But he knew Shula was now in an uncomfortable spot. And Huizenga, a tough-minded businessman who once sealed a contentious negotiation by grabbing his opponent by the balls and squeezing, had no qualms making some people uncomfortable.

Accustomed to winning Super Bowls, Miami fans had grown critical of Shula because he was routinely qualifying for the playoffs but not winning big in the postseason. Shula's new wife, Mary Anne, perhaps seeing the passing seasons and criticism wearing on Shula, advised her husband to retire. And yet football and Shula was an enduring love affair. And he wasn't sure he wanted to break it off after three decades.

A week earlier on December 22, Shula had said he intended to "coach and honor my contract" in 1996. The statement at the time put to rest questions about Shula's intentions. Then he told his players on December 31 before sending them off into the offseason that he would return. Three days later on Wednesday afternoon, he even sent word to the *Miami Herald* through spokesman Harvey Greene that "nothing has changed" regarding his status for 1996.

But amid those seemingly decisive words, Shula was wavering. He knew he'd have to refurbish his coaching staff and then his roster. And what was the end game anyway: a one-year shot that might not work out?

Huizenga didn't aggressively push Shula out. But the same man, who three years later talked Jimmy Johnson into staying when he wanted to leave and a decade later convinced Nick Saban to come to Miami when he really didn't want to, never tried to coax Shula to stay.

Huizenga instead greased the ground underneath the coach with an undisclosed financial inducement to leave and then slid him out the door. Huizenga made leaving easy and staying hard.

And Shula opted for the easy thing. "We're going to make this a happy day," Shula ordered at the press conference in which he announced he was stepping down. "I made this decision, and when you make a decision, then you do everything to make that decision work. This is the decision, and I'm not going to second-guess myself. I'm at peace with myself. I know there have been disgruntled fans. I'm aware of that. But I want to concentrate on the positive, not the negative."

33 Zach Thomas

Zach Thomas measured Shawn Jefferson as he closed on the New England Patriots receiver for yet another tackle. Jefferson had taken a handoff on a reverse and should have been looking downfield for headhunting linebackers, but his eyes were instead fixed on the football because he had already fumbled twice. And suddenly... *Kaboom!* Jefferson was motionless on the turf, and the ball was loose again. Thomas had raced seemingly out of nowhere, cracked Jefferson in the helmet, and was standing over the semi-conscious player savoring the collision. This was the first game of Thomas' professional career, and this play was the perfect statement for what was happening in 1996: Thomas had blindsided the NFL.

Like that tackle Thomas was a surprise to everyone in the summer of '96 when Jimmy Johnson began his first training camp as the Miami Dolphins coach. Johnson expected a good season. He had a veteran quarterback in Dan Marino and a young defense that also had its defensive quarterback of sorts in veteran middle linebacker Jack Del Rio. Then camp began. And the short, stocky rookie selected in the fifth round to play special teams was showing up on the practice tape. A lot. And then the Dolphins played their first preseason game, and that same rookie was playing, well, better than Del Rio.

The day after Miami's first preseason game, Johnson cut Del Rio. The veteran of 11 NFL seasons announced his retirement. Thomas, who is all of 5'11", had sent the accomplished Del Rio there. "The bottom line is that Zach Thomas was making plays," Johnson said. "He has quickness, he's an instinctive player, and he makes plays…Jack Del Rio would still be here and still be our starter were it not for the play of Zach Thomas. It was probably as difficult a cut as I've ever made. When you look at a professional, Jack Del Rio is everything you want from a player. He was giving me everything. But I've got to do what's right for this football team. Zach Thomas was making more plays."

Thomas, though, was not a prototypical player. He joked about being short and having no neck. And that's how the rest of the world saw him initially. Take the day early in camp when he found a new barber in Fort Lauderdale, Florida. His barber asked what Thomas did for a living.

"I play football," Thomas said.

"What high school you play for?" The barber asked.

"I'm not in high school anymore," Thomas said.

"You play for the Hurricanes?" The barber asked excitedly.

Thomas admitted he didn't exactly look the part of a starting NFL linebacker. But that was part of his charm. Thomas was different. Transparent. Humble. When Thomas made the team, he and teammate Larry Izzo rented an apartment 10 minutes from Miami's training facility. It featured Post-it notes and football posters for decor. "Gotta have a roommate," Thomas said. "Don't want to be shelling out a grand a month by yourself."

Similarly built, Izzo and Thomas soon were nicknamed Fred and Barney—of *The Flintstones* fame—by their teammates. "I guess 'cause we're short and stocky, and we hang around together," Thomas said. "I don't have much to say about it except that I'd rather be Barney because I always liked Betty better than Wilma."

Despite a promising future that we now know included seven Pro Bowls and five first-team All Pro selections, it wasn't until that '96 regular-season opener against New England that Thomas finally believed he had arrived. "We were singing the national anthem. It was the best feeling in the world," Thomas said. "I remember it like it was yesterday, playing the Patriots, Bill Parcells was on the other sideline, and it was a good win. Just knowing that I made it, it's all kind of like a fog to me now, but I enjoyed the whole ride."

34 The Mud Bowl

The fans stormed the field, which itself is appropriate after a game played mostly in a downpour. The grass that long ago turned into a mud pit was now a place for a carnivalesque, horn-blowing celebration. Some folks were frolicking in the mud like happy hogs. Some picked up Dolfan Denny on their shoulders and marched him around, kicking up slop with every triumphant step. How could such an ugly gray day have felt so perfectly uplifting? How could a decade filled with too much darkness have led to what everyone thinks is the new dawn for the franchise?

It was the afternoon of January 23, 1983, and the Miami Orange Bowl was the scene of what looked like a medieval Scottish festival—complete with a quagmire courtesy a cold, pounding rain. In a time when artificial turf and air-conditioned domes were coming into vogue, this game was primeval football at its finest. The Miami Dolphins defeated the New York Jets 14–0, and the Mud Bowl joined NFL lore.

The players wore mud over their uniforms. The fans wore plastic garbage bags as raincoats. Dolphins coach Don Shula stood at a podium after the game with dirt he picked up while hugging his players smeared all over his shirt. "Today was the greatest day ever," Shula declared.

This was the man who won a Super Bowl in guiding his team to *the* Perfect Season. But this was also the man whose franchise was finally emerging from the shadow of now distant consecutive Super Bowls and back into the limelight. The Dolphins didn't get to the playoffs in 1975. Or 1976. Or 1977. They missed the postseason again in 1980 and succumbed to the San Diego Chargers in that wonderful (terrible) overtime marathon in 1981.

But this victory in the AFC Championship Game meant the Dolphins were going back to the Super Bowl 10 years after their last Super Bowl win in 1974. "I'm starting to see in this team the beginnings of what made our 1970s Super Bowl teams great," defensive end Vern Den Herder said.

This was the time of the Killer Bs. But this game is mostly about a defensive player not part of that hive: A.J. Duhe. Though he had two interceptions in six seasons before this game, he intercepted three Richard Todd passes within 18 second-half minutes. Todd finished with five interceptions, and the Dolphins limited the Jets to a paltry 139 yards. Duhe's first interception led to a seven-play, 48-yard touchdown drive that ended with a seven-yard run by Woody Bennett, a former Jets player. Duhe then anticipated a screen pass, intercepted the pass, and cruised in from 35 yards out for a fourth-quarter score. That play was the lasting highlight of a victory that propelled the Dolphins into Super Bowl XVII. "That game meant so much to so many people," Duhe said. "Don't get me wrong. It meant a lot to me. It's crazy. It's easy for me to remember exciting plays. But fans remember it frame by frame."

As if watching an NFL Films replay, the play lives on. Duhe jumps, catches the pass behind the Jets line of scrimmage, bobbles it, grasps it again, and heads for the end zone. He holds the ball aloft as he crosses the goal line. "I was trying to get past [tackle] Marvin Powell to pressure Todd," Duhe said. "Then I saw [Bruce] Harper coming out of the backfield, so I decided to drop back. It was a poor play as a defensive end but intelligent for a linebacker."

Before the game Jets coach Walt Michaels complained to a sideline reporter that Shula ordered the field not be covered despite the threat of rain. That, Michaels suggested, slowed down the Jets' speedy offense. Yes, it rained, but Shula, who built a career around a cornerstone of integrity, denied any conspiracy.

The Jets that offseason forced Michaels to resign in favor of Joe Walton. With whispers of the Mud Bowl controversy still echoing in the New York press, the Dolphins and Jets met twice the next season. The combined score of those two Dolphins victories was 66–28. In the first of those two games, the Miami defense that intercepted Todd five times in the Mud Bowl intercepted him six times to win the road contest. It was clear and sunny.

35 The Kellen Winslow Game

It took four hours and three minutes to play. It featured nearly 14 minutes of overtime, an NFL-playoff record 79 combined points, and an NFL-playoff record 1,036 yards that led to 10 touchdowns and three field goals. At least 16 different players on both teams suffered some sort of cramps or spasms during this marathon game. More than that required liquids pumped intravenously to treat dehydration. It was the Epic in Miami. The San Diego Chargers defeated the Miami Dolphins 41–38 on that 79-degree evening of January 2, 1982. "A great game," a sweat-drenched Don Shula told reporters afterward. "Maybe the greatest ever."

Sports Illustrated called it "The game no one should have lost." And certainly it may have felt that way in the hours after it happened because so many of players were simply happy to survive. The enduring memory of this one is a picture of a totally spent Kellen Winslow being helped off the Orange Bowl field with one arm over the shoulders of tight end Eric Sievers and the other arm over the shoulders of offensive lineman Billy Shields. Winslow had delivered a performance for the ages, catching 13 passes for 166 yards with a touchdown and a blocked field goal that saved the game for San Diego in regulation. "I remember telling our guys: hit him harder, get him down," Shula said. "But he kept getting up and kept making plays."

"The Dolphins were determined to try to stop him," Dan Fouts told NFL Films. "The Dolphins did a good job, beating him up, trying to get him out of the game. They did get him out of the game for a short time because of different injuries and dehydration and everything."

Winslow being pushed down and repeatedly getting up is a metaphor for this game of peaks and valleys. Because what promised to be a close game between two division champions and between a team with an explosive offense and a team with a stingy defense, mostly resembled a blowout in the first quarter. Until the team whose hopes were strewn on the canvas got up.

The Chargers took a 24–0 lead in mostly on mistakes by Miami's special teams, and the game seemed to be a Miami embarrassment. But Shula moved to salvage the half if not the game when he benched David Woodley and inserted Don Strock at quarterback. And when Strock came in the game, the inept Dolphins exited, and the championship Dolphins emerged. "The truth is my first thoughts were: *I don't really want to go in this game. Why am I going in?*" Strock joked. "But seriously the Chargers had an average defense back then. So I knew we were going to throw the ball and have a chance to score some points. And I loved throwing the ball and scoring points."

Strock had started a game and had thrown 130 passes during the season. But the Chargers had not prepared for him. They'd prepared for Woodley's running and play-action looks. Strock brought a classic drop-back style to the game. In just more than 12 minutes and three possessions of the second quarter, Strock led the Dolphins to two touchdowns and a field goal. Miami suddenly was back in the game, trailing only 24–17 at halftime. But this wasn't just about the rally. It was that final touchdown before halftime that lit the night sky around the Orange Bowl.

Shula sent in the play—*86 Circle Pro Lateral*—with four seconds to play and the Dolphins sitting at the San Diego 40. The play had been in the Dolphins' playbook for years but had never been used. "We practice it every three weeks or so," said wide receiver Duriel Harris. "We hadn't worked on it this week. I was surprised when Strock came into the huddle and called it."

The play called for Harris to run a 15-yard curl coming back for the ball. Halfback Tony Nathan trailed him, and when Harris made the catch, he lateraled back to Nathan, who, of course, scored to complete the 40-yard play. "Hall of Fame!" NBC play-by-play man

Don Criqui exclaimed to the national audience as Nathan scored untouched. "Hall of Fame football play!"

"It was halftime. We're in the locker room—what—10, 15 minutes?" Strock said. "And the whole time we could hear the place roaring because of that play and how we came back."

The Dolphins rode their momentum to a 38–31 lead with only five minutes to play. And then on what seemed to be a drive that would be a dagger to heart of all San Diego, Andra Franklin fumbled on second down from the Chargers 21-yard line. The most remarkable comeback in NFL playoff history was first in jeopardy and then lost when the Chargers recovered and drove 82 yards for a tying touchdown. After the Chargers tied the game at 38, the Dolphins had 58 seconds to rally (again). And they did exactly that. Uwe Von Shamann got a chance to win it with four seconds remaining. But his potential game-winning kick was tipped at the line by Winslow. "It was the biggest thrill of my life," Winslow said.

Overtime. In that fateful fifth period, Chargers kicker Rolf Benirschke missed a 27-yard field that ruined San Diego's chance to end it. The kicker had never missed a game-winning field goal in his career, but this miss gave Miami new life. Minutes later Von Schamann had another chance to win it. This time it was with a 34-yard field goal, but that was also blocked. "That second block was hard to swallow," linebacker A.J. Duhe said. "You thought you were going to win it right there and didn't. That was a letdown, and we couldn't recover."

The Chargers eventually got the game-winner off Benirschke's foot when he drilled a 29-yard kick on the next possession. Players from both teams laid on the field. Some Miami players walked around in stunned silence. "My back, my hamstring, my calves all cramped up right after that kick," Winslow said. "I felt like I was going to die, but that game was just wonderful."

36 A Bolt of Lightning

Even in the twilight of his career, Don Shula clung to the hope of getting his hands on a football team that could win a Super Bowl. And for one afternoon in January of 1993, that team seemed to finally be in the coach's grasp. Unveiled before a national television audience and the second-largest crowd ever at Joe Robbie Stadium was a Miami Dolphins team with an explosive offense, a punishing defense, and opportunistic special teams working in unison to make postseason history. Again. Finally.

The team Shula thought worthy of sending him and quarterback Dan Marino back to the NFL's biggest game was only four quarters from stamping its ticket for that return. The Dolphins had pummeled and even punished the San Diego Chargers in a surprisingly convincing 31–0 playoff win. And that game had Shula and South Florida thinking that maybe, just maybe, glory days were back again. "I take a lot of satisfaction in our team being where it is," Shula said. "There are only four left, four pretty good football teams, and I take a lot of pride in being one of them. But I don't want it to end here. I want to be one of those two." Then Shula held out two fingers before slowly folding one back and saying, "And then…No. 1."

Why not? The Dolphins were mere hours from the most lopsided playoff win in the team's fabled history and the biggest playoff defeat ever for the Chargers. Miami's offense, which had failed to score 20 points in five of its final six regular-season games, unlocked its handcuffs and delivered a 21-point second quarter. The defense caused five turnovers on four interceptions and a fumble recovery and never allowed the Chargers inside Miami's 40-yard in 15 possessions. "We dominated," Shula said, grasping for words that could best describe the whipping.

The 21 points the Dolphins scored in the second quarter set a team playoff record at the time. All of the scores came via Marino throwing touchdown passes of 30 and nine yards to Keith Jackson and one yard to Tony Paige. All those scores followed San Diego turnovers.

"We felt like all season long, especially when we hit a couple of slumps, that the defense was pretty much pulling the offense along," safety Louis Oliver said. "We just kept telling ourselves that once they get it going, we'd be tough to stop. Well, you saw what happened out there today. Dan [Marino] and those guys dissected them like surgeons."

And what was so pleasing to Shula was that his team, an intriguing mix of veterans and youngsters, got big plays from both. Rookie cornerback Troy Vincent had two interceptions in what was his finest game of the season. Second-year linebacker Bryan Cox also had an interception. Third-year left tackle Richmond Webb faced Leslie O'Neal one-on-one the entire game and he limited the Chargers' defensive end, who'd collected 17 sacks that season, to only two tackles, and neither of them were sacks. "San Diego has a great defense and they hit people," Marino said, "but they didn't get to me at all today."

Jackson, who had joined the team in September as one of the NFL's first unrestricted free agents, suddenly looked like Marino's favorite target on those two touchdown catches. It was a wonderful balance that showed up in a stat book. Miami rushed for 157 yards and passed for 167 yards while the defense delivered the franchise's first playoff shutout in a decade and only the third in team history. "The young players forgot everything they'd ever heard about being nervous in big games and just played at another level," Jackson said. "I guess nobody informed them they were supposed to feel some butterflies."

But Vincent did feel sick for three days before the game. He battled some sort of stomach ailment that prevented him from eating anything other than one chicken sandwich the night before the game. He was still so dehydrated on gameday that he required an IV at halftime.

And still he had those two interceptions that signaled to everyone the first-round pick the Dolphins invested on him months before was money well spent. "Troy played a whale of a game, and it makes you feel good as a coach that a young player like that can overcome some adversity leading up to the game and respond like he did on such a big stage," Shula said. "He played great. There's no question."

In the weeks before this game, the narrative circulating around some NFL circles was that the game had passed Shula by. There was talk the coach could not win in the postseason since defensive coordinator Bill Arnsparger left Miami after the 1983 season. And Arnsparger, ironically, was now San Diego's defensive coordinator. "That was just a ridiculous accusation," Arnsparger said. "People were knocking Don unjustifiably this year. He's as astute a football coach now as he ever was. As usual, he prepared his team very well for us. I know this may sound ridiculous, considering Don's accomplishments, but he really doesn't get the credit he deserves."

After the game Arnsparger made his way to the Miami locker room to congratulate Shula and offensive line coach John Sandusky and others. Though the Dolphins would actually succumb to their AFC East rival, the Buffalo Bills, in the AFC Championship Game, Arnsparger wished them luck the rest of the way. "They've got a fine team," he said. "They look like the team Don has wanted for a long time."

37 Super Bowl XVII

In a perfect world where the Perfect Season franchise wins all its games, the enduring snapshot of Super Bowl XVII could be that routine 21-yard pass David Woodley throws to a virtually uncovered Jimmy Cefalo that the receiver turns into a stirring 76-yard touchdown in the first quarter. Or perhaps the memory that would speak loudest is Fulton Walker's 98-yard kickoff return, in which the Washington Redskins kickoff team parts like the Red Sea as Walker rockets through the opening to take back the lead and momentum before halftime. That's how the Miami Dolphins' first Super Bowl appearance of the 1980s *should* be remembered.

But there's that pesky reality thing that separated Don Shula and the Dolphins from continuing their Super Bowl dominance a decade after they first burst onto the championship scene. Super Bowl 17 (for those who can't stand Roman numerals) in Pasadena, California, was instead a highlight reel of Redskins moments that raised Joe Theismann and John Riggins and the Hogs to prominence. And rather than being a watershed moment for the Dolphins, it was instead the moment Shula understood he needed great quarterback play to win another Super Bowl. "It could have been a great story," Shula said, following the 27–17 loss on January 30, 1983. "But now it will only be on the Redskins. I realize better than anyone else that after a Super Bowl they're only going to be talking about one team, and it won't be the Dolphins. We had a fine season and we have to turn this loss into a learning experience, which is the only positive thing I can possibly say about it."

Any other positives Shula could think of were lost in a horrible second half during which the Redskins dominated by scoring 17 unanswered points as the Dolphins were shut out. Woodley did not complete a single pass out of the eight he threw in that deciding half, and the Dolphins managed only 34 yards of offense and only two first downs. The young quarterback was all of 12 years old when Miami drafted Theismann out of Notre Dame in 1971. And although Theismann never played for Miami because he bolted for the Canadian Football League, he definitely left marks in team history that day. The first mark was in striking a vivid contrast to Woodley.

While Theismann moved the Redskins with consistency, Miami's quarterback completed a dismal four passes out of 14 all game for a total of 97 yards. The Dolphins did not lose because of Woodley, but they had no chance to win with him. "Woodley hung the ball out there for Cefalo a little too long at the end of the third quarter, and Mark Murphy makes the interception," Shula said. "So we try to get our running attack going and can't do it, and they're making the big plays against our pass attack, too. We went deep a lot because I thought we could throw long with them crowding us the way they were. It just didn't click. We just go three and out, three and out, three and out."

The performance left Woodley a marked man because it was the second consecutive postseason he finished as a benched and ineffective starter. The next spring—when Dan Marino fell to the No. 27 overall pick where the Dolphins were slotted—the selection was equal parts brilliance and necessity for Shula. "After it was over, it was just such an empty feeling for me," Woodley told the *Miami Herald*. "You get so up for a game like that, and afterward there's a void where the feelings were."

Few remember Shula actually benched Woodley in this Super Bowl. He brought in Don Strock, as he had multiple times before, hoping the reliever would rescue the situation. But Strock had no significant opportunity because the Redskins owned time of possession in the second half. "We like to play ball control," Shula said. "We got ball control—in reverse."

And that brings up the actual moments everyone recalls from this game. Both involve the Redskins offense. And the Dolphins defense. And the Redskins getting the better of the situation both times. The first moment came with the Redskins on their own 18-yard line with two minutes remaining in the third quarter. Theismann attempted a first-down pass, and Dolphins lineman Kim Bokamper batted the pass in the air. And as it floated there for a moment, it seemed as if Bokamper would catch the ball and possibly score. At the very least, it seemed like it would give Miami the ball inside Washington's 10-yard line with a chance to build on 17–13 lead late in the third quarter.

But just as the 6'6" Bokamper got his hands on the football, the 6' Theismann knocked it out of his grasp and to the ground. A photo of the play was all over the Los Angeles newspapers the next day. Theismann completed 15-of-23 passes for 143 yards and two touchdowns, but the most important play he made was his tip of the seemingly no doubt Bokamper interception. "I guess I'm a better defensive back than quarterback," he said.

"As soon as I saw it up in the air after I blocked it, I thought, *All right. Touchdown*," Bokamper told the *Herald* the next day. "Then Theismann came, and I couldn't believe it. I didn't even see him coming and I don't know how he got there. He made a hell of a play. He saved the game for them."

Riggins won the game for them. Washington's befuddling and simultaneous array of pre-snap motion helped Riggins seem like a sledgehammer coming out of a NASA science experiment. "We didn't do too much original," Theismann said. "We went John left, John left, John left, and threw in John right occasionally. But with all the motion we show defenses, there's a lot of confusion before we hit them with something so simple."

Riggins rushed for a then-Super Bowl record 166 yards. He busted a 43-yard touchdown run for a 20–17 lead in the fourth quarter. The picture of him running over Dolphins cornerback Don

McNeal, the last defender on that fourth-down play, is iconic everywhere except in South Florida—and perhaps Dallas. "I'd be calling out changes. Then they would [motion], and I'd try to call those, and they'd snap the ball," linebacker A.J. Duhe said. "In that fourth quarter, we were on the field so long. And when they can get the ball to Riggins that much, something has to give."

The 1982 Dolphins were a fun team that South Florida embraced. And Shula told his players he was proud of their accomplishments. But in classic Shula form, winning was always respected. So when Miami held a ticker tape parade days after the Super Bowl, the coach ordered the few players who had returned to town to stay away. Shula unapologetically explained to the crowd that "ticker tape is for champions."

38 Bob Kuechenberg: Greatest Hall of Famer Not in the Hall of Fame

It's fair to say Bob Kuechenberg was an acquired taste even for Miami Dolphins fans.

He didn't appreciate Dan Marino very much and didn't mind saying so. "Eventually after two, three, or four years, defenses learned how to stop him," Kuechenberg said of the legendary Dolphins quarterback. "Force him to throw short and take away the deep stuff. After that he wasn't patient enough. It made him like any other quarterback. Eventually he'd make a mistake."

When first-round draft pick Ted Ginn was struggling to catch the football, which was—after all his job—Kuechenberg minced no words. "He's an embarrassment and a coward," Kuechenberg growled. "Guy's got alligator arms."

Kuechenberg was a straight shooter who often had his own franchise in his sights. It made some folks cringe. But that never changed the fact that the man was one of the best offensive linemen ever to play in the National Football League. "This man has been a superstar and a Hall of Famer for a long time already," his former coach Howard Schnellenberger told the *Miami Herald* in 2003.

Kooch, as Don Shula called him, came to the Dolphins in 1970 after being discarded by the Philadelphia Eagles and Atlanta Falcons, two teams nearly hopeless themselves at the time. He stayed through the 1984 season by becoming—in the words of Hall of Fame quarterback Fran Tarkenton—"not just the best guard in football but the best who ever played the game."

Kuechenberg, however, is not in the Hall of Fame. It doesn't have to do with whether he deserves it. He does. But voting politics and a million other things have kept him out, making him possibly the greatest Hall of Famer who isn't actually in the Pro Football Hall of Fame.

Sounds like an opinion, doesn't it? Well, of course it is. Opinions are what made Kooch interesting.

But this opinion is backed up by irrefutable facts. Consider: Kuechenberg was a six-time Pro Bowl player, which is a lot but is surpassed by the eight times he was a finalist for the Pro Football Hall of Fame. Kuechenberg was a finalist each year from 2002 to 2009, putting him in the same company with 14 others selected as a Hall of Fame finalists eight or more times. Kuechenberg, however, is the only one of that illustrious group not in the Hall of Fame. He played in 215 games, including 19 in the postseason. He played 14 seasons. And in all that time and over approximately 14,000 snaps, he was flagged for holding 15 times.

In 1972 fullback Larry Csonka gained 1,117 yards, and halfback Mercury Morris gained 1,000 yards. That made them the first pair of running backs in the same backfield to gain 1,000 yards. "Bob was my roommate for 10 years. He was like a brother," Hall of Fame center Jim Langer told the *Miami Herald* in 2019. "You always hear about what kind of man you want to have next to you in the foxhole, and it was Kooch. [Offensive line coach] Monte [Clark], Larry Little, the whole offensive line, we were all pretty intense guys. There was no one more intense on what that team was about than Kooch."

He played mostly as a left guard during his career, but Kuechenberg also started at left tackle for much of 1978 and all of 1979 despite being undersized for the position at 6'2", 253 pounds. He was so proficient at both positions in 1978 that he was named All-Pro as a guard by the Associated Press and *The Sporting News* and All-Pro as a tackle by *Pro Football Weekly*. "It was about the most unselfish thing I've ever seen," Shula said. "I asked him to go to tackle after he made the Pro Bowl six times as a guard. His answer was, 'Coach, if that's what you need.'"

Kuechenberg broke his left arm on a kickoff (yeah, he played special teams, too) in the penultimate game of the 1973 regular season. After drilling out bone marrow to insert a 10-inch alloy rod and wrapping the arm in a plaster cast to stabilize it, doctors told Kuechenberg he was out for the rest of the year. After missing the last regular-season game, Kooch was back in the lineup for the playoffs.

Playing with that broken arm, Kuechenberg dominated Minnesota Vikings defensive tackle Alan Page, that season's Defensive Player of the Year, in Super Bowl VIII. Page had one tackle in the game. "We were going where Alan Page wasn't," Csonka said. "Bob was taking Page the way he wanted him to go, and then we were running opposite that. And the result was that I was coming through the line unscathed."

Kuechenberg called it a career after the 1983 season. He had played in four Super Bowls. He had filled his resume with excellence. And what did this outspoken man do as he went off into retirement after a stellar career? He contemplated his service by complimenting the men he played next to over his 14 seasons. "I played inside the best," he said with satisfaction. "Langer and Dwight Stephenson on my right, maybe the two greatest centers in football history. And two good 79s on my left, Wayne Moore and Jon Giesler. It was great, just great."

39 Super Bowl XIX

The Miami Dolphins were a confident bunch on Super Bowl eve in January 1985. They had shredded opponents and the record books in crafting a 16–2 record and felt they had advantages over the NFC champion San Francisco 49ers because, well, Don Shula had won more Super Bowls than Bill Walsh, and Dan Marino had thrown more touchdowns than God. "I slept like a baby the night before that game," special teams and linebacker coach Bob Matheson said. "I had some experience dealing with Super Bowl games as a player and I felt we were well-prepared and had a nearly unstoppable offense. I wasn't worried at all."

Complete with a creepy *Hounds of the Baskerville*-type fog that encompassed Stanford Stadium that January 20th, Matheson's good night of rest turned into a nightmare for the Dolphins the next afternoon. The Dolphins lost the game 38–16, and it really didn't feel as close as the score. How could this happen? How could a team that set or tied 27 NFL or team records in the season go out in a whimper?

Well, it didn't look like that initially. The Dolphins actually led 10–7 in the first quarter after Marino completed 9-of-10 passes for 103 yards. His only incompletion came from a pass that was tipped at the line. The Dolphins marched down the field for their touchdown using a no-huddle attack that caught the 49ers in their base defense. But that was it. Miami's championship hopes would soon unravel as the 49ers scored 21 points in the second quarter.

Bill Walsh attacked Miami's inside linebackers, particularly rookie Jay Brophy. But it wasn't inexperience that made Brophy a bad matchup against San Francisco's running backs, particularly Roger Craig. "We were just too slow," defensive coordinator Chuck Studley said. "Brophy and Mark Brown were primarily run stoppers. They were good at that. But those guys have pass coverage responsibilities, too. And that day it was not good."

The Dolphins missed Bill Arnsparger that day. Arnsparger was the architect of the No-Name Defense and then the Killer Bs in 1982. He had left before the '84 season to become the head coach at Louisiana State. Joe Montana directed only seven of his 24 completions to wide receivers. All the others were to backs or tight end Russ Francis. Craig caught eight passes for 82 yards in Super Bowl XIX. It was triumph of tactics for the San Francisco coaching staff. Walsh outcoached Shula. Studley didn't adjust. "The fog also spread like virus through the Dolphin coaching brain trust," *Miami Herald* columnist Edwin Pope wrote.

On defense the 49ers went onto the field with six defensive backs to cover the secondary, four down linemen to pressure Marino, and only one linebacker—Keena Turner. Marino and the Miami offense had burned defenses that tried single coverage with the Dolphins receivers on the outside that year. One-on-one was almost always a bad idea against either Mark Clayton or Mark Duper. "When we get single coverage on the outside," Marino said, "we're going to win those matchups most of the time.

So Walsh decided not to repeat what had already failed in a season, in which Marino threw for an NFL record 5,084 yards. The Dolphins then failed to run the ball with any effectiveness against only five players in the tackle box. They gained 25 rushing yards that day. San Francisco had 211. And then there was this: Marino, a maestro throughout the season, was struggling to merely play chopsticks. Easy passes he usually completed were either behind receivers or often too low. He completed only one of six passes the first 13 minutes of the second quarter, providing no answer while the 49ers riddled the Miami defense with 21 points. "I made some bad throws," Marino said. "And they dictated some things to us, playing five, six, and seven defensive backs."

Marino was sacked only 13 times in 16 regular-season games and not at all in the postseason before Super Bowl XIX. He was sacked four times by San Francisco. But for all of the great strategy the 49ers employed on defense, it was their offense that carried the day. When it was over, the 537 yards the 49ers gained was the most ever in a Super Bowl. Montana's 331 passing yards were also the most ever in a Super Bowl.

Marino was the NFL MVP in 1984. Montana was the Super Bowl MVP. As the NFL Films historical retelling of the game said, "Dan Marino's year turned into Joe Montana's day."

Afterward, Marino and Montana filmed a commercial for Diet Pepsi. Marino congratulated Montana for a draw play in the second quarter. Montana offered to buy Marino a beverage. "That's the least you can do," Marino said smiling.

Marino took a swig and, as Montana was leaving, said, "Joe, next year, I'm buying."

Instead it was the last time Marino, Shula, or the Dolphins played in a Super Bowl. "We just believed we would have more opportunities to go back and play for a championship," Marino said. "That was only my second year in the league so many of us thought it would be like that for a long time. Maybe we didn't have enough respect for how hard it was to even reach the Super Bowl."

40 The Wildcat

His team has just been dealt its second loss in as many games to open the 2008 season, and this one was an embarrassing 31–10 blowout. Knowing his plan for starting the season and his head-coaching career was already in shambles, Tony Sparano was desperate. And out of that desperation came a season-saving notion: the Wildcat.

So on a dimly lit charter flight from Arizona to South Florida, Sparano called on quarterback coach David Lee to save him. To save the Miami Dolphins. To save the season. "I brought him up to the front of that plane," Sparano said in October of 2008. "We just chatted a little bit."

Sparano asked Lee to draw up the details with offensive coordinator Dan Henning for implementing an old-school set of offensive plays that looked something like the winged T but was actually much more refined. Lee used the formation previously while he was the offensive coordinator at the University of Arkansas and months earlier had suggested their implementation to Sparano.

The Dolphins were about to throw a Hail Mary by turning to the Wildcat. Two days later, when players arrived for the first practice of the week on Wednesday, Lee presented the plays to the offense. "He was talking about it, explaining it, and then he was like, 'So, who wants to be the one to handle the ball?'" Ronnie Brown, a running back, said.

Brown had never taken a center snap. Not in high school. Not at Auburn University. But he looked around the hushed room and decided to break the silence by responding, "I will."

"Thinking about it, most guys when they're playing around, they want to be the quarterback," Brown said. "To actually have a chance to do it in the NFL, I'll do it. I'll volunteer for it."

The Wildcat package born of genius and desperation had its trigger man. But it didn't have the team's confidence. "I saw what we were doing in practice that week," linebacker Joey Porter said, "and I'm thinking, *Really? Have things gotten this bad? This is what we've come to?*"

The Dolphins went into their next game, which was on the road against the mighty New England Patriots, with four Wildcat plays. One of those was a pass designed to go from Brown to tight end Anthony Fasano. And the plan came with a caveat. "We were going to run it, and if it didn't work the first time we tried it, we were going to shelve it," Sparano confided.

It worked the first time. And the second time. And several other times. The Dolphins ran plays out of the Wildcat formation six times and gained 119 yards against the Patriots. They scored four touchdowns using the Wildcat that afternoon. The team that once deciphered Dan Marino's audibles in a playoff game was stumped. Coach Bill Belichick huddled his bedeviled defenders around the bench and frantically drew assignments to no avail. "I saw the highlights of that," Sparano said in a private moment later that week. "It made me smile at little bit."

Brown scored four touchdowns, three of which came on Wildcat direct snaps, including a 62-yard run. He also threw the planned Wildcat pass to Fasano for a 19-yard touchdown. It was awesome! "What is that play called?" A reporter asked Ricky Williams afterward.

"It's called the Wildcat," Williams said.

Using the momentum of the Wildcat package and perhaps benefitting from New England's confusion on defense, the other 51 plays the Dolphins ran gained 342 yards.

"I don't like to think it's a trick play," Williams, said. "I don't look at it as razzle-dazzle."

Indeed, the Wildcat was far from trickery. It was mostly about physicality. The beauty of the package was that it supplied the offense with as many or one more blocker than the defense could account for. And the man taking the snap was a running back rather than a pass-oriented quarterback. "We outnumber the defense in the box," Brown said. "It's really that simple."

The morning after the Dolphins upset New England, coach Houston Nutt's phone began ringing in his University of Mississippi office. Nutt was previously the head coach at Arkansas, and Lee was his offensive coordinator. NFL men with questions about how to implement or stop the Wildcat package were on the line. Nutt took some of those calls but immediately called the Dolphins to warn them. "He and David Lee are very close, and Houston said, 'Understand we're rooting for the Dolphins. We're not going to give away any of this information to anybody else,'" Henning said. 'I said, '*Riiight.*' There's only one way you can keep a secret between three people; you've got to kill two of them."

The Dolphins actually lost two of their next three games after that first Wildcat game. But they kept the package and even refined it. And it helped the team win 10 of its final 11 games and the AFC East in 2008. "The whole reason for this was just to give our players something that they can kind of put their arms around and think that, *This is our deal. This is going to give us an advantage one way or the other,*" Sparano said. "It's not a short-term fix. It's something that, as I've said, we have several other pieces to this puzzle if we want. We may not use them and we may use them. It just depends on what we see and how we do it."

41 The Fake Spike

Mark Ingram was correctly thinking his days with the Miami Dolphins were practically over in late November of 1994. He was right to worry. Because after starting the season's first eight games with modest results, Ingram lost his job to O.J. McDuffie in game nine, walked off the team the next day to protest, and was inactive the next week against the Pittsburgh Steelers.

Ingram was a big free-agent addition the year before and a Super Bowl hero for the New York Giants before that. But the man, who often quoted scriptures, had fallen from grace with the Dolphins. "Times like I've had recently will get to a man if you let it," Ingram said. "You keep your faith in God, you keep praying, and let that help carry you through."

A possible answer from heaven? The Fake Spike.

Some people call this the "Clock Play" because that was the call in Miami's 1994 playbook. And it is iconic because it not only lives in Dolphins lore, but is also part of New York Jets infamy, which everybody outside of New York loves.

The two teams were locked in battle for first place at the time. Miami's 7–4 record led the AFC East, and New York was 6–5 and one game back. The Dolphins, however, were reeling because they'd lost two consecutive games and now trailed the Jets 17–0 at the Meadowlands.

Eventually, the Dolphins climbed back into the game and trailed 24–21 with 2:34 to play. They got the ball at their own 16, following an interception, and drove 76 yards in seven plays for a possible tying field goal or go-ahead touchdown.

After a completion to the Jets 8-yard line and only 38 seconds left, the Miami offense hurried to the line of scrimmage. "Clock!" Dan Marino yelled pointing to the turf, "Clock!"

The Jets understood that meant Marino was going to spike the football. Fans around the world understood the same thing. "He tried to make it seem like that," Jets cornerback Aaron Glenn said. "I thought he was spiking the ball."

Except before that season began, backup quarterback Bernie Kosar brought the fake spike play to Miami from his days with the Cleveland Browns. And when Marino was running (or more accurately jogging) to the 8-yard line just before the fateful play, Kosar suggested it to Marino over his radio headset. At the line of scrimmage, Marino saw Ingram get one-on-one coverage against Glenn on the outside and he nodded to the wide receiver. Ingram took off at the snap and got open. After taking the snap from under center, Marino didn't spike the ball as expected. He threw the game-winning touchdown pass to Ingram instead. Miami prevailed 28–24.

The Dolphins didn't have much use for the quarterback sneak during the time Marino was their quarterback. But this play proved they had a sneaky quarterback. They had Marino, who had appeared in a movie and several television commercials. "I am," he said the day after the victory, "an accomplished actor."

The Dolphins had tried "Clock" against the Minnesota Vikings two months earlier in a 38–35 loss. One Miami lineman didn't block, and a Vikings defensive tackle broke through, forcing Marino to throw the ball away. The Jets provided no such pressure. Their defensive linemen barely got out of their stances. "One of them was yelling at the refs, 'Hey, they called 'clock!' Where's the flag? Where's the flag?'" Dolphins offensive lineman Jeff Dellenbach told the *Miami Herald*. "Like if we called it, we had to do it."

Glenn, ironically, was perhaps the lone New York defender not completely fooled by the Fake Spike. He actually ran with Ingram and had decent coverage, but the pass from Marino's quick release zipped right into the receiver's hands. "[Expletive] Marino!" Ingram heard Glenn exclaim.

The Jets were devastated. The Dolphins sideline erupted. Miami left the Meadowlands in first place in the AFC East. New York coach Pete Carroll called the loss "staggering," and it was for his team. The Jets would not win another game the rest of the season, and Carroll, who was fired after the season, never won another game for the Jets. "I enjoy talking about it," Don Shula told ESPN in 2014, "but never with Jets fans. I don't talk to Jets fans in South Florida. Or in New York. Or in the United States."

42 Nat Moore

The Miami Dolphins were struggling to win games in the late 1960s, but defensive back Jimmy Warren still found time to visit schoolchildren during the season to share his story of rising out of his native Ferriday, Louisiana, in the 1930s and '40s to earn a scholarship playing football at the University of Illinois and then earn a career playing in the NFL. Warren visited Edison High School, which was located in a Miami neighborhood that was starting to battle the rise of poverty, in hopes of inspiring the kids listening to him. Nat Moore was listening. And he was inspired. "It made me think that if he could rise out of his situation, then I could rise out of my situation," Moore said 50 years later. "It made me think I could make it playing football or doing whatever else I was gifted to do."

Moore was indeed gifted in his ability to play football. But he was also somehow anointed by fate to follow his time on the field with the Dolphins by becoming an executive with the team in a career that has spanned 45 years and is still going strong. "I jokingly call him Elmer's because he is the glue that keeps the history and the tradition and the people that built this organization together," club president and CEO Tom Garfinkel said. "I don't know that there's a person on the planet that loves the Miami Dolphins more, who cares more. There might be someone who loves the Dolphins as much, but no one loves this team more."

The love affair began in 1974 when Don Shula drafted Moore, a running back at the University of Florida, in the third round. That same year the burgeoning WFL franchise planned for Jacksonville, Florida, also selected Moore and wanted to sign him. So what came next was, well, something of a negotiation. "I took less money to come home and play for the Dolphins compared to what Jacksonville was offering me," Moore said. "We're talking to Coach Shula and we were probably $40,000 to $50,000 off from what I was being offered in Jacksonville. We started talking about the Dolphins, and they made the point about being in three straight Super Bowls and having won the last two and going back to the Super Bowl. He says, 'If we go back to the Super Bowl, you're going to make another $25,000, so we're not that far off because we're going to do that anyway. You need to add that into that figure, and it doesn't look so bad.' My goal was to get to the Super Bowl. Everywhere I'd been, I'd been a star, but I was a team guy that happened to be a star. Whatever the team needed me to do, that's what I would do. So they wanted me to just return kicks that year. But eventually everybody got hurt, and I started playing."

At the end of that rookie season, Moore had one of his signature career moments. In the Sea of Hands playoff game against the Oakland Raiders, the Dolphins delivered the first blow when Moore returned the opening kickoff 89 yards for a touchdown and a 7–0 Dolphins lead.

The final Raiders player who had a chance to catch Moore on that kickoff return touchdown, was Warren—the man who years earlier as a Dolphins defensive back had encouraged Moore to chase his dreams. "When I returned the kick against Oakland, it was like, 'Yes, we're off to a good start. I'm going to get that 25 grand this year.'" Moore said. "Well, we know it didn't work that way. And it showed me that nothing is promised in this league. No matter how hard you work, it doesn't guarantee anything. It puts you in the position you could be successful, you could get to the Super Bowl, but it doesn't actually put you there."

Moore spent the next seven seasons catching more passes than anyone on the team. Today he is third all time with 510 receptions behind only Mark Clayton (550) and Mark Duper (510). In 1982 the leadership role Moore had earned began to pay dividends. During an NFL players' strike, Moore and Don Strock led the squad during player practices for 56 consecutive days. "Because of what we had learned and the way we worked, we continued to work," Moore said. "We didn't need the coaches. It was also a way of us staying close. It was also a way for us to keep up with what was going on in negotiations to the point some of us went to New York just to sit in on the negotiations."

The Dolphins went to the Super Bowl that strike-shortened season. But Moore caught only eight passes. "I was the back coming out of the backfield, but then Tommy Vigorito came in and started to play well. Well, guess what? They wanted to play Tommy on third down," Moore said. "And so we made a pact that Jimmy Cefelao, Duriel Harris, and myself would play two downs each. Well, I'm playing first and second down, and we're running the ball. So I don't catch a lot of balls that year, but I make a lot of key blocks and I make catches when we need it. I learned at that point: it's not about how much I do with the ball in my hands. It's about what I do as a leader on this football team. And if I'm not willing to sacrifice, how can you expect or ask others to sacrifice?"

Moore was always willing to sacrifice. Who doesn't remember the Helicopter Catch against the New York Jets in the Meadowlands?

It's an iconic and all-time play. And it looks quite painful. "We'd run that same play earlier. Dan Marino hit me going through the seam, and on the way down, I hit my elbow, the ball pops out, I'd fumbled the ball," Moore said. "And Coach Shula yells, 'Hang on to the football! We'd been better off if you didn't catch it because we could have punted it away.' Coach Shula was a mentor and always will be. He makes an impression on you at all times. So I caught the next pass, same route, same play, but now we're going in, and I've got a chance to score. I'm thinking, *I'm going to show Coach Shula*. So I start to go over Ken Schroy and I'm going to leap over him and land in the end zone and be a hero. As I'm halfway over, Kirk Springs, the cornerback who was covering me, hits me on the side, and I just start spinning. The irony of that whole move is I landed soft, didn't get hurt, didn't realize what had happened. But the only thing I was thinking was, *Whatever you do, don't let go of the dang football!* I jumped up, ran to the sideline, and I was pissed off because I didn't score. I saw it on TV that night after we got back and I'm thinking, *Holy mackeral, you could have hurt yourself.*"

Moore worked on behalf of the South Florida community throughout his career, and the team's community service award is named after him. But his service to the team went beyond that. He has been a club vice president, a special advisor, and now serves as senior vice president in charge of special projects and alumni relations. He helped bring together the leaders of the Seminole tribe of South Florida with the Dolphins, and that eventually led the tribe, which owns Hard Rock corporate and its casinos, restaurants, and hotels, to put its name on the Dolphins' refurbished stadium in north Miami-Dade County as part of a naming rights deal worth $250 million. "I know a lot of people, and that's part of that platform the Dolphins have given me through the years," Moore said modestly. "I play a lot of golf. I go to a lot of events. And in the process, you meet people and develop relationships. To me there's nothing better than to take two entities that I know and put them together and hopefully they can work something out."

43 Dwight Stephenson

A full two years after that awful moment, Don Shula, a man known for expending precious little time focusing on the past, was in his office at the Miami Dolphins old training facility in Northwest Miami-Dade County looking back on what might have been. Shula has waited on a visitor who passed a colorful painting of center Dwight Stephenson doing what made him great: dominating the line of scrimmage. The artwork includes three words that speak of his excellence: "The Winning Edge."

When the admiring visitor mentioned the portrait, Shula sighed deeply, perhaps recounting in his mind how things should have gone and how different those possibilities were from what actually happened. "Losing a player like that to an injury like that is the most depressing and devastating thing that could happen to any football team," Shula said. "And we know because that's what happened to us when we lost Dwight."

Stephenson retired from football in September of 1989. He had spent the previous 21 months trying to recover and rehabilitate from a catastrophic moment that left him with a torn anterior cruciate ligament, torn lateral collateral ligament, and damaged nerves in his left knee. The career-ending injury against the New York Jets in December of 1987 was a painful and premature loss of talent and leadership for the Dolphins. But it was more than that: "He was the best offensive lineman in the league," Dan Marino said. "He might've been the best ever to play the game."

Stephenson was gifted and unmatched as an NFL center from 1980 to that fateful day in '87. But because Stephenson reached such heights—five consecutive Pro Bowls—and turned an often anonymous position into one highlighted by opposing coaches and pundits alike, the question wasn't whether Stephenson was good. The question was whether he was the greatest. "The greatest center I ever coached," Alabama coach Paul "Bear" Bryant said of Stephenson.

In his book *By A Nose*, Buffalo Bills nose tackle Fred Smerlas, who directly opposed Stephenson, wrote: "Before he tore up his knee, the best center in modern-day football."

Said Dolphins offensive line coach John Sandusky: "We had Dan Marino and we had Dwight Stephenson, who was the Dan Marino of centers."

Stephenson was inducted into the Pro Football Hall of Fame in 1998, but we'll never know how great Stephenson could have been. "He was in his prime," linebacker Matt Millen told NFL Films. "You wish he could have played more so we could enjoy it more."

There is also debate about whether the play that prematurely cut short Stephenson's career was even necessary. Stephenson had just turned 30 a month before the Dolphins played the Jets on December 7, 1987. In a game the Dolphins were dominating, running back Troy Stradford fumbled, and as a defensive back was returning the ball for a touchdown, New York defensive lineman Marty Lyons blindsided Stephenson. Miami's center laid on the field. "I knew I was hurt," Stephenson said. "But I didn't think my career was over."

Some Dolphins players were enraged. Lyons had something of a reputation among Miami players for playing to the whistle and sometimes a little beyond. Many said the block was not illegal but also unnecessary. Others were less subtle. "If Lyons was involved, it was probably a cheap shot," guard Roy Foster insisted.

"Their players and coaches were yelling 'cheap shot' at me right there on the field," Lyons told New York area reporters the day after the game. "But if I had wanted to cheap shot him, I wouldn't have been down on one knee, trying to call for their trainer and their doctor. I wouldn't have stayed out there with him for several minutes. And I wouldn't have walked into their locker room to see him afterward."

Lyons and Stephenson were friends. It was a bond forged from their days at the University of Alabama. "When I went in to see Dwight," Lyons said, "I told him how bad I felt, that I didn't try to do anything intentional. Dwight told me that it was a good clean shot, that he got hurt when he caught his leg. Two other Alabama guys were in the trainer's room with us, Tony Nathan and Don McNeal. They didn't complain. They know me, they know I wouldn't do anything like that on purpose. I'm sorry it happened, but I couldn't say that if the same situation came up, I wouldn't do the same thing again."

If Stephenson felt any rancor, he never let on. "Marty was shook up," Stephenson said later. "He's a good guy. I hold no grudge. We played together three years at Alabama. He was a year ahead of me. He told me he didn't even see me on the play. He just reacted. I'm one of the last people he would want to cause any harm. We're pretty close."

That response was so Stephenson. He rarely spoke and when he did he never complained. It was a style fashioned from a lesson taught by his college coach. "Bear stressed the importance of showing class," Stephenson said. "When things aren't going so well, you still have to show your class. That's very important."

44 The Killer Bs

The developing excellence of the Miami Dolphins defense in the early 1980s was recognized by the media pundits in South Florida, and soon many of them were looking to hang a nickname on the unit. One came up with No-Names II. *Nope.* Another reporter trotted out New Names. *Really?* "We have the type of defense where it might be hard to put an identity on us," nose tackle Bob Baumhower told the *Miami Herald* in 1983. "Killer Bs is about the only thing I've heard that fits. But the thing is: we play so well as a team, together, everybody. There's no one area that stands out."

What stood out was their names. At one point in the early 1980s, seven of the 11 starters on the Miami defense had surnames that began with the letter B.

Doug Betters
Kim Bokamper
Bob Baumhower
Bob Brudzinski
Glenn Blackwood
Lyle Blackwood
Charles Bowser
Jay Brophy
Mark Brown
Bill Barnett was a backup defensive tackle, Don Bessilleu was a reserve defensive back for three years, and Bud Brown came later.

Still lacking a nickname, Miami's defense began earning recognition in 1981 when it allowed the fewest points in the AFC. The unit allowed the second fewest points in the entire league in 1982 and the fewest points again in 1983. By '83, when Dan Marino was drafted, the Dolphins were known for their stifling defense. And the stifling defense was known as the Killer Bs. "We had a different style when I first got to Miami," Marino said. "It was about the defense. We had a lot of guys with last names that started with B. They went to the Super Bowl the year before. Because I was drafted later in the first round, I got an opportunity to go to a team that was pretty well-established. I tell people all the time: I think that's why I got off to a pretty quick start."

In the last month of the 1982 regular season, as the Dolphins made a push to Super Bowl XVII, the Killer Bs dominated games, particularly in the second half. They allowed one field goal after a turnover at their 23-yard line and another field goal in the snowplow game at New England. That's it. The Dolphins outscored opponents 40–6 in that span. "Bill Arnsparger got the credit for that," Betters said. "He's a guy who can think on his feet. If something isn't right early in the game, he gets it fixed the next series or at worst by halftime."

Arnsparger was perhaps the greatest assistant coach in Dolphins history. His fingerprints were on defenses that played in five of the first eight Super Bowls—two with the Baltimore Colts and three with Miami. And his ability to teach and adjust on the fly was unparalleled. He eventually designed the defenses on Miami's first four Super Bowl teams. "I give them one or two points they can think about and get addressed the second half," Arnsparger said. "That gives us a chance to win games late, and we have."

Although Arnsparger was the tactician for the defense, the vision for the unit and indeed the entire team came from Don Shula. "Coach Shula always had the big picture in mind," Baumhower told FOX-10 News in 2013. "When we came in every year to training camp, we were coming in to win the Super Bowl. He had a vision for us."

The Killer Bs embraced their new nickname late in '82 and throughout the '83 season. They donned aqua and orange striped pants (bees, get it?) and posed for a Killer Bs poster that sold moderately well in South Florida. "I can recall being out on the field and doing a poster," linebacker-turned-defensive lineman Bokamper said. "Every now and then, I see one of those posters and cringe at the thought of doing the thing."

More important than posters and media attention was the manner in which the Killer Bs approached games. And their style matched their nickname. "We had a swarming defense," cornerback Don McNeal said.

The Killer Bs prided themselves on being physical. Baumhower certainly was. Betters, Brudzinski, and Bokamper were. And the Blackwoods basically collected concussions in those heady days—to opponents and themselves. But the unit also played intelligently. They studied. They anticipated. "There are certain teams when you play against them that you know it's going to be more a challenge mentally than physically," former Chargers quarterback Dan Fouts told NFL Films. "And with Miami it was always that way. They seem to be right there in the huddle with you sometimes as if they're able to read your mind."

The Killer Bs basically got the Dolphins to the Super Bowl in that 1982 season and played a feature role in Miami's return to the game in 1984. But that latter Super Bowl—the 38–16 loss to the San Francisco 49ers—was a significant disappointment for the unit. The 49ers gained 537 yards, and players afterward questioned the use of man-to-man coverage throughout a game, in which Joe Montana was mostly throwing short or intermediate passes to running backs and tight ends. "Our guys are running man-to-man, their backs are turned, and [49ers running backs] are catching the ball underneath them and running forever," safety Mike Kozlowski told *The Washington Post* the day after the loss. "Any time that happens, you're beat. The stuff that shouldn't hurt you was killing us."

That game signaled the decline of the Killer Bs. Arnsparger was gone by then. Players began aging. Soon most of the Killer and the Bs were gone from Miami's defense.

45 Jimmy Johnson

It began with smiles, as many new loves do. And great hope. With respect. And even a little intrigue. The Miami Dolphins' courtship of Jimmy Johnson started in July of 1994 when one of owner Wayne Huizenga's representatives called Miami attorney Nick Christin to ask if the man, whose days as the Dallas Cowboys coach ended months earlier, would be interested in replacing Don Shula in Miami.

Christin, Johnson's representative, immediately called his client and friend, and the two spoke of the possibility. But two days later on July 21, 1994, Huizenga signed Shula to a contract extension through 1996 and vehemently denied any interest at all in Johnson. "Subsequent to that call, I have found out that Mr. Huizenga's representative was acting alone," said Christin, who declined to identify the so-called lone wolf. "He was calling us without Mr. Huizenga's permission. I guess he thought he could be a hero."

Or a prophet.

Because whether that Dolphins employee was acting alone or not (he probably wasn't based on circumstantial evidence) that call shows how far back Johnson was on the Dolphins' radar. And that spark kindled an intrigue that would burst into a raging full-court press by the Dolphins to hire Johnson 18 months later. While the January 1996 press conference signaling the Shula era's end dominated media coverage in South Florida, Huizenga discussed a possible Johnson hiring. "Obviously, his name is at the top of the list," Huizenga said. "When the time is right, either he'll call us, or we'll call him."

That call came within hours. Huizenga was keenly aware of what he termed as a "groundswell" among Dolphins fans wanting Johnson. After all, J.J. had won a national championship as coach of the Miami Hurricanes and then won two Super Bowls as coach in Dallas. Just as importantly, Johnson seemed comfortable replacing legends. He replaced Howard Schnellenberger after the coach won a national championship in Miami. He replaced Tom Landry, who was an icon across the entire NFL as well as in Dallas. Johnson would be a fit to replace Shula, Huizenga thought, because big shoes were a perfect fit for him. "He's a winner, he's a great coach and great personnel man, and he's a commanding presence," Huizenga said. "What's there not to like?"

Huizenga and Johnson met on exactly the one-week anniversary after Shula and Huizenga had agreed on a new direction for the franchise. Huizenga arrived first and was waiting for Johnson and Christin when they arrived at the Dolphins facility in Davie, Florida, about an hour later. Pleasantries led to a tour of the camp and then lunch. And while Huizenga was getting the measure of Johnson, this meeting was equal parts the coach feeling comfortable with his prospective new owner because Johnson and his previous owner Jerry Jones didn't exactly agree on everything. Huizenga, who had demanded Shula fire most of his defensive assistants only days before, convinced Johnson he was not a meddlesome owner. "The biggest issue was knowing that we could become the very best," Johnson said. "I wanted to see that commitment."

Johnson and Huizenga didn't talk money directly. That would happen with Christin later. The conversation was about Huizenga doing everything necessary, spending whatever was necessary, and staying out of the way as much as necessary to make the Dolphins champions. Huizenga agreed to everything. "Wayne walked out of the room, and Nick said, 'When he talks like that, you don't even want to ask for anything,'" Johnson said. "And we didn't."

The sides agreed Johnson would become the Dolphins new coach by 2:00 PM on the day of that first meeting. But it was not announced. Huizenga, a closer throughout his business career, let Johnson sleep on it overnight before having a press conference the next day. As Johnson and Huizenga walked out of the building, they joked they were within a hair of an agreement. "One of the big issues is Jimmy has to shave his head," the bald Huizenga said as he and his new coach posed for a slew of curious reporters.

Johnson answered: "And that's a big hang-up."

Huizenga handed the keys to the franchise to Johnson and in doing so couldn't have picked someone more unlike Shula. The image-conscious Shula once yelled at a reporter when the scribe wrote that his hotel room on the road was always stocked with beers for himself or guests. "You make it sound like I'm a drunk," Shula barked.

Johnson let it be known he loved Heinekens. And admitted he allowed himself one "binge" night a week for beer when dieting.

Shula went to church daily. Johnson's sons once said they didn't know if their father believed in God. Shula was stoic in postgame news conferences after losses and quickly put losses behind him. Johnson sometimes turned beet red and even wept during press conferences. And he clung to losses for days, making himself and everyone around him miserable.

The next day on January 11, 1996, Johnson put on a blue suit and one of his two diamond-studded Super Bowl rings. He met with Shula's assistants and promised to interview them all despite the fact he'd eventually fire most of them. Then he met with support staff, administrators, and their assistants. None of them would be fired, he promised. He then pointed to his championship ring and said, "Get back to work and let's get one of these."

46 Flipper

Flipper was pretty cool. And Flipper at a football stadium celebrating a Miami Dolphins touchdown is the stuff of NFL lore. That's how it was in the 1960s and again in the late 1970s in Miami. It was a different time then. Nobody thought anything of transporting a 350-pound bottlenose dolphin from its lagoon at the Miami Seaquarium and moving it eight miles to a 37,000-gallon tank in the east end zone of the Orange Bowl—just so Dolphins fans could be entertained and the game's atmosphere could be improved.

Back then even Richard O'Barry, who captured and trained all five of the dolphins that played Flipper in two movies and 88 TV series episodes, didn't voice any complaints. That was before he became an activist vehemently opposed to the capture of wild dolphins. A different time indeed.

The Dolphins probably needed Flipper early in their existence. Crowds at the Orange Bowl sometimes numbered in the 20,000s. This was before Don Shula. And Hall of Fame players. And the Perfect Season. By the time the franchise turned around with Shula's hiring in 1970, Flipper had been cast out. In 1968 the city of Miami and the Seaquarium decided they no longer would pay for tank repairs and transportation costs. Known for counting the cost of paper clips used by his office administrators—yes, he really did this—team owner Joe Robbie also refused to foot the bill.

So Flipper went back to Flipper Cove at the Seaquarium. But in the late '70s, the parties made accommodations, and Flipper returned to the Orange Bowl once again. She visited every football Sunday into the early 1980s before the Dolphins moved to their new stadium in north Miami-Dade County.

The show ended. A tradition passed. But Flipper lives. The Seaquarium, a gorgeous 38-acre tract of land bordered on both sides by Biscayne Bay and in the shadows of Miami's glitzy skyline, is still Flipper's home. You can see her anytime the facility is open, which is 365 days of the year.

Flipper came to the Seaquarium in 1963. Filmmaker Ivan Tors shot the *Flipper* pilot and scores of series episodes there over the next few years. Two movies were also filmed at the Seaquarium. The fish stand featured in the show is today used by dolphin trainers at the Seaquarium.

You can visit Flipper and even get downright interactive with other dolphins at the Seaquarium. For $160 you can get into a tank and shake hands, share a kiss, and even use training signals to have the dolphins perform various behaviors. For $220 visitors can actually swim with the dolphins and go for a ride around the pool by holding on to a dorsal fin. Flipper isn't celebrating Dolphins touchdowns anymore. She's not on a weekly TV show or doing movies anymore. But the show at the Seaquarium has endured.

47 The Ricky Williams Experience

In the spring of 2001, Ricky Williams was on the telephone with a *Miami Herald* reporter, telling him he'd like to be traded from the New Orleans Saints to the Miami Dolphins. The story of Williams wanting to leave hit the newsstands the following morning, and as with many things involving the enigmatic running back, craziness ensued.

The Dolphins called the Saints inquiring about Williams. The Saints told the Dolphins they could not trade Williams because of salary cap constraints. The Dolphins told the Saints they're not interested anyway. The Saints called Williams asking if he wanted to leave. Williams, who lived in South Florida, denied any desire to leave New Orleans. Dolphins coach Dave Wannstedt told reporters the story was overblown. Then Wannstedt met privately with the reporter who spoke to Williams the previous day and asked about that conversation before admitting he'd love Williams on his team. One year later the Dolphins sent four draft picks, including two first rounders, to the Saints to acquire Williams.

Welcome to the Ricky Williams experience.

Following this supremely talented player's days with the Dolphins was more like following a journey than a career because Williams was intelligent, confused, brave, cowardly, interesting, complex, selfish, and often surprising. He was—in short—very different. He was the most intriguing figure ever to cross the Dolphins landscape. None of this would have mattered if Williams wasn't amazingly gifted. And he was, which is the reason he won the Heisman Trophy and has a statue commemorating that accomplishment outside Darrell Royal Stadium on the University of Texas campus.

Williams came into the NFL in appropriately weird fashion. Saints coach Mike Ditka traded all his available draft picks so he could select Williams. Then Williams and the coach posed on the cover of *ESPN The Magazine* depicting the two getting married—with Williams wearing a wedding dress. Williams was a good player for the Saints, gaining at least 1,000 yards in two of three seasons. He became great his first year in Miami when he rushed for 1,853 yards, averaged 4.8 yards a carry, and scored 17 touchdowns. His next season in 2003 was not as good. His average dipped to 3.5 yards per carry. He felt overused. He felt underpaid. The Dolphins didn't make the playoffs despite his 1,372 rushing yards.

In the spring of 2004, Williams was at a crossroads. He didn't love the idea of replaying the frustrations of the previous season. He didn't really respect Wannstedt anymore. And he had many, many other things he wanted to do. So Williams retired. At age 27. A week before training camp was set to open. "I just don't want to be in this business anymore," Williams told the *Herald*. "I was never strong enough to not play football, but I'm strong enough now. I've considered everything about this. Everyone has thrown every possible scenario at me about why I shouldn't do this, but they're in denial. I'm happy with my decision."

Williams said he wanted to go off and study philosophy, the world, himself. He said he wanted to find himself, and that meant losing the NFL. It all made sense for about two weeks, and then it became clear there was also another reason. Williams had tested positive for marijuana in the offseason and would have faced a mandatory suspension and lost paychecks totaling $1.7 million—over half his salary. Eventually, Williams admitted the positive tests played a larger role in his retirement than he originally indicated. Williams said, however, there were "a hundred reasons" for his retirement and that his desire to smoke marijuana outside NFL regulations was merely one. "I didn't quit football because I failed a drug test," Williams said.

Williams convinced friends that July that his departure from football was not a whim. But within five weeks, he was open to returning. He was living out of a tent in Australia, where he was bitten by some insect he described as a caterpillar, causing so much pain and swelling in his legs he could hardly walk for days. Against that backdrop Williams called Wannstedt and Dolphins general manager Rick Spielman to gauge their interest in letting him return. The conversations did not go well from Williams' perspective. Wannstedt wanted Williams to apologize for abandoning his team. No one promised to drop an $8.6 million judgment the Dolphins won against Williams for what was essentially breach of contract.

The 2004 season was a 4–12 disaster. Wannstedt was fired after nine games and a 1–8 record. The coaching staff had already endured something of a mutiny. The locker room was often divided and sometimes disinterested. Desperate to correct course, owner Wayne Huizenga, convinced (begged) Nick Saban to take over. And the new coach, who would quit on the franchise after two seasons, struck up a good relationship with the player who quit on the franchise after two seasons.

Williams returned in July 2005. He was still a character. He conducted a nationally televised press conference announcing his return while barefoot. But he was contrite about abandoning the team—at least publicly. "I realized by making that decision, I affected the team in a negative way. I upset a lot of the fans," Williams said. "I'm very regretful that people were hurt in the process of me doing that. I do realize that to a lot of people it comes off as being very, very selfish. So I do offer an apology to all the people who were negatively affected by my decision."

Williams had studied philosophy. He could debate existentialism. He absorbed Hindu while he lived in an ashram in India. He had fed various passions but had never come to the knowledge of the truth. In April of 2006, Williams was suspended after failing his fourth drug test. That suspension was supposed to be lifted in the spring of 2007 but was extended into November when Williams reportedly failed another test, his fifth.

The Dolphins never expected Williams back on their roster. They had yet another head coach in Cam Cameron, and he'd talked to multiple teams, including the St. Louis Rams, about a trade before that fifth positive test became public. Cameron didn't like Williams. But the Cameron, who thought Williams never again would play in Miami, also believed Ronnie Brown would last an entire season and Jesse Chatman would back him up, and both were injured now. So Williams came off suspension and played one game—against the Pittsburgh Steelers. Williams carried six times before linebacker Lawrence Timmons stepped on him and Williams tore a pectoral muscle right off the bone. By year's end, Cameron was fired.

But Williams was about to enjoy three more years in Miami, the longest uninterrupted span in his Dolphins days. Bill Parcells took control of the organization, and he and Williams got along marvelously. Credit Williams for that. He didn't judge Parcells based on his age or history with other players but for how he was treated. And Parcells treated Williams like the great worker and football player he had always been. In 2008 Parcells and Williams negotiated a contract extension among themselves without any agents. "My relationship with authority figures was strained in the past," Williams said. "Now I realize they write the checks."

Williams played for the Dolphins through 2010. He was integral in the Wildcat package of 2008. No one has run the ball for Miami more than Williams, and he finished his time as the franchise's second leading rusher behind only golden-era fullback Larry Csonka. His 228-yard game against the Buffalo Bills in 2002 is a club record. Fans even changed "Run, Ricky, Run!" when he was at his best.

48 The Snowplow Game

Then-Indianapolis Colts head coach Ron Meyer was sitting on the home team's bench at the RCA Dome an hour before a game against the visiting Miami Dolphins in 1991 and he was being careful not to catch Don Shula's attention—much less walk on the field and possibly get near the legend. A visitor asked why an NFL head coach, who leads big men with big egos, seemingly was shrinking from even a casual, passing encounter with an opposing coach? "Because that's Don Shula, and I'm pretty convinced he hates me," Meyer said. "The guy hasn't forgotten what happened 10 years ago, and I don't feel like being yelled at right now."

It actually had been only nine years since that snowy, 22-degree day in Foxborough's old Shaefer Stadium that Meyer sealed his fate with Shula. Meyer was the New England Patriots coach then, and his team handed Shula and the Dolphins a 3–0 loss in a game in which the teams passed for 89 yards *combined*. But it wasn't his struggling offense or even the score that irritated Shula as much as how it happened. Because he believed the Patriots, at Meyer's direction, cheated. And they used a John Deere tractor to do it. Hence, the name of the infamous "Snowplow Game."

In a scoreless game with four minutes and 45 seconds left in regulation, the first-year Patriots coach sent kicker John Smith onto the snow-covered field to attempt a 33-yard field goal. But soon the coach, who had earlier seen Dolphins kicker Uwe Von Schamman have a 45-yard kick blocked when his footing slipped, called timeout. Meyer then ran down the sideline and ordered Mark Henderson, a convicted burglar working for the Patriots as part of a work/release program, to clear a path for Smith. Henderson got on his tractor and brushed a half-moon swath to expose green turf where ice and snow had been moments before. "He was waving and screaming, and he said, 'Get on that thing and do something,'" Henderson told the *Boston Herald* in 2007. "The tractor was still running. So I went out on the 20-yard line like I was going to do my normal thing, which was to clear the yard markers, and I swerved over where [holder] Matt Cavanaugh was and I made what looked like a sidewalk of green."

Patriots players in the huddle applauded as Henderson worked. Eventually, Smith got good footing, the ball sailed through the uprights, and New England won the game. "If I had it to do over again, I would dive in front of the snowplow," Shula said years later. "I just tried to get the officials' attention when that guy plowed the snow away. I was bewildered by what was happening in front of my eyes."

The nickname for the game itself is a bit of a misnomer. "First of all," Henderson told the *Herald*, "it wasn't even a snowplow. People always call it the 'Snowplow Game,' but it was a small John Deere tractor with a brush on it. It was artificial turf, and that was a brush I used to clear the snow."

When a Miami sportswriter told Henderson that Shula was upset about the incident, Henderson said, "Well, what are they going to do, throw me in jail?" That was a funny retort, considering Henderson had been arrested in multiple states. But it wasn't funny in Miami. Shula called it "the most unsportsmanlike act I've been around." "The snowplow didn't come on the field for us," Shula said of Von Shamman's earlier field-goal attempt. "Our kicker slipped and fell, and we lost the game 3–0. I called the commissioner that week and told him it was the most unfair act that had ever happened in a football game. He agreed. So I asked him what he was going to do about it. He said, 'Nothing.'"

That game is remembered fondly in New England to this day. Current Patriots owner Robert Kraft has interestingly referred to it as "one of the greatest moments in Patriots history."

The John Deere tractor even hangs from the rafters at the Patriots Hall of Fame at Patriots Place in Foxborough, Massachusetts. This franchise has won 21 division titles, 11 conference championships, six Super Bowls. And that tractor hangs from a rafter as proudly as those banners do.

In other places the game lives in infamy. "I don't know if I look at that as a good point in my life or as a tremendously bad point," Meyer told NFL Films. "I'm sure if you were the other coach on the other sideline, you would say it was a black mark, but I know one thing: I can live with myself knowing it wasn't an attempt to deceive or it wasn't an attempt to cheat anybody."

A month after the snowplow game, the Patriots visited the Dolphins in the Orange Bowl for a first-round playoff game. It was 76 degrees and sunny, so the Dolphins had fake snow made at a local ice plant and put it on a sideline near the west end zone, along with a John Deere tractor and some random guy who wore a black-and-white striped jumpsuit. Yeah, the NFL was a lot more fun then.

The Dolphins won that playoff game 28–13.

After that season the NFL amended their rules to prohibit plows or tractors from clearing patches on the field to improve the footing of any player. In 2017 the league made it impermissible for the ground crew or other non-players to clear a path prior to a field goal, punt, or kickoff.

49 The 1985 AFC Championship Game

The entire Earth expected the Miami Dolphins and Chicago Bears to play each other in Super Bowl XX. It was destined from that moment the teams met in December, and Don Shula's team handed the big, nasty Bears their only loss of the season. The matchup made so much sense: the team that authored a Perfect Season, that went to the Super Bowl the season before, that had no fear of Chicago's angry 46 Defense vs. the most dominant team of the 1985 season.

The problem is those pesky New England Patriots ruined the whole thing.

The Patriots were a good team in 1985. They won 11 games, but back then the Patriots were still the inconsistent franchise folks remembered as having not won a playoff game since 1963 and they would have to win three road playoff games, including a trip to Miami's Orange Bowl, to reach the Super Bowl. The Dolphins, meanwhile, had never lost in the AFC Championship Game in five previous tries. Shula owned AFC Championship Games. So

Dolphins vs. Bears should have happened except the Patriots ended up winning 31–14 on January 12, 1986. "I'm sorry we don't have the opportunity to play the Bears," a dejected Dan Marino said afterward. "We have the type of people that: if we had won, we could have won everything. But we just couldn't do anything tonight."

How could this happen? How could one afternoon derail fate? Start with six Dolphins turnovers. It began on Miami's first offensive play when running back Tony Nathan fumbled on his own 20-yard line. That led to a Patriots field goal. In the second quarter, Marino fumbled a snap from center at his own 37-yard line, and that led to a Patriots touchdown.

The Dolphins had trailed the Cleveland Browns 21–3 the previous week in a conference playoff game but rallied for a 24–21 win. They had similar comeback hopes despite trailing 17–7 at halftime in this one. "What did I say at the half?" Shula said, repeating a reporter's question. "That we'd played about as bad as you can play and we still had a chance to get back in this ballgame, 'bout the same thing I said at the half of the Cleveland game."

But Lorenzo Hampton fumbled the opening kickoff of the second half, the Patriots recovered at Miami's 25-yard line, and converted the mistake into a touchdown. Then they led 24–7. "It's so damn disappointing after fighting and scratching," Shula said, "to leave the ball on the ground like that."

The Dolphins, though, had come back from the brink all year long. Marino held out for 38 days and missed all of training camp before joining the club for its season's opener. So the Dolphins started slow and were bogged down by the loss of four starters, including Mark Duper, for significant portions of the season. But the Dolphins rallied from a 5–4 record and won their last eight games, including the playoff victory against the Browns. They were the AFC East champions. This team had not quit all season. "We were moving the ball," Marino said. "We can score three touchdowns with a quarter left in the game. We've done it before. You don't ever think the game's over when it's still on. You don't say, 'We're out of it.' But we just left it on the ground too much. They got a lot of turnovers."

The turnovers put the Dolphins in a hole. But the hole became a grave when the Patriots exposed the Miami defense. Defensive coordinator Bill Arnsparger, a master of second-half adjustments, was no longer in Miami, and new coordinator Chuck Studley's unit simply wilted.

The Patriots rushed for 255 yards. They snapped the ball 71 times on offense and ran the ball 59 of those times. "We missed a lot of tackles," safety Glenn Blackwood said. "We couldn't seem to hit their running backs."

The Patriots offensive line also nullified the Dolphins' pass rush. Quarterback Tony Eason was rarely pressured and never sacked. "I don't even remember being touched all day," Eason said.

Shula, who spent a career looking ahead to the next challenge, was so disappointed his team "didn't battle," he admitted to not sleeping that night. The next day he was graceful but realistic about the looming Super Bowl matchup that would not include his team. "The Patriots represent our conference, and I'm proud of them," he said. "But the Bears aren't going to let anybody run on them the way the Patriots ran on us."

The Bears trounced the Patriots 46–10 in the Super Bowl. It was the most lopsided Super Bowl result ever at the time.

50 The New Left Side

In the spring of 1990, Don Shula hired longtime friend and former San Francisco 49ers and Detroit Lions head coach Monte Clark as the team's director of pro personnel. And the marching orders for Clark were immediately clear. "All I heard when I got here was we have to have more muscle," Clark said during the 1990 season. "We have to be a more physical football team. I think we're getting to that with Webb and Sims."

Indeed, Richmond Webb and Keith Sims brought that. Those names go together in Miami Dolphins history as much as Jim Langer and Larry Little. No, the two offensive linemen of the 1990s didn't reach the Hall of Fame heights their former day Miami alumni did, but fans, who followed the team in Don Shula's last decade, know Webb and Sims stood for excellence. "They mean everything right now," John Sandusky growled before the 1991 season. "We bet they'd be pretty good. We invested high picks on them. So far so good."

The Dolphins went into the 1990 draft knowing they needed a left tackle. Jeff Dellenbach had filled the spot well in 1989, but the team thought of him more as a versatile swing player than someone to line up against Bruce Smith twice every year. Shula wanted a cornerstone to protect Dan Marino. "Well, we have a quarterback that we need to protect a little bit," Clark joked. "So how about we find the best player we can to do that."

The Dolphins found that player in the unassuming Webb. Miami drafted him with the ninth overall selection. And the amazing thing is the Dolphins didn't expect Webb to be available. "We thought for sure he'd be gone in the top five," Clark said.

If Webb wasn't available with the No. 9 overall selection, Clark said Miami's backup plan was to trade down with the idea of picking Sims in the first round.

Back then the NFL was already comfortable with 300-pound offensive tackles, and Webb was that. But 6'6" offensive tackles were still hard to find. And Webb was 6'6" and 307 pounds and would eventually reach 325 pounds. Guards, meanwhile, were rarely above the 300-pound mark. But Sims was a 6'2", 310-pound left guard who wore a size 56-long jacket and moved like a much smaller man. "I don't know why everyone makes such a big deal about my size," Sims said upon arriving in South Florida. "It's really getting to be a drag. I've been over 300 pounds since I was a senior in high school and I really don't feel like it's going to be a problem."

It wasn't a problem for Sims because he had not allowed a sack as a senior at Iowa State and immediately beat out Roy Foster for a starting job.

Linked by the draft, Webb and Sims soon seemed joined at the hip. They walked out to their first practice side by side with Webb on Sims' left. They practiced that way. They played that way and usually they walked off the field that way. (Even their locker stalls at training camp and at both at home and road games were predictably side by side.) "Never really noticed that," the soft-spoken Webb said in 1994. "I guess it's a natural thing."

As rookies Webb and Sims took the first snap of their first practice with the starting offensive line. And they started every preseason game. And they started every game both were healthy for during their rookie seasons, which was 13 games because Sims missed three starts with an injury.

Webb and Sims were often in the same sentence. Mentioning one led to a mention for the other. But they were vastly different people. Sims was outgoing, outspoken, unafraid to show his emotions. He was 20 minutes late to his first Dolphins meeting because he was taking a physical and he was open about it. "They had to check *all* of me," he joked.

Webb was reserved, soft-spoken. Boyhood coaches wanted to see him be more aggressive, even angry, but Webb rarely showed that side growing up or during his NFL career. "They wanted me to do a lot of growling and grunting," he said. "That wasn't me, still isn't. I play my game and let that speak. It doesn't mean I'm not aggressive."

Webb's assignment from the moment he stepped on the field until 2000 when he played his final game in Miami was to protect the quarterback's blind side usually one-on-one. The Bills boasted Smith, a future Hall of Famer, during that time, and every year Webb battled Smith—often besting him—the matchup was *mano a mano*. No wonder Webb went to the Pro Bowl seven consecutive seasons from 1990 to 1996. "He's the best in the NFL," Clark said in 1995 when he returned to his duties as Miami's offensive line coach.

The Webb-Sims combination was so successful for the Dolphins that they tried to replicate it in 1995. The team that drafted Webb in the first round and Sims in the second in 1990 selected Billy Milner in the first round and Andrew Greene in the second of 1995 to fill their right tackle and right guard spots. "Of course," Clark said, "we hope lightning strikes a second time."

It didn't. Both players were gone after one year. Webb and Sims, meanwhile, were still going strong on the left side.

51 Bryan Cox Hates Buffalo

It was bitter cold. The natives, who hated his guts, were hurling objects to bruise his body and racial slurs to hurt his feelings. The level of contempt he felt for the tormentors in the stands was surpassed only by the revenge he wanted to exact on his foe on the field. This was Bryan Cox in Buffalo. Perhaps the most volatile, intelligent, violent, passionate player ever to don a Miami Dolphins uniform, the linebacker spent the last week of his last regular-season with the team praying to play the Buffalo Bills in the playoffs. God answered. But not the way Cox hoped.

But first one had to understand how Cox got to this mind-set in December of 1995. And to understand that, one has to travel back to Cox's second season in 1992. That was a breakout year for Cox. The former fifth-round selection in his second season surprised everyone with 14 sacks. It was about more than just the sacks with Cox because his physical style was contagious. And a Miami defense that rarely intimidated and often lacked life needed whatever infection of toughness and backbone Cox brought. "Bryan gives it everything he has," Don Shula said. "The negative is that sometimes he loses control. When he loses it, it's tough to control him. But ordinarily he works hard at holding his temper. It's hard for people to realize all the good things. He works hard in the community, in meetings, and the practices. He's the ideal player you want on your football team."

The ideal player hated losing. And that's exactly what the Dolphins often did against the Bills in the early 1990s. The Bills beat Miami in three of four games, including in the AFC Championship Game in January 1993 at the start of Cox's career. Making matters worse: when the team traveled to Orchard Park, Miami players were sometimes greeted with batteries thrown at them or epithets slung at them. It made Cox crazy, and in September of 1993, 10 days before that season's first trip to Buffalo, he let everyone know. "I don't like the Buffalo Bills as a team, I don't like them as people, I don't like the city, I don't like the people in the city, and I don't like their organization," Cox said. "I'm sure they share the same sentiment toward me, but I don't care. I wouldn't care if any of those people fell off the face of the Earth."

Cox also held a special place in his heart for Bills players. "Some of them think they're so much better than anybody else," he said. "They think they're better than the average person simply because they're football players. There's this arrogance about them, and those type of people I don't like and choose not to associate with."

What happened next can only be described with a more 21st century term: Cox's words went viral. Switchboard operators at Joe Robbie Stadium spent time the next week fielding long-distance calls from Buffalo residents who were offended by the comments. One of the callers demanded Cox's home phone number. And that was the mood the afternoon of September 26, 1993 when the Dolphins and Cox traveled to play the Bills for the first time that season. During pregame warmups, some Buffalo fans yelled racial slurs at Cox, who is black. Others threatened to kill him. And so minutes later, when the Dolphins ran out of the tunnel onto the field for kickoff, Cox defiantly raised both arms and gave the crowd a twin middle finger salute. NBC happened to go live from its pregame show to Rich Stadium just in time to catch Cox's display.

NBC color analyst Paul Maguire, who once played for the Bills, joked, "He's just showing the Bills' fans that the Dolphins are 1–1."

The Dolphins won the game 22–13, and Cox provided a tone-setting sack of Jim Kelly on the game's second play. By game's end he added four tackles, an assist, a deflected pass, and several pressures. Attention on Cox also led to two other sacks. "We all love Bryan," teammate John Offerdahl said. "He says what a lot of players and coaches are thinking but don't say."

Cox was fined by the NFL three days later for shooting the crowd the birds. In announcing the fine, commissioner Paul Tagliabue said, "This kind of behavior will not be tolerated. To the fans in Buffalo and to those who witnessed the gestures replayed on television, we extend our apologies on behalf of the league and its players."

Cox also apologized to youngsters who may have witnessed the gestures on television. But even the apology came with a broadside rip at Buffalo. "It's not in the best interest of myself as a professional and a role model to have made those gestures," Cox said. "But the only thing I regret, I'm saddened by, and feel bad about is that kids across the country may have seen me do something that I wish they hadn't seen. I'm *not* apologizing for making the gesture to those idiots."

The dislike between Cox and Buffalo soon grew into something more. Cox criticized the NFL investigation that led to the fine because no one even talked to him to ask why he had made the gestures. The league reduced its initial $10,000 fine to $3,000, but Cox nonetheless sued the NFL, charging it forced him to work in a racially discriminatory atmosphere. He won, and the league wound up paying his legal bills

In December of 1995, the Dolphins visited the Bills, and it wasn't pleasant. Cox and Buffalo fullback Carwell Gardner got into a fight on the field, and both were ejected. As he left the field with a security escort, Cox was showered with trash and trash talk from the stands. Cox spit on the Rich Stadium turf and was once again caught on camera. More fines ensued. "It was at the ground," Cox said, explaining his spitting, "to say the hell with all of you."

Amid all of this acrimony, the Dolphins needed multiple scenarios to play out the final weeks of the '95 season so they could qualify for the playoffs and get a rematch against the Bills. "If I get my wish and God is listening to my prayers, we'll be back up in Buffalo in two weeks," Cox said. "I'm not afraid of those people. I want to go back there."

Cox got his wish. The Dolphins played the Bills in the first round of the playoffs. They lost 37–22 in what would be Shula's final game. It was also the last game Cox played for the Dolphins.

52 Cameron Wake

The Miami Dolphins brain trust met after the 2008 season, and the debate raged about whether to sign an unproven talent out of the Canadian Football League. "I like what he has done and I like what he can do," general manager Jeff Ireland said.

"I like what he might do for us also, but that's a lot of money they're asking, considering he's not proven anything in the NFL," assistant director of pro personnel Brian Gaine said.

Bill Parcells, lingering in the shadows of the ongoing debate, finally chimed in. "Do you like him? Yes. Do you think he'll be a good player? Yes," Parcells said. "Well, then go sign the guy already. You've got to gamble sometimes, gentlemen. Let's get this done."

Within days of this January 2009 meeting, the Miami Dolphins signed Derek Cameron Wake to a four-year contract worth $2.6 million with $650,000 in guarantees. Over the next decade Cameron Wake—yeah, we tossed the Derek—earned nearly $52 million from the Dolphins and delivered 92 sacks and five Pro Bowl appearances in return. Wake was named to the Dolphins 50th Anniversary Season All-Time Team and ranks second in sacks in team history.

So, yeah, Wake burst onto the scene as surely as he crashed NFL pass protection schemes. "I know I can play," Wake said the first time he spoke to Miami reporters. "And I know what I can do. Every time I step on the field, I want to show people that I belong and that I can play and produce. That's the mentality I took to the CFL and that's the mentality I'm going with to the NFL."

The fact Wake had to play in the CFL for two seasons and dominate, leading the cold-climate league in sacks both seasons, was curious. Wake played collegiately at Penn State. And he was a good player, collecting 191 tackles while playing linebacker at Linebacker

U. Wake also tested well before the 2005 draft, running a 4.55 in the 40-yard dash. And still he wasn't drafted. *Did you kill somebody, Cam? What gives?* "That's the first question I asked," Wake said. "I had no idea. I know I wasn't a dominator or crazy All-American in college. But I tested with any of the names at linebacker and at defensive end at the combine and during workouts. So I don't know. That's a good question."

Wake caught on as an undrafted free agent with the New York Giants. But he was cut before the regular season began. He was out of football entirely in 2006 and took a job as a mortgage broker. "Definitely wasn't something I appreciated," he said of his time away from football. "Not being in football, I was sitting at home on the couch watching people I played with and played against all my life. I know what it's like to not play. I know what it's like to be at home hoping and wishing I could play. It's something I can carry with me the rest of my life."

After he collected 39 sacks for the British Columbia Lions and was CFL Rookie of the Year and Defensive Player of the Year twice, Wake got the NFL's attention. Four teams aside from the Dolphins showed serious interest in signing him before the 2009 season, and the Indianapolis Colts seemed to be leading the way. So why Miami? "I wanted to eliminate all the fluff," Wake said. "It wasn't about whoever offered the biggest deal. It was about the coaching staffs, the opportunity, the organizations. Miami put themselves above the others in those things even if it wasn't by much."

Wake spent much of the 2009 season sitting behind Joey Porter. He played some on special teams, but his explosiveness was obvious when he did get on the field to play defense. The next season in 2010, Wake was one-man apocalypse for NFL offensive tackles, collecting 14 sacks. "Things have clicked for him," head coach Tony Sparano said. "He's worked at becoming a premier pass rusher, and that work is obvious on gameday."

Perhaps Wake's signature moment came against Cincinnati in 2013. The Dolphins and Bengals were tied at 20 in overtime. And halfway into that overtime period, Wake blew through a block and dropped Bengals quarterback Andy Dalton in his own end zone for a safety. It was a walk-off safety. Wake beat a guard for the sack because the Dolphins had blitzed, and Phillip Wheeler was blocked by the tackle, who typically was assigned to Wake. This was only the third game-ending safety in league history. "I have a picture of it in my home," Wake said.

Just as Dolphins history can be measured by the eras of their quarterbacks—with Bob Griese and Dan Marino as the two most significant markers—the same can be done with Dolphins pass rushers. Bill Stanfill. Vern Den Herder. Doug Betters. Jason Taylor. Cameron Wake.

As Taylor's career was winding down, Wake's was spooling up. And the Hall of Famer recognized it because game recognizes game. "I've been around a long time, and he does things that amaze me," Taylor said in 2011. "It's those young, fresh legs, good cartilage in his knees. I always joke watching tape, seeing Cameron dip underneath somebody, kind of getting pushed around, then he'll spin around and pop off the ground. He easily does things that older guys can't do anymore."

Wake collected 11½ sacks while starting only 11 of 16 games in 2016. He added 10½ in all 16 starts the following year. After the 2018 season, in which Wake delivered six sacks in 14 games, he became a free agent. Multiple teams showed interest in the 37-year-old, and he signed with the Tennessee Titans.

53 The Shula Bowls

The historic significance of father coaching against son in a head coach matchup was not lost on anyone in 1994 before the first Shula Bowl. But in a private moment, the winningest coach in NFL history was thinking as much like a dad as a coach. "I want to win the game for the Miami Dolphins organization. I have that responsibility," Don Shula said. "But it hurts that Dave is having a tough time getting that team going. And I get no satisfaction from possibly adding to those tough times for him."

The first father vs. son coaching matchup in NFL history—the Shula Bowl—was not exactly a wonderful time for the Shulas. That's how it is when the family business gets in the way of family blood. On the business side, Don Shula was obviously concerned about his own team, winning, and making the playoffs. But he recognized Dave Shula's Cincinnati Bengals were 0–4 and taking fire from critics. And the prospect of extending that losing streak and adding volume to the criticism stung. "It was a very hard week for the Shula family. It was a very hard week for Don," his wife, Mary Anne said. "It was very hard for Don to read the articles, to read the negative things written about his son."

Don Shula was respectful and even complimentary of the Bengals before the game as an indirect way to lift Dave. And he used his trademark sense of humor to turn the conversation to the happy topic of family rather than the painful topic of football. "Everyone's in David's corner. I've already been warned," Don said. "But I've got Mary Anne. She's going to be with me."

The Dolphins dispatched the Bengals 23–7 in what was otherwise an unremarkable game on a dreary Ohio evening. And afterward Don Shula walked to the middle of the field to hug his son, the opposing coach. "I just told him how much I think of him," Don said. "I know how hard he has worked. It's tough when you're on the losing end. I've been there."

"I'm glad I got to see family and friends," David said. "I appreciate them all coming in. I'm glad they got to be part of it. But in the end, we're 0–5 and we lost another football game."

A scheduling quirk found the Dolphins visiting the Bengals again 364 days later. Again, the Dolphins were vying for a great season with a 3–0 start. Again, the Bengals were trying to reach some level of relevance with a 2–2 mark. David Shula tried to out-coach his dad in this one. He emptied his bag of tricks to keep the Bengals close. Running back Eric Bieniemy and receiver David Dunn threw option passes on one drive, and quarterback Jeff Blake faked a draw and threw a lateral on another.

The game pulsated with four lead changes. But a missed field goal in the closing seconds sealed Cincinnati's fate in a 26–23 loss. Moments later, a crestfallen David Shula got another tender cheek-to-cheek hug from his father at midfield. "It was a tough loss for Dave, about as tough as you can get—when you get into a situation like that when you seemingly have the game won and then you lose it right at the end," Don said, sounding more like a father than a winning coach.

David Shula was named Bengals head coach at age 32. His youth suggested he was on the same victory-lined path his famous father took when he first became a head coach at age 33. But David soon proved he is no Don. He could do little to overcome the ghastly lack of talent—especially at quarterback—the Bengals put on the field. Where Don coached Hall of Famers Johnny Unitas, Bob Griese, and Dan Marino, David sent Jeff Blake and David Klingler into his huddles.

It proved an impossible act to follow. David was fired after four-and-a-half seasons in Cincinnati with a 19–52 record. He surpassed John McKay, who coached the expansion Tampa Bay Buccaneers, as the fastest coach to 50 losses in NFL history. After a 22-year break from coaching—years he spent running the Shula's Steak House empire—David Shula returned to the sidelines in 2018 as the receivers coach at his alma mater Dartmouth College. "He's as happy as he's ever been," Sharon Shula said of her brother. "Coaching is in his blood."

54 Thanksgiving Snow Game vs. the Cowboys

A thermometer held up against the battleship gray sky read 0 degrees that Thanksgiving Day morning in 1993. Keith Byars looked out the window of his Dallas area hotel room and saw the overnight snowfall turning to ice. It wasn't supposed to be like this in Dallas and certainly not for the Miami Dolphins, who had spent the previous couple of days practicing in South Florida's inviting sunshine and pleasant breezes. But here they were for a nationally televised holiday game against the defending Super Bowl champion Dallas Cowboys. Seeing a couple of people slip and slide as they walked outside, Byars had one lingering thought. *Football weather*, he said to himself.

Within hours the Dolphins loaded their party onto three busses and began their 20-minute trip to Texas Stadium. They were escorted, as was the custom, by police on motorcyles who cleared the way and ensured the party's safety. But on the second turn of what was supposed to be a routine ride, one of the three cops hit a patch of black ice, skidded, and took a spill. The three Dolphins busses came to a slow, methodical stop as everyone looked for signs the cop was alive. "I'm fine," the officer shouted as he got to his feet and began inspecting his wrecked cycle. "Go on without me."

Down the highway the Dolphins' buses and their two escorts continued. And within a couple of more minutes, a second cop also took a spill. Don Shula, riding in the first seat on the passenger's side, was as sympathetic as the next guy, but on gameday he was all about winning, and getting to the stadium on time and going through a proper pregame ritual was part of winning. So without hesitating Shula barked orders at the driver, "Keep going. He'll be all right."

A Dallas-area historian noted he had never seen snow on the ground at Texas Stadium since it had opened in 1971. A winter weather advisory warned travelers of hazardous conditions on bridges and overpasses throughout the day. Snow, sleet, and rain poured through the stadium's iconic roof opening and caused the tarp that covered the field to freeze to the artificial surface. Ground crew chief Bruce Hardy, who had been in charge of the facility for a decade, called the conditions the worst he had experienced. Hardy's crew couldn't remove the tarp by hand in some areas of the field so a forklift was brought in for the job. But even that was ineffective when portions of the tarp ripped where it had stuck to the field. Cowboys receiver Alvin Harper took a nasty spill while warming up before the game and had to be helped to the locker room. And *then* things got crazy.

The Dolphins came to town down to their third starting quarterback after Dan Marino and Scott Mitchell were felled by injuries. Marino had a torn Achilles, and Mitchell had a separated throwing shoulder. So against Dallas' offense that boasted Troy Aikman, Michael Irvin, and Emmitt Smith—three future Hall of Fame players—the Dolphins answered with...Steve DeBerg.

DeBerg was 39 years old at the time. He'd been cut in October by the Tampa Bay Buccaneers after he threw one touchdown and three interceptions in three games. He was picked up as a free agent by the Dolphins because, well, where else could one find a chain-smoking, hard-drinking, horse-race-loving quarterback with moxie in mid-November? After throwing two touchdowns without an interception in his Dolphins debut four days earlier, DeBerg was about to throw for 287 yards and direct a game-winning drive against the defending champions. But DeBerg was neither the hero nor goat this day.

This is about Byars. And kicker Pete Stoyanovich. And center Jeff Dellenbach. And, yes, Leon Lett.

Despite field conditions that made professional athletes move like people wearing ice skates for the first time, Byars showed no fear. The snow, ice, and frigid temperatures took him back to his childhood in Dayton, Ohio. And so when he took a handoff that he ended 77 yards later in the end zone, Byars celebrated the success as he had as a child by dropping onto his back and making a snow angel. "I was a kid watching the Cleveland Browns play in the snow a lot," Byars said. "Snow like this—me and my friends would go outside and imitate what we just saw. We would play like we were the Browns playing in the snow."

The veteran fullback outran everyone to the end zone, even though it took him 12 seconds to travel those 77 yards. "To me it was just like it was green grass out there," Byars said. "It was just like it was 75 degrees and sunny out there—only better."

After 59 minutes of play, the Cowboys had erased Miami's early advantage and clung to a 14–13 lead. But a late drive by the Dolphins kept their hopes alive. And Byars kept the drive alive with two big catches that put Miami in position for a 41-yard field goal attempt. After team Bible study the previous night, Byars had told some teammates something amazing was going to happen. He told them he was going play a big part in the next day's game. He just felt it. "I told the guys I felt inside that I would make something happen with a big play of some sort," Byars said. "I felt something big was coming."

He was right because after the last of Byars' seven catches for 80 yards, the final 15 bizarre seconds of the game turned certain disappointment into sheer joy for Miami. Stoyanovich's 41-yard attempt was blocked by Dallas defensive lineman Jimmie Jones, and the ball slithered inside the 10-yard line where three Dolphins offensive linemen surrounded it. All the Cowboys had to do was watch the play from afar to win the game. Indeed, owner Jerry Jones was seen celebrating the apparent victory on the Dallas sideline the moment Jimmie Jones blocked the kick.

But Lett, a stellar defensive tackle, for some reason went sliding into the ball, leading with his size 16 EEE shoes. "You could hear the thump, and as soon as I heard it, the scramble was on," Dellenbach said. "We all knew if we could get the ball, we could have another chance."

Guard Bert Weidner tried to fall on the ball, but all that did was push it toward the goal line. Then Dellenbach fell on it at the 1-yard line as his momentum carried him into the end zone. In his second season as an NFL referee, Ed Hochuli met with his crew as a group of Dallas players tried to sway them to award the Cowboys the ball. But Hochuli correctly awarded Miami the ball and had it placed at the 1-yard line. Then the ball was placed at the 7-yard line. And then it was put back at the 1-yard line.

And each time the spot was changed, holder and backup quarterback Doug Pederson used a towel and his hands to clear away the snow and ice from the spot he would soon put the ball down for Stoyanovich's fateful kick. "One of their guys kicked some [snow] where my hold was supposed to be, and I just kicked it back toward him," Pederson said. "I felt like Billy Martin kicking dirt on an umpire."

With three seconds left, Dellenbach's snap was good, Pederson's hold was good, and Stoyanovich's kick was true. Dolphins 16, Cowboys 14. "I feel like something of a hero, but at the same time I feel so thankful that we had fortune on our side today," Stoyanovich said.

"We go a whole game playing decent. Then we get three seconds on the NFL bloopers show," Dallas defensive back James Washington said.

The moment stuck with Lett. It probably always will. He didn't speak to reporters afterward and stayed out of sight for days even as there was speculation he'd be cut by coach Jimmy Johnson or alienated from teammates. "If you work in a chemical plant, you better know your chemicals," Dallas cornerback Kevin Smith responded when asked about Lett's knowledge of the rules. "If you're a doctor, you've got to know doctoring. We're getting paid a lot of money to read the fine print."

The following Monday after playing hide-and-seek with the local media for days, Lett released a statement through the Cowboys' public relations office. "I'm deeply hurt for my teammates because of the judgment error I made at the end of last week's game," Lett said. "In my efforts to try to help our team win, I made a poor decision. Hopefully, my performance in the future will in some small way make up for my mistake."

Years later, Lett claimed to know the rules about touching a ball that had been blocked and called the moment "a brain freeze."

The Dolphins left that game with a 9–2 record. After the Buffalo Bills lost that weekend, they led the AFC East and boasted the NFL's best record. The Cowboys had lost two in a row and were 7–4. But the Cowboys didn't lose another game that season as they rallied and went on to win their second consecutive Super Bowl. Ravaged by injuries at quarterback, linebacker, and the secondary, the Dolphins didn't win another game. They finished 9–7 and missed the playoffs.

55 Marino Tears His Achilles

Minutes before a forgettable Miami Dolphins practice in 2017, Dan Marino was warming up. He was in his late 50s and nearly 20 years removed from playing his last NFL game, but that arm that thrilled thousands in the 1980s and '90s was still golden. The spirals were tight. The velocity was obvious. And that quick release had not slowed over time. That moment was a glimpse of what Marino could once do. And it also makes this point: the greatest quarterback in franchise history didn't leave the game because he was betrayed by his right arm.

It was because he was forsaken by his legs. And if you need to get specific, it was mostly his right leg, the one with the surgically repaired Achilles tendon that Marino ruptured in October of 1993. The facts about that long ago Achilles injury have mostly faded. Marino's heroic comeback the next year is like a fog at sea and it kept us from seeing how Marino's 17-year career was about to run aground.

Go back to that moment in Cleveland decades ago. On a second-and-16 play from the Browns' 20-yard line, Marino threw a 10-yard completion to Terry Kirby. But while eyes were on Kirby being pushed out of bounds, Marino was writhing in pain on the ground. "I thought I'd gotten kicked by the rusher," Marino said. "I was told I wasn't. There was a sharp pain in the back of my ankle just as I threw the ball. It felt like I'd been shot."

The Achilles tendon on his right foot unraveled and flew up his calf like a window shade run amok. It was ruptured, and Marino's season was over. The next day team physicians Dan Kanell and Peter Indelicato performed surgery at Imperial Point Medical Center to repair the Achilles. The results were not great. He required additional surgery March 31 to remove bone spurs in the front of that right ankle.

Marino came back in 1994 amid questions whether he could regain his form at age 33. Yeah, um, dumb questions because Marino threw 30 touchdowns that season—the first time he reached that mark since 1986. In the season opener, Marino threw five touchdowns. He threw for 473 yards. He even had a 10-yard run for a first down. Marino completed passes to seven different receivers, including a 35 yarder to Irving Fryar on fourth and 5 with 3:19 to play. On a day New England Patriots quarterback Drew Bledsoe threw four touchdown passes, that fourth-down score was the difference in the game. "Dan's back," Don Shula proclaimed.

Except he wasn't. Sure, the statistics looked the same and sometimes even better than before. But Marino didn't look the same. Or feel the same. He was often in considerable pain. He admitted the "quickness and burst" in his drop, setup, and throwing motion had not fully returned. By then Marino had no cartilage in his left knee so he wore a metal knee brace. And he was fitted with a special shoe and brace to protect the right Achilles. Along with those big pads players wore then, Marino trotted onto the field each gameday looking like a semi-truck prepped for a drag race. "Are you asking me if I'm at the place I was when I got hurt in Cleveland last year? The answer is no," Marino admitted during the season. "It might be a while before I get close to that."

The 1994 season came and went, and Marino was still searching for answers to the problem even as reporters were naming him Comeback Player of the Year. "You can see the right calf has not developed like it should," Marino said. "Most of the time it's not noticeable in the way I play, but I feel a difference."

Marino's right calf was smaller than his left, a product of post-surgery atrophy. Tests performed by the team's medical staff confirmed what was obvious to the eyes: the right calf was only 80 percent as strong as the left. Marino could not stand on the toes of his right foot and struggled to do so the rest of his career. That affected his torque. And the whole thing eventually made a quarterback, who was never extremely mobile, a target.

Marino considered another Achilles surgery in January 1995. He visited a specialist in New York. But he decided against the procedure because it would have meant another long rehabilitation and possibly missing part, if not all, of that season. He chose to continue rehabbing the leg to try to regain what he had lost. "The doctors told me it was ruptured pretty bad, and I might take longer than most people to recover," Marino said. "It's not where it was before I was injured and I'm not so sure it will be back to that, but I've got to try and work at it and try to get it to that point."

It never happened. To this day Marino's gait is different, and that right calf looks different than the left.

56 Jason Taylor Almost Quits

There was so much at stake for Jason Taylor the summer of 1997. The Miami Dolphins had invested a third-round draft pick on Taylor only months earlier, which signaled coach Jimmy Johnson had high hopes for the defensive end but realized the player was not yet fully ready for the NFL. And that first week of training camp proved to everyone—including Taylor—both were fair.

Taylor was allowed no entitlement that first training camp. He wasn't gifted first-team snaps. He wasn't allowed days off or even practice repetitions off during the scheduled two-a-days. Taylor had to work. And fight. And improve so he could prove worthy of his spot. And one week into the whole deal, Taylor was in a dark place. Thoughts of quitting—hatched days before—had grown into a temptation that needed only the affirmation of one person, Taylor's mom, Georgia Taylor. "After about the fifth day of training camp my rookie year, after the heat, the two-a-days, Jimmy yelling, I called my mom and said, 'You know, Mom, I don't know if this NFL thing is for me.'" Taylor said. "I told her I didn't think I could do it anymore. I told her I was seriously thinking of quitting."

And that stark revelation was met with a pause on the other end of the line before it was answered with career-saving wisdom. "She said, 'Well, you can come home and get a job or go in the military. Or you can get your butt back to bed and get to practice in the morning.'"

The military had long been an option the Taylors considered a way to improve their lives. His former adoptive father was in the military. One of his sisters was in the military. "It was an option," Taylor said. "But I thought about it and got up the next morning and went to practice. And I didn't think about that nonsense again."

The Dolphins are glad of that. Taylor put together a Hall of Fame career that included 139½ sacks, which was sixth all time when he retired. And now that Taylor's 17-year career was over, that lone thought of quitting the game was overshadowed by thoughts of missing the game. "Those three and a half hours you can't replace," Taylor said. "You cannot find anything in life to replace it. It's an extraordinary time, and the bigger the game, the pressure, the more physical, the game is always more fun. Yeah, those times are intoxicating. The nasty, physical, chippy games? Yeah. More fun. Your head's on a swivel because people are taking shots at you. There's pushing and shoving after every play. Those battles are fun. And I think those kind of battles bring your team closer together, too."

Taylor played his final game in 2011. He's since worked in the media on both television and radio. He runs the Jason Taylor Foundation in South Florida. He has coached his sons in high school. But none of that has fully helped him detoxify from the game he calls "intoxicating." "How do you detoxify? You go to football rehab—the golf course," Taylor said. "You go frustrate the hell out of yourself. You get your [butt] whooped by a game. You try to get good at something else. I use it as a business networking thing. The foundation has a tournament. You meet great people, and the big, competitive side of you gets a small way to compete. I also like to play with my boys. That's fun."

It needs mentioning that after that night, in which quitting was a serious consideration, Taylor bowed to a competitive spirit that always had him pushing for something better. It was as if he embraced the opposite of quitting. But now he apparently understands that approach might not have been the answer either. "I tell my kids, I tell the kids I coach: if I could go back and do it over, I'd enjoy the process more," Taylor said. "I never enjoyed the process because I was so focused on the destination. So you kind of miss the journey sometimes. The good times, the crappy times, the locker room times, the bonding times of sitting around, even the grind, I'd enjoy it more. I think maybe I missed the boat a bit on the process. I missed little stupid stuff that you take for granted every day during your career. And then it's over. I miss those times."

57 Saban Leaves for Bama

In November of 2004, as names of candidates for the Miami Dolphins' soon-vacant head coach job made the rounds, Nick Saban wanted everyone to know he was thrilled to be coaching at Louisiana State University. "I'm happy with the job that I have at LSU and I'm not interested in doing anything else," Saban said in a statement released by the LSU sports information office. "I'm happy here, and my family is happy here. I don't know anything about any other jobs."

One month later Saban signed a five-year contract to become the Dolphins' coach. And so it was two years later, in December of 2006, that Saban turned to a familiar play from his career advancement playbook. Rumors of Alabama's interest in the struggling Dolphins coach were rampant for weeks, and finally on December 21, Saban was peppered with questions about that job during a press conference. "I don't know how else I can say it, guys," Saban told reporters as his voice rose. "I've said it three different occasions. I don't know how else I can say it. I don't know why you keep asking. I don't control what people say. I don't control what people put on dot com or anything else. There's no significance in my opinion about this, about me, about any interest I have in anything other than being the coach here."

He was then asked why he wouldn't just say, "I'm not going to be the Alabama coach?" Saban responded, "I think I just said that. Did I not say that? How didn't I say that?"

Because he had not used those words, one reporter answered. So Saban did just that. "I guess I have to say it: I'm not going to be the Alabama coach," he said.

Two weeks later, on January 3, 2007, after his agent and then he met with Alabama athletic director Mal Moore and after Saban's wife, Terry, expressed to her husband how she didn't love living in South Florida and preferred a small town, Saban accepted the Alabama job.

As Saban rolled away from his South Florida house with Moore, Dolphins owner Wayne Huizenga asked reporters and fans for suggestions on what to do next. South Florida football fans immediately vilified Saban; some called him Satan for years to come. The media wasn't much kinder. Even people, who were tied to the franchise, bashed the departing coach. "He's a scoundrel and a skunk. And those are his good points," former Dolphins guard Bob Kuechenberg said.

"Obviously, he lied," former coach Jimmy Johnson told South Florida's 790 The Ticket. "He's playing word games with the media. His agent, Jimmy Sexton, was negotiating with Alabama. He knew that. He comes back and says, 'I have not talked to Alabama.' No he hasn't, but Jimmy Sexton has done all the talking."

Saban had kept some assistants from interviewing for promotions with other teams, telling them they needed to be loyal. And now he was on a speakerphone with members of that same staff telling them he was leaving. "I called eight, 10 guys and probably got a hold of six or eight of them," Saban said. "I left messages for other guys. I emailed every guy on the team…A few guys called back."

In an interview with the *Miami Herald* days later, Saban vainly tried to defend his own honor and portray himself as a victim. "I'm disappointed that I'm being victimized a little bit here," Saban said. "That's really not the person I am. If you look at 35 years of work that I've done in this profession and my marriage and everything else, that's not who I am. That's not what I've done. I've never been a guy to lie, cheat, and steal anywhere, never, ever. But now all of a sudden, I am."

But what about that lie, Nick? What about saying, "I will not be the Alabama coach?" "When you lie to somebody, you're trying to deceive them," Saban said. "I wasn't trying to deceive anybody. I was focused on the season and I was working."

Saban admitted he was sorry—but not about how he handled the whole lie thing. He was sorry about how he failed to properly dodge the fateful question with spin. "I really do regret that I was pinned into the corner," Saban said. "I regret that there was not some kind of way that I could answer a question [like] that."

58 Winning the AFC East While Wearing Towels

Picture a royal coronation with all its stately pomp and trimmings. Now imagine the king juggling, then fumbling the crown just as it's handed to him. And imagine that by the end of the ceremony, the king is wearing nothing more than a towel wrapped around his waist. That's how the AFC East division crown was handled and then handed over to the Miami Dolphins on Christmas Eve of 2000. "Twenty years from now," Dolphins defensive end Trace Armstrong said afterward, "it will be fun to say you were a part of this."

The Dolphins were a good team in 2000. Dave Wannstedt's club was 11–5 and won the AFC East for the first time in six years. But before that could happen, the Dolphins had to beat the New England Patriots in the season finale in dank Foxboro Stadium. It didn't seem a tough assignment because the Patriots won only five games that year. Except the Dolphins trailed at halftime. And after three quarters. And they needed 10 points in the final quarter to save the day. Kicker Olindo Mare connected on a 49-yard field goal—his longest of the season—to give Miami its 27–24 victory margin.

As game-winning field goals go, this one was unorthodox in its timing because it came after the Dolphins called their final timeout with 15 seconds left to play. Had coach Dave Wannstedt been patient and let the clock run down to, say, three seconds, Mare's kick would have been the final play. But the questionable clock management gave the Patriots nine seconds to take a kickoff and snap one play from their 40-yard line. And that's when things got all sorts of bizarre.

Dolphins defensive lineman Jason Taylor chopped at New England quarterback Drew Bledsoe's arm as he threw his final pass. The ball bounced in the dirt, after which Bledsoe picked it up and tried to run with it before eventually throwing it forward in a futile last gasp.

Referee Johnny Grier first ruled it a fumble. *Game over. The Dolphins were AFC East champs!*

But then Grier ruled it an illegal forward pass, a penalty that ran 10 seconds off the clock. *Game over. The Dolphins were AFC East Champs!*

Everyone headed to their locker rooms. Then Grier had to change his mind again. Because as he and his crew reached their dressing room, the buzzer on his belt went off. The replay booth wanted Grier to take another look at the so-called final play. Grier watched the play and decided he had erred. Incomplete pass. Jerry Seeman, the NFL's senior director of officiating, called from New York to tell Jack Reader, the officiating observer in the press box, that the game wasn't over. It was the Patriots' ball with three seconds to play. *Game on. The Dolphins were not AFC East champs.* "We were in our locker room when the officials came in and said there were three seconds left," said New England coach Bill Belichick. "So I got the team together, and we walked back out on to the field."

But there were no Dolphins in sight. AFC East championship hats and T-shirts had been distributed to players in their locker room. Wannstedt, wearing one of those hats, had already talked to the team and reporters. Owner Wayne Huizenga had delivered a congratulatory speech. Players were in the showers. "They really didn't want to come back on the field," Grier said of his first visit to the Miami locker room. "I could understand that."

Wannstedt wanted nothing with continuing the game and argued that point with Grier. "My guys were undressed, untaped, dressed in their street clothes," Wannstedt said. "I was concerned about the safety of my people."

Grier agreed with this argument and sent everyone home for Christmas. "We got out on the field, and I talked to Johnny, and he said, 'Well, there are three seconds left, and there should be another play, but we are not going to have another play for safety reasons,'" Belichick said.

But Seeman wasn't having it. He directed Grier to finish the game. And Seeman said if the Dolphins didn't play, they would be subject to forfeiting the game. Grier relayed that message, and that turned the Dolphins locker room into a beehive of activity. Taylor got his teammates going. He had been knocked unconscious during the game and went down in such a manner that linebacker Derrick Rodgers thought Taylor had died. Now alive and well, Taylor went into the crowded shower area and told teammates to suit up again. "Everybody thought he was kidding so he could cut in line to take a shower," linebacker Zach Thomas said.

Eleven Dolphins defenders, many of them showered, put on their game-soiled uniforms and went back onto the field without tape or braces to protect their wrists, ankles, or knees. Some didn't even put on pads. Offensive players, including tight end Jed Weaver, guard Kevin Donnally, and others, paced the frigid sidelines wearing nothing but shower clogs and towels draped around their waists. Patriots wide receiver Terry Glenn said offensive coordinator Charlie Weis told New England players, "If we score, it will go down in history as one of the great plays of all time."

The Patriots came back out with Michael Bishop as their quarterback. The strong-armed Bishop was New England's designated Hail Mary thrower. He snapped the ball with those controversial three seconds remaining, scrambled around long enough to let receivers get downfield, and uncorked a harmless floater that came off the side of his hand.

Womp, womp, womp.

Game over. Dolphins were the AFC East champs—a full 35 minutes after everyone thought they won the title the first time. Thomas sprinted into the Miami locker room, yelling, "Repeat, repeat!"

59 Signing Keith Jackson

Hall of Famer Bill Polian knew how to build a football team. He was the architect of the Buffalo Bills that went to four consecutive Super Bowls. He got the expansion Carolina Panthers to the NFC Championship Game in their second season. He built the Indianapolis Colts into a powerhouse that reached two Super Bowls and won it all in February 2007. But in September of 1992, he was annoyed the Miami Dolphins were beating him in free agency with the signing of tight end Keith Jackson only four days after the system began. "My gripe is not with Don Shula," Polian told *USA TODAY*. "My feeling is to have it [free agency] happen at this point in the season, regardless of who he signed with, is disruptive to competitive balance."

Polian was comfortable with the balance of power in the AFC East because his team had been better than the Dolphins the two previous years and had gone to the Super Bowl in the 1990 and '91 seasons. But the NFL witnessed a seismic shift in the autumn of 1992 when federal judge David Doty granted four players—Jackson, Webster Slaughter, Garin Veris, and D.J. Dozier—the ability to sign with new teams.

The door to unfettered free agency was ajar. And the Dolphins aggressively pushed it open four days later by signing Jackson to a four-year, $6 million contract that included a $1.5 million signing bonus. "You need to do anything you can to get a good football player in your organization," Shula said. "He's an excellent player."

The signing made the Dolphins free-agency pioneers. And it temporarily shifted the balance of power away from Polian's Bills and to Shula's Dolphins. Jackson arrived in Miami four days before an October 1992 game between the undefeated Dolphins and undefeated Bills in Orchard Park. He didn't know the entire play-book on gameday, but Shula used the tight end in passing situations during the Dolphins' 37–10 victory. Jackson caught four passes for 64 yards, including a 24-yard score that Dan Marino had originally intended for Mark Clayton, who at first was a little peeved Jackson snatched his reception out of the air. But then Jackson turned the catch into an electric score, and Clayton was the first to greet Jackson in the end zone to celebrate.

It was an exhilarating time. The Dolphins had Clayton, Mark Duper, Bobby Humphrey, Marino, and had just dropped a three-time Pro Bowl tight end into the mix. In the ensuing weeks, Jackson caught everything Marino threw in his general vicinity. He was affable, started his own luncheon series on Tuesdays, and even president-elect Bill Clinton said that he had begun rooting for the Dolphins because he wanted to see his fellow Arkansas native do well. "I didn't make a mistake, and people were sitting back wondering if I'd ever make one," Jackson said. "But then it happened, and everyone jumped on it."

Jackson fumbled against the New York Jets. He tipped a pass that resulted in an interception in the rematch with Buffalo. He dropped a sure touchdown against the New Orleans Saints. He fumbled against the San Francisco 49ers. Nonetheless, he finished second on the team with 48 catches and five touchdown receptions in 1992.

His success led the Dolphins to only increase their appetite for free agents. And in 1993 Miami added Keith Byars, Ron Heller, Mark Ingram, and Mike Golic. A year later they signed five more free agents, including quarterback Bernie Kosar. The team even made a run at Deion Sanders, giving him a Dolphins jersey embla-zoned with the No. 2—his number at Florida State—during his free-agent visit to the team facility. "Coach Shula has made the decision we're going to try to be at the forefront of free agency," club executive Bryan Wiedmeier said.

60 Thanksgiving Game vs. the Cardinals

After two bench-clearing brawls on the field resulted in 20 players from each team being fined a then-NFL record $14,000, after Conrad Dobler was ejected for taking cheap shots and shoving an official, after several Miami Dolphins players tried to shove a reporter into the showers in their locker room, *then* the attention for what really happened could be placed on the man who wore horn-rimmed glasses behind his facemask.

Thanksgiving Day 1977 was a strange one, all right. Oh, it was magnificent for the Dolphins as they thoroughly whipped the St. Louis Cardinals 55–14 in front of a sold-out Busch Stadium and a national television audience. But it was also a weird game—at once memorable and forgettable. And regrettable.

Consider that this was Bob Griese's finest game. His finest hour, perhaps. Yes, he was the quarterback of the Perfect Season team and the great team that won Super Bowl VIII. He also was inducted into the Pro Football Hall of Fame and had his No. 12 retired. But this game, this performance, was unparalleled. He had six touchdown passes. And he threw only 23 passes and played only three quarters. "People had been writing us off because they didn't have faith in us," Griese said. "We have faith, though. We had to win. This was a pressure situation, and everyone was down on us, but we won. That's the significant thing—not whether it might have been the best game I ever played."

Three times before in his career, Griese had thrown four touchdown passes in a game. He and John Stofa shared that distinction in the team record books. But this game Griese had four touchdowns by halftime. (Dan Marino would throw six touchdown passes against the New York Jets in 1986 to share the record with Griese to this day.)

Griese threw three touchdown passes to Nat Moore and one each to Duriel Harris, Andre Tillman, and Gary Davis. He did it against a team that had won six consecutive games and was the hottest team in the league. "I didn't feel like it was going to be that easy," Griese said. "But you never know when you're going to get that kind of execution. It's hard to say why things go right in some games and not in another."

In his first season wearing glasses during games, Griese almost tied the NFL record of seven touchdowns in one game, but his last pass fluttered off Loaird McCreary's fingertips in the third quarter. "Yes," he said. "I knew it would have tied the record."

The Dolphins set some team records that day. Their 55 points still stands as the record for most in a game, surpassing the 52 scored in 1972 against the New England Patriots. Their eight touchdowns still stand as a team record in one game. Their 34 first downs set a record that stood until 2014. "What they did was kick the holy hell out of us," Cardinals coach Don Coryell said.

He meant the football stuff. The extracurricular stuff offered a much more nebulous result because, well, no one wins football fights.

That drama began, of course, with St. Louis offensive lineman Dobler. *Sports Illustrated* dubbed Dolber the "meanest man in Pro Football" in 1976. The Dolphins thought he was just a dirty player. And that's exactly how it looked when Dobler chop blocked Vern Den Herder as the Dolphins defensive end was engaged with a Cardinals tackle. The play resulted in a knee injury that ended Den Herder's season. Dobler also drew a personal foul penalty two plays later.

And then it was on. "Dobler is an average to below-average player who's a cheap shot son of a bitch," Dolphins offensive lineman Bob Kuechenberg told the *Miami Herald*. "He's mediocre until somebody's back is turned. There's no place for him in this game."

Dolphins linebacker A.J. Duhe and Dobler engaged in some verbal sparring before it got more physical later. And, yes, it got more physical later. "I was telling him, 'I guess we're knocking your butts out of the playoffs,'" Duhe said. "He kept saying, 'I'm going to get you out of here before it's over.' He means he's going to go for your knees. He hit Vern in the knees. I'm laying on the ground one time, and he comes in and piles on like—*pow*—like the dog that he is."

Tim Foley, one of the softest spoken players on those 1970s Dolphins teams and a prominent member of the Fellowship for Christian Athletes, was incensed after this game. "He makes his living being a slob," Foley said. "He's in there trying to hurt people. It's a real lowlife way to play. I'd be embarrassed being that guy's teammate."

Dobler, by the way, was ejected mostly because he shoved one of the game officials. He later discussed the matter with some reporters and not others in the St. Louis locker room. So, yeah, he was as inconsistent as his play. He told the *St. Louis Post Dispatch* that one of the Dolphins' "tall linebackers spit on my helmet and hit me in the head." As to the official, Dobler assured everyone that he would write him a personal letter of apology.

In the Dolphins' postgame locker room, several players were upset with *Hollywood Sun-Tattler* sports editor Ed Plaisted because he had written a piece predicting Don Shula and the Dolphins would "not be giving thanks" (remember it was Thanksgiving) after being "manhandled" by the Cardinals. A scuffle broke as Kuechenberg reportedly tried to throw Plaisted into the showers. Dolphins offensive line coach John Sandusky intervened—thankfully.

61 The Revenge of the Bills

The franchise that owned much of the 1970s had a new look by 1980. The No-Names from the famed Super Bowl defense were gone, giving way to new names. Wide receivers Paul Warfield and Howard Twilley were gone, and the Miami Dolphins opened games in double-tight end sets 12 times in 1980. Even future Hall of Fame quarterback Bob Griese had become a backup. The new decade signaled new times and not necessarily good times for the Dolphins, at least not immediately. And there was no clearer indication that things had changed than the decade's regular-season opener at Buffalo.

The Dolphins swept the Buffalo Bills in the 1970s. Despite the greatness of O.J. Simpson running, the development of Joe Ferguson passing, and the advent of the Electric Company blocking, the Bills lost 20 consecutive games against Miami. That's every single meeting over 10 years. But on September 7, 1980 at a sold-out Rich Stadium, the Bills beat Don Shula's team 17–7 behind 131 combined yards by Joe Cribbs. And that game didn't just foreshadow change but rather screamed it.

Little did we know it would eventually lead to revenge. That wouldn't come until the 1990s because the Dolphins and Bills generally went back in forth in the '80s. "They won some; we won some," Shula said in 1990. "These two teams have a history."

History was about to get less kind for Miami. Over the next six seasons, the Dolphins made the playoffs four times. And the Bills eliminated Miami from the postseason on three of those occasions. By the end of that six-year run in December of 1995, the Bills were on a decline from their four straight Super Bowl appearances, and the Dolphins...were shaking from Shula's seismic decision to retire.

"A lot of things happened up there and down here against Buffalo," linebacker Bryan Cox said almost prophetically in 1994. "We're in each other's way."

It began in 1990, a year that would set a tone for what was about to happen. The Dolphins, a good team, beat the Bills early that season. The Bills, a great team, won late in the year and in the playoffs—when it mattered most. That's exactly how it was that year when the Dolphins beat the Bills 30–7 that first meeting. Buffalo was about to launch an AFC dynasty, but nobody told the Dolphins, who dominated the game so thoroughly that Buffalo coach Marv Levy surrendered with eight minutes to play by removing Jim Kelly from the game. "The Miami Dolphins are no joke anymore," safety Louis Oliver proclaimed. "We can play with anyone in the league. We pounded them today. It feels great!"

The feeling was fleeting. The regular-season meetings soon became an afterthought because it was all about the postseason for these two teams. The Bills wanted to establish something those years. Once they did, they wanted to keep going back to the Super Bowl.

The Dolphins had similar goals. Shula wanted to return to the Super Bowl one final time. Dan Marino wanted to return. Shula wanted a ring for Marino.

The Louis Oliver Game

That 1990 season all came down to a January 12, 1991, meeting in snowy, frigid Orchard Park, New York. Defensive coordinator Tom Olivadotti, who typically played a bend-but-don't-break defense, decided he wanted to blitz Kelly. Except that idea meant the Dolphins would have to cover Andre Reed or James Lofton man-to-man. And Olivadotti decided Oliver, a safety, could match up against Reed and sometimes Lofton. In the snow. In single coverage.

He couldn't.

Reed caught three passes for 96 yards and a touchdown in the first half. Lofton caught four passes for 84 yards and a touchdown.

Both touchdowns were yielded by Oliver. He was benched at halftime. In the second half the Dolphins played cornerback Paul Lankford on the receivers, and the offense scored as often as the Bills. But Miami's fate was sealed. "You've got to have corners out there on me. You can't have safeties, and I had Louis Oliver," Reed said. "It doesn't make sense. Anybody knows that when you put a safety on a receiver one on one, it's going to be a mistake. Oliver is not really a cover guy. It didn't work out."

The Screen Pass Game

In the 1992–93 season, the Dolphins had perhaps their best last chance to get to a Super Bowl. They hosted the AFC Championship Game in January of '93, and again the defense failed miserably in a game that has its own depressing name.

The Bills had used a couple of innocuous screen passes in a November victory against Miami. And somebody obviously remembered because they came back with at least half-a-dozen screen passes this game. All of them were successful. "In 15 years at NBC," analyst Bob Trumpy said on the broadcast, "I don't ever remember seeing a game that employed the screen pass more."

The Bills used receiver screens. They threw screens to running backs Kenneth Davis and Thurman Thomas. "We got that from the Houston Oilers," Thomas bragged afterward. "They run it a lot. We were just going to go where the empty spot was, and it worked all day for us."

Olivadotti never adjusted, and the Bills won 29–10.

The Thomas Plows Olivadotti Game

The last of the three elimination games Buffalo served Miami in the '90s came on December 30, 1995. It was supposed to be about two coaches in their 60s looking for new wrinkles. No one imagined Levy's plan would be to play old-fashioned ball, battering and bruising the Miami defense to the tune of 341 rushing yards.

Thomas gained 158 yards. Some guy named Darick Holmes gained 87 yards. And another unknown named Tim Tindale, who rushed for 65 yards in a career spanning three NFL regular seasons, gained 68 yards against the Dolphins that day.

The Bills had a 27–0 edge in the fourth quarter before the Dolphins managed their first touchdown. The 37–22 final suggested a more competitive game than it actually was. It ended up being Shula's last game. "From the start of the game, it was obvious we couldn't stop them, and we couldn't get anything going ourselves," Shula said. "We never challenged. That's the way this team will be remembered."

62 Order a Steak at Shula's

The server at this rustic restaurant in this sleepy northwest Miami-Dade County town had brought to the table a side of beef the size of a man's head. The serving reminds one of that slab of dinosaur the cartoon waitress threw on Fred Flintstone's ride to open the show every Saturday morning in the 1960s. At the original Shula's Steak House in Miami Lakes, named after the coach and located in the town where the coach lived for decades, you are presented 48 ounces of sizzling porterhouse cut of pure angus in all its 2,400-calorie glory.

Perhaps in a manner similar to how players of yesteryear faced the legendary coach calling them out, you can understand the pressure of the Don Shula challenge. As folks in adjacent tables stare, the objective is to devour that massive slab of meat so you can go down in restaurant history. People across America have taken on the challenge of eating that enormous porterhouse. At last count some 40,000 hearty souls had completed the demanding and delicious task. Adam Richman, a Miami Dolphins fan, conquered the 48-ouncer in a record 20 minutes in 2010 when he was on the Travel Channel. The restaurant claims some dude named Taft Parker completed the challenge over 347 times because, well, Shula won 347 games. Parker completed the challenge for the 100th time in 2001 with Shula by his side, and the coach gave Parker a commemorative football for accomplishing the feat.

That day Parker started with the shrimp cocktail, followed by the steak soup, which was really a Hungarian goulash right from a recipe Shula's grandmother wrote. Then came the porterhouse—cooked rare—along with an extra helping of mushrooms. Did we mention Parker was 5'11" and 280 pounds on the day he marked this milestone? Parker said that the football Shula gave him that day read, "Dear Taft, I'll pay for the angioplasty." No idea if he was kidding.

Shula's Steak House, a must visit for Dolphins fans, boasts 21 restaurants in seven states, though the numbers expand and contract because the restaurant business isn't quite as consistent as Shula's players once were. The chain promises an expansion to 30 locations by the end of 2020. There's Shula's Steak House, Shula's 347 Grille, Shula's 2, Shula's Bar & Grill, and Shula Burger. The original is in Miami Lakes. It was there well before it was ever named Shula's. "After home games sometimes my dad and mom would go have dinner there," said Sharon Shula, one of Shula's five children. "They would go so often eventually it led to the restaurant becoming the first Shula's."

That happened in 1989. Back then the angus and other beef the restaurant used was sourced from a herd that was less than a mile away on the west side of State Road 826. *Talk about fresh.* Black angus cows remain the star of the show even if that original herd is long gone, and that field now houses a school. Shula's uses black angus beef in its trademarked Shula Cut, which among other things, is always center cut, hand selected, and aged 28 days.

Shula doesn't run the day-to-day operations. He never really did. Wife Mary-Anne was the CEO for years before she retired. Son David was a partner and brand ambassador until he returned to his true love, which is coaching. But whenever the coach shows up at his restaurant, it's a draw. He likes the attention and gets it.

The only down side? While the place has lobster bisque and French onion soup on the menu, the Hungarian steak soup is nowhere to be found anymore. It was apparently retired like a former Dolphins star whose time on the roster had ended.

63 Tragic Deaths

Romantics remember the early 1980s as a time when the Miami Dolphins came close to rekindling the glory of the previous decade. Don Shula's team went to one Super Bowl running the ball with Andra Franklin in 1982 and then lucked into a star passer named Dan Marino in the following year's draft. It felt everything was going right. But the franchise endured pain amid all that promise.

In four summers starting in 1981 until 1985, the Dolphins mourned. Car crashes claimed the lives of linebacker Rusty Chambers, running back David Overstreet, and the wife of linebacker Charles Bowser. Heart disease killed linebacker Larry Gordon. Three players, each an integral part of the team's plan, were suddenly snatched away by fate. Four families, all young and vibrant, with children to raise, parents to nurture, and wives to love, were torn apart by death. "I can't remember any team having losses like this year after year," Shula said in 1985 after Camilla Bowser was killed in a head-on auto accident at the age of 25. "The only thing you can do is continue on and do the best you can. You can't feel sorry for yourself and your football team in a case like this because of the great loss to the family of the player."

The tragedies were disparate in that they involved different people in different circumstances. But they were all connected by the heartache they caused. Chambers, a linebacker acquired in 1976 as a free agent, died July 1, 1981, on the outskirts of Hammond, Louisiana. The car he was riding in, which was driven by a friend, ran off a highway and flipped. Chambers died instantly. Chambers, 27, had been the Dolphins' leading tackler in 1978 and 1979 and the first defensive starter Shula ever claimed off the waiver list. The Dolphins wore a black patch with No. 51 on their helmets. They donated all the money collected from fines to his family.

Gordon, another linebacker and No. 1 draft choice in '76, died on June 25, 1983, after jogging near Phoenix. In a 1987 victory against the Oakland Raiders, Gordon intercepted three passes, blocked an extra point, and had eight tackles. Shula called it, "the greatest game I've ever seen a linebacker play."

It was 101 degrees in his native Phoenix that fateful day Gordon died. He waited until dusk before asking his 16-year-old cousin Eric Lamar to drive him to a suburb where he liked to jog. After a mile of jogging with Lamar keeping pace in the car, Gordon stopped and leaned against the car. Then he climbed into the passenger side. "He looked like he couldn't catch his breath," Lamar told the *Miami Herald* in 1985. "He said, 'Just drive the car, man,' and then he collapsed." Lamar told the paper he pulled the car to the side of the road and gave Gordon mouth-to-mouth resuscitation before taking him to the hospital. Gordon was dead two hours later as a result of idiopathic hypertrophic subaortic stenosis, a progressive obstruction of the left ventrical chamber of the heart.

Overstreet, a running back and also a No. 1 draft choice, died on June 24, 1984, when he lost control of his Mercedes in the Texas town of Winona and crashed into a gas station. Shula had hinted to reporters he expected big things from Overstreet in that coming season. The coach drafted Marino in 1983, but in the '84 offseason, told *Sports Illustrated* "the keys are David Overstreet and Dan Johnson."

Overstreet had in fact been told he would be Miami's starting running back in 1984 and had gone to visit a family member and also celebrate the news. On the return trip, Overstreet, whose blood alcohol level was over the legal limit, reportedly fell asleep, and his car struck a row of gasoline pumps. The explosion charred Overstreet's body so badly his wife could only identify him by his hands, and authorities relied on dental records.

In October of 1985, the team was preparing for a game when news came that Bowser's wife had been involved in a head-on collision about 15 miles from their training facility. By the time the player reached Pembroke Pines General Hospital, his 25-year-old wife and mother of their five-month-old daughter was dead.

Four heart-wrenching tragedies in five years numbed players and made Shula hate the weeks leading to training camp because he knew players were still away from his watchful influence. "It's the time of year," Shula told the *Miami Herald*, "when you hope the phone doesn't ring. This time of year, no news is good news."

The Dolphins dealt with the pain of those losses and persevered. But the frustration of losing men and women so young, important, and dear to them lingered. "Who knows why this happens?" Shula said. "You see it happen all the time: something negative happens to the good people, to young people who can be a real asset to society, and the people who are out dealing drugs live to be 90. It's hard to take."

64 The Replacements

Early in the autumn afternoon practice, Don Shula was at his usual spot for individual drills with his running backs. Shula threw each runner the football as they hurtled toward him. The legendary coach then suddenly raised either his left or right arm to signal the direction where the player should immediately cut before a collision ensued. It looked like a typical practice, but the difference was that the Miami Dolphins coaches were on the field with their replacement players.

The 1987 NFL season, which was supposed to debut a new stadium for the Dolphins, had been derailed by a players' strike. And club owners, unwilling to give up television revenue during the walkout, signed replacement players to fill their rosters and promised the games would go on. So the team that once won championships with a No-Name Defense now had a no-name roster of replacement players.

Shula fired the football at one of his new runners and then signaled to go left. The player instead stumbled and fell at the coach's feet. "Keep your feet under you!" Shula demanded before muttering under his breath, "This isn't going to be easy." Before this week was over, Shula had found something to be upbeat about. "I'll tell you this: the center-quarterback exchange has been real good the last couple days," he said smiling.

When players went out on strike, Dolphins personnel men Charley Winner and Chuck Connor went to work finding fill-ins. They found players who had been cut in training camp a month before. They found guys who'd played in the league years before. One defensive end came in after his career had been cut short following a failed knee surgery. His leg bowed out at a strange angle below the knee, but he was a starter nonetheless. The Dolphins signed wide receiver Floyd Raglin, but he left camp because he got a chance to play a football player in a movie and viewed that as more stable work than being an actual player on Miami's replacement squad.

The Dolphins signed former Texas A&M tight end Richard Siler. Unbeknownst to them, he was awaiting trial on a second-degree murder charge in Daytona Beach, Florida, and was free on a $7,500 bond. The club found out as they were leaving for a game in Seattle and actually got the judge to remand Siler into their custody so he could travel out of state. That one didn't last long because Siler broke his ankle in that first replacement game and was cut. He was later convicted of manslaughter in that Daytona Beach incident for which he served one year. State records show in later years he was convicted of vehicle theft, cocaine possession, and resisting arrest with violence. And in 2014 he was convicted in federal court of identity theft, for which he was sentenced to 12 years and 10 months.

The Dolphins had Dan Marino throw 44 touchdown passes in 1986, but then Kyle Mackey was their starting quarterback for a few games the following year. Mackey, a record-setting Texas high school quarterback, was the son of Dee Mackey, who had played for Shula with the Baltimore Colts. When the Dolphins called about crossing the picket lines, Mackey had already turned down half-a-dozen other teams, but he agreed to come to Miami after talking to Shula. "We had a long conversation," Mackey said. "I had a lot of respect for Coach Shula and still do. We talked and finally I said, 'They're going to play whether I'm there or not. I might as well take the opportunity and try to show what I can do to play in the NFL.'"

While coaches and replacement players prepared for what would be a three-game tenure, Miami's regular players picketed at the entrance to St. Thomas University where the Dolphins had their practice facility. After picketing for maybe an hour every morning, the players then drove to a nearby college and held an impromptu practice. The regular players often had other unions join their pickets. Musicians from the South Florida Philharmonic—members of the AFL-CIO—even showed up. "I played the drums when I was young," Marino told one of the musicians.

The real players quickly grew frustrated their pickets weren't getting enough attention. So they decided to march into camp, effectively trespassing on private property. "We might get arrested," Marino told offensive tackle Ronnie Lee as they marched. "That's all right," Lee answered, "I've been arrested before. Stick with me."

Eventually, the games were played. And the replacement Dolphins were 1–2. They lost at the Seattle Seahawks and then beat the Kansas City Chiefs at home. That game was the Dolphins' first regular-season game at their new North Miami-Dade Stadium—named Joe Robbie Stadium at the time and now called Hard Rock Stadium. The first Dolphins win at the facility was that day's 42–0 beating of Kansas City. There were 25,867 fans in the stands, and before the game was over many were chanting, "Stay on strike! Stay on strike!"

The last of Miami's three replacement games came on the road against the New York Jets. The strike had been a disaster for the players' union and had collapsed when many players crossed the picket lines. The Jets had nine regulars in uniform the final replacement weekend. The Dolphins had only one, defensive back Liffort Hobley. The Jets defensive line that day included starters Mark Gastineau, Barry Bennett, and Marty Lyons. "We decided as a group that on the very first play our right tackle was going to punch Gastineau in the mouth," said Miami center Greg Ours, who was working in an Ohio tow-truck shop when the Dolphins called weeks earlier. Not surprisingly, a fight ensued.

Mackey threw five interceptions. But he also threw a touchdown pass that helped tie the game at 31 with 1:01 to play. Mackey was so thrilled that he celebrated by hugging the first person he saw: referee Dick Jorgensen. The game went into overtime, but the Jets eventually won 37–31. The replacement Dolphins finished 1–2, and the 1987 season ended when the Dolphins missed the playoffs by one game. But the weeks of work with the replacements didn't leave Shula bitter. "I couldn't be prouder of those guys," Shula said.

65 Sammie Smith and Bobby Humphrey

Sammie Smith had spent the last five minutes at his locker stall with his head buried in his hands, weeping. And then he was summoned to Don Shula's office. "You've got to find a way to get past this," Shula said. "You've been important to our team in the past and you will be in the future. Don't let this define you. This will pass."

It was perhaps the singular moment that Miami Dolphins fans openly turned on one of their own. Smith, a first-round pick in 1989, fell out of favor with the fanbase because he fumbled at the goal line against the Houston Oilers earlier that afternoon in October of 1991, and that was too familiar because he had fumbled at the goal line the previous week against the Chiefs in Kansas City. But the misbegotten carry against the Oilers cost the Dolphins a fourth-quarter touchdown in a 17–13 loss. Unlike the K.C. fumble, this one cost the Dolphins a victory. Echoing through the stadium were chants of "Sa-mmie sucks! Sa-mmie sucks!" Smith's parents, wife, and 4-year-old daughter were sitting in those stands amid the angry bedlam.

Afterward, Smith assured Shula he'd rebound and everything would soon be back to normal. But nothing felt normal anymore. Security had to escort Smith to his car in the players' parking lot. A couple of teammates whispered concerns that Smith had lost his confidence. The running back's fate with the Dolphins was sealed after the season. Smith was traded in May 1992 to the Denver Broncos in exchange for running back Bobby Humphrey. It was a welcome exchange for both players. "It's good that I got out of Miami," Smith said the following spring. "That place wasn't right for me."

Smith wasn't long for the NFL. He played three games and gained 94 yards for the Broncos before suffering an abdominal injury. After having surgery he never played again.

In 1996 Smith's idyllic retirement imploded when he entered a guilty plea in federal court to two counts of drug trafficking. He'd been arrested in Apopka, Florida, with seven kilograms of cocaine worth an estimated $154,000. Orange County Sheriff Kevin Beary said there were videotapes showing Smith selling drugs to undercover agents. Smith served a seven-year federal prison sentence for possessing and distributing cocaine. In prison Smith rediscovered his Christian roots. "I had lost my way in my life," Smith told the *Miami Herald* in 2016. "I got disconnected from God and had to find my way back to him. Once I did, my life improved immediately. God will define what my legacy is. What he has done in my life is a testament to his power, and I hope that is what people will say about me. I made some bad choices in my life that created rough patches for me, but when I put my trust in God, he helped me to find my way back."

After the Smith trade, the Dolphins tried to enjoy what they hoped would be the better end of the deal. Humphrey had been unhappy in Denver and even held out for contract reasons. In Miami he showed up with a great attitude and free spirit. The Dolphins used him as both a runner and pass catcher out of the backfield. And he exceled at both. He averaged 4.6 yards per carry and led the team with 54 receptions. "He's productive," Shula said of Humphrey after that first season, "but there are the other things."

The other things included Humphrey being late to meetings, practice, the AFC Championship Game against the Buffalo Bills, and missing a team flight. Then things got worse after the season. Humphrey's '93 offseason included: an arrest and charge of cocaine possession, being shot in the leg by "a friend" while driving in the same car, and holding out from training camp for over a month because of a contract dispute. Obviously unhappy with the player, the Dolphins gave Humphrey permission to seek a trade.

Only two years earlier, he was coming off his second consecutive 1,000-yard season and was in the Pro Bowl. Now, no team tried to trade for Humphrey. "I'm ready to put all that behind me," Humphrey said after all the incidents. "This is a different Bobby Humphrey. I'm here to tell Coach that I'm going to give my all to playing football, and that what has happened won't affect me. I've grown and changed a lot in the last couple of months. With God's help, I know I can help the Dolphins next season."

Nope. Humphrey, 26 at the time, injured his knee and went on injured reserve. He never played a regular-season down in the NFL again.

66 The Patriots Knew the Dolphins' Signals

Sitting in the first-class cabin of the charter flight home from an embarrassing 17–3 playoff loss to the New England Patriots in 1997, Jimmy Johnson was watching a video replay of the game when *that* play streamed before his eyes. It was second and 5 for the Miami Dolphins at their own 38-yard-line. The offense was at the line of scrimmage when quarterback Dan Marino audibled. And immediately New England linebacker Todd Collins reacted by signaling to his defense where the ball was going. Marino threw a quick slant, and Collins intercepted it and ran 40 yards for a touchdown.

It was Miami's first possession of the second half, but this game was over because not even Marino can beat a defense that knows the

Dolphins' offensive plays before the snap. And the Patriots knew. No question. Johnson was already seething when he admitted as much in a sideline interview before the game. He saw it only days earlier in a 14–12 loss to the Patriots in the regular-season finale. And after seeing it again on tape, he turned his wrath to offensive coordinator Gary Stevens. "How many times do I have to tell you?" Johnson yelled as he slung a miniature video player at Stevens, who was sitting in a nearby row.

"It was getting really loud," said former Dolphins player and longtime play-by-play man Jimmy Cefalo. "They were trying to close the curtains, but we heard it."

The game, the play, the whole episode start to finish was an embarrassment. And Stevens paid the price. The Dolphins got home from the December 28 game, and Johnson fired Stevens a couple of weeks later. He announced the change 32 days later. But not before more hijinks ensued

Stevens swore the Patriots did not know his audibles. "There's no way," Stevens said. "They do know we audible, and Danny likes to throw on those, but they don't know exactly what we're throwing." Stevens said Collins was guessing when he signaled his defensive teammates that the Dolphins were about to throw that slant. That play was the 46 audible in Miami's playbook. "We called the same audible two times earlier in the game and instead of throwing the slant we ran the ball twice," Stevens said. "Later in the game, we were going to throw deep on the same audible. They guessed on that one play by playing the percentages."

The coach's opinion is in the minority. And the coach's opinion is, well, wrong because the Patriots admitted they knew. "We had a pretty good fix on their calls," Patriots safety Willie Clay said. "Keith Byars helped us out on those, and the Dolphins didn't change them too much. The prime example was the interception. When they saw we were going to blitz, they changed their play, and then we checked out of the blitz into the perfect defense for that play. We knew what was coming, checked, and they walked right into it."

Byars played for the Dolphins from 1993 until he was cut four games into the '96 season. He joined the Patriots and apparently did not forget the Miami offense. "I know a lot of football, I'm an intelligent player, and I have good retention," Byars said sheepishly. "Of course I know the Miami Dolphins' offense."

Stevens was cornered. And that's when he apparently tossed a Hail Mary to try to save his job by telling a *Miami Herald* reporter that he'd done the best he could that season with limited resources. Except he said it more colorfully. "You can't make chicken salad out of chicken [expletive]," he said in the lobby of the team practice facility as he was leaving one evening. "Name me a great player we have besides Danny. You can't. We were No. 2 in the passing game. No. 2 in the passing game! How did we do it?…We had to throw. We couldn't run. And do we have a great running back? No."

The next day Stevens denied throwing his players under the bus. And then he kind of, sort of repeated himself. "We did it without any great players except for Danny," Stevens said. "That doesn't mean I'm blaming them for anything. It's a credit to those players and to the coaching staff. We don't have a great back. That's not to discredit Karim Abdul-Jabbar or Bernie Parmalee. But they're not Emmitt Smith. We have talent, just not a lot of great talent. The only great talent we have is Dan Marino. The rest are good football players. Some of them can become great in the future, but they still have to work before they get there."

Stevens would not work with them. He was fired February 3 after nine years as Miami's offensive coordinator. He coached quarterbacks the next three years with the Oakland Raiders and ended his career coaching the Atlanta Falcons receivers. The Dolphins revamped their offense under new offensive coordinator Kippy Brown but scored 18 fewer points than they had the season before.

67 Flutie Flakes

After winning his first playoff game as the Miami Dolphins coach, Jimmy Johnson was dancing (sort of) and celebrating the moment. The elation possessed him, and Johnson grabbed a box of cereal he had placed inside the Dolphins locker room and smashed it against the side of an equipment trunk, sending the contents flying in every direction. Johnson stomped on the cereal, and some players joined the flake-stomping, locker-room frenzy.

The animated closed-door celebration was weird but worthy of Miami's stirring 24–17 playoff victory against the Buffalo Bills in January of 1999. It was a heart-stopping win that culminated a week of contemptuous banter between the teams and sent the Dolphins into the postseason's second round. And Johnson's rambunctious cereal killing was symbolic of the game's most consequential play. With 17 seconds left in regulation, Dolphins defensive end Trace Armstrong sacked Doug Flutie, leaving the Buffalo quarterback sprawled at the Miami 5-yard line and exposing a fumbled football to fate. Defensive lineman Shane Burton smothered the fumble, dashing Buffalo's comeback and sealing Miami's victory. It was Buffalo's fifth turnover of the day.

The problem with this celebration, Johnson would soon learn, was that what he perceived as a harmless postgame bash was seen as an attack on a charity by some others. The cereal, you see, was Flutie Flakes. Flutie had branded the Flutie Flakes after his popularity in Western New York skyrocketted upon becoming the Buffalo quarterback. And all the profits from Flutie Flakes went to the Doug Flutie Jr. Foundation, which was named after Flutie's autistic son and works toward treating autism. "As far as I'm concerned," Flutie said when word of the Miami locker room hijinks reached him in the Buffalo locker room, "that's like stomping on my son."

The player who stomped Flutie on the Bills' last play was actually nowhere near the Flakes celebration. Armstrong was still on the Dolphins bench. He had his head between his legs and was gasping for breath. He was so wiped out that defensive line coach Cary Godette had to help him stand and carry his helmet. "I needed to rest," said the 33-year-old Armstrong, who was Miami's second oldest defensive contributor at the time. "I didn't know if I could make it [into the locker room] if I tried to walk right away. Even when I was out there before the last play, I didn't know if I could go another play."

Armstrong's absence didn't postpone the party. Miami defensive backs gleefully did a jig on the cereal. "I ate a little bit, spit a little bit out, and stomped on it a little bit," said cornerback Sam Madison, who earlier that week foreshadowed the Flakes fracas by saying he would like the Dolphins to shove them down Flutie's throat. Dolphins cornerback Terrell Buckley said he didn't partake of the Flutie Flakes that were scattered over the locker room floor after the game. "I'm a Frosted Flakes man," he said with a wide grin.

Miami's joyous outpouring was understandable as a release of a decade's worth of frustration. The Bills dynasty of the early 1990s had long since ended, but Thurman Thomas and Andre Reed and other players of that era remained on the Buffalo roster. And they all talked of dominating the Dolphins for a decade. The rivalry was no longer about Dan Marino vs. Jim Kelly. The rivalry had become about Flutie saying neither Madison nor Buckley could cover Buffalo receivers Reed and Eric Moulds, and Madison called Flutie "a little short dude" who didn't do "anything spectacular."

Days after the Miami celebration, Johnson realized it might not be a great look for him to stomp on a cereal when the proceeds went to a good cause. So he wrote Flutie a letter of apology. "We were obviously very happy winning the playoff game, and it wasn't anything negative toward anybody," Johnson said. "I wrote Doug a letter and said that. I would never do anything negative toward any charity, and everyone knows how much respect I have for Doug Flutie. He's an outstanding quarterback."

Flutie was gracious about the apology. "That was totally blown out of proportion," he said. "The media has a tendency to do that. When you win a game, you can do anything."

But Buffalo coach Wade Phillips wasn't quite so forgiving. In October of 1999 in the next season, the Bills beat the Dolphins on *Monday Night Football.* "I didn't go in and stomp on a can of hair spray, but we're excited about the win," Phillips said.

68 Jimmy Johnson Quits...Twice

Jimmy Johnson stomped off a field adjacent to the team's practice facility in the middle of a training camp practice on an August 1999 morning and then he went inside the cafeteria that overlooked the field, yelling obscenities at two *Miami Herald* reporters. The Miami Dolphins coach reached into a back pocket of his polyester shorts and pulled out a crumpled article he cut from the newspaper and read passages he highlighted in yellow marker. "Johnson is spending more time away from the office," Johnson said, reading the article aloud. "That's not [expletive] true. I'm in the [expletive] office just as much now as I ever was," Johnson yelled, directing himself to the *Herald's* Jason Cole, who authored the article. (By the way, it was true.) "He skipped the Senior Bowl in January and an NFL coaches meeting in Atlanta," Johnson read before continuing his tirade. "That's not [expletive] right either. You're calling my [expletive] reputation into question. My [expletive] work ethic is the same as it's always been, you [expletive] and you're a [expletive] for putting this [expletive, expletive] in the [expletive] paper, you [expletive]. Why did you write this [expletive]?"

And that's where I stopped counting Johnson's words that started with "mother." Surprised by the withering assault, Cole stammered and struggled to answer. Then Johnson turned to me and added, "And you, if you don't get your [expletive] guy in line, I'm going to call your [expletive] publisher and let him know you two [expletives] don't know [expletive] about [expletive], and you should both be fired."

And with that the 1999 season, which ended with Johnson quitting his job as Dolphins coach, was off to an attention-grabbing start.

This scene has its genesis eight months earlier. On January 13, 1999, after a trying '98 season that ended with the Dolphins again unceremoniously bounced from the playoffs, Johnson quit the first time. That day Johnson chaotically packed possessions in his office into a dozen or so boxes. He told team president Eddie Jones he was quitting and then he went out for a few beers with assistants and head trainer Kevin O'Neill to celebrate his new freedom.

The move was a surprise to many, but it's understandable why Johnson wanted out. His mother and father had been fighting various maladies for several years, and that had turned more urgent when Allene Johnson fell and broke her hip in December 1998. She died days later at age 77. This personal loss had a profound effect on Johnson. The coach had been all about football for decades. He had often chosen the sport over family. But now Johnson was re-thinking priorities. And football was losing ground. He wanted to be closer to his father, C.W. Johnson. He wanted to bridge the gap with his two sons after years of nurturing a relationship with football over a relationship with them. He wanted to enjoy his life instead of being so damn miserable after every loss.

So Johnson walked out the door. But he left it ajar rather than closing it completely. And when Dolphins owner H. Wayne Huizenga, who was away at a baseball owner's meeting, returned to South Florida and offered Johnson concessions just so he'd stay, the coach changed his mind. About those concessions Huizenga offered: Huizenga would hire longtime Johnson assistant Dave Wannstedt, who had been fired as Chicago Bears coach, to help Johnson in Miami. Johnson could coach only home games if he wanted and let Wannstedt coach away games. Or Johnson could pass all coaching duties to Wannstedt and serve as Miami's general manager. Johnson could do his general manager work from his home if he wanted. And Johnson wouldn't have to make a final decision on quitting until January 14.

When he arrived at his nearly cleared-out office that morning, quarterback Dan Marino was waiting outside. "Dan sat down with me at length, and he said, 'Coach, we are so close,'" Johnson said after eventually announcing he was staying. "He said, 'We are really close to getting to where we want to be.'"

The 37-year-old quarterback still saw Johnson as his best hope for finally winning a Super Bowl and had been surprised by the coach contemplating a departure. "I was shocked when I first heard about Jimmy possibly not coming back and I told him I hoped that wasn't true," Marino said.

The first time Johnson quit was a surprise to Marino, but those who knew the coach understood the reasons. Yes, family played a role. "Jimmy told me he was ready to retire and wanted to start enjoying himself," C.W. Johnson, the coach's father, said in 1999 from his home in Port Arthur, Texas. "He said the season wore on him. I told him I was glad, and that was the best news I had heard in a long time."

It wasn't just the season that wore on Johnson. The job wore on Johnson. And Johnson wore on Johnson because he didn't just coach the Dolphins. He hoisted the entire franchise on his own shoulders and tried to carry it to success.

Soon after Doug Blevins was hired as Miami's kicking coach in 1997, the Dolphins faced a difficult decision at the end of training camp: keep incumbent Joe Nedney or go with newcomer Olindo Mare. "We have to make a tough decision on this one," Blevins told Johnson.

Johnson took his new assistant aside and said, "Doug, *we* are not going to make a decision. *I* am going to make a decision. This is not a democracy where we take a vote. You can have an opinion, but my opinion is the only one that counts."

Johnson, the general manager, made all the personnel decisions. Vice president of football operations Bob Ackles held the cards for the club during contract negotiations, but Johnson directed him when to raise and when to fold. If there was a trade to make, Johnson picked up the phone, dialed the number, and did the haggling. In the weeks before a draft, Johnson jotted down which players he liked and kept the sheet in his desk. Only he decided which names went on the paper, and no one else in the organization saw the list. Johnson decided who sat with him in the war room on draft days and even determined where people sat. When disagreements between coaches and scouts broke out, Johnson mediated to appease both sides. He'd compromise on behalf of both men. And when they left, he'd slot the player wherever he thought was right without either man seeing the result because, remember, Johnson decided if they could enter the war room or not.

So Johnson did a lot. Probably too much.

And if 1998 pulled on him, the 1999 season was the final jerking of the chain. His father was battling cancer, he wanted to spend time with his sons, he was feuding with Marino, who was no longer playing like a star, and the prospects of accomplishing his goal of winning a Super Bowl seemed no closer than when Johnson arrived in 1996.

Johnson told club president Eddie Jones that December that he was considering quitting. So, in his mind, Johnson was pretty much done by then. Sure, the Miami season extended into a playoff berth and even a victory against the Seahawks in Seattle. But after a humiliating defeat to the Jacksonville Jaguars in January of 2000, Johnson had endured enough. The day after that 62–7 playoff loss, Johnson said his final good-byes to players. He then bid farewell to the job with a 790-word statement he made at a press conference. His words were filled with as much relief as regret. He took no questions. "We gave it our best shot, and it didn't work out," Johnson said.

That press conference served a dual purpose because it also introduced the Dolphins' new coach. And that, along with the talent he drafted and history he plotted over four seasons, was Johnson's Dolphins legacy. Because after winning zero division titles, zero conference championships, and zero Super Bowls in Miami, Johnson was able to name his successor: Wannstedt.

69 Marino's Final Game-Winning Drive

The Miami Dolphins were broken the first week of 2000. The team had lost five of the regular-season's final six games. Superstar coach Jimmy Johnson and superstar quarterback Dan Marino had feuded throughout the season primarily because the coach didn't think Marino was great anymore, and the quarterback basically thought the same thing about the coach. Marino agent Marvin Demoff, who'd famously strategized the quarterback's entrance into the NFL in 1983's first round, was already designing his client's possible departure from Miami. Johnson was already certain he was quitting (again) after the season. Defensive assistant Dave Wannstedt already had designs on the Miami coaching job.

And on the outside, Don Shula was reportedly interested in returning to the Dolphins. Shula called ESPN's report "speculation," but he didn't deny it. "I think [the reporter] said that. I didn't say it," Shula said. "I'm not out there soliciting anything. They're playing a season and have a good chance to do well. I'm pulling for the Dolphins to do well. I'm not out there actively seeking anything."

Amid all this drama, Johnson asked the media to give it a break. "Let us put the soap opera on the back burner for one week," said the man who authored much of the soap opera. "Let's focus in on Seattle. Let's ask the players questions about Seattle."

Oh, yeah, the Seattle Seahawks. The Dolphins were in the playoffs.

Everyone knew they limped in. Marino had nursed a bulging disk and cervical bone spur for much of the season, and his 12 touchdowns and 17 interceptions were symptoms of those maladies. Johnson had nursed his gameplans before games, demanding the team run the ball more, pass the ball less, and rely on the defense but often abandoned those plans on gameday.

So the Dolphins, who had been 8–2 on November 21, took a 9–7 record to the Kingdome for a wild-card game.

This gameplan had wrinkles, and the Dolphins went against their tendencies and relied on the defense. But all that planning and great defense still had the Dolphins down 17–13 with 9:09 to play. And that's when, amid the tension of the playoffs and the melodrama of the season, the Dolphins did what they'd done in much better days: they let Marino be Marino. On a third and 17 from their own 8-yard line, Marino completed a 31-yard pass to Tony Martin. "I thought they'd just call a draw play and put the game in our hands," linebacker Zach Thomas said.

On a second and 7 from Seattle's 49, Marino hit Martin again for 20 yards. "I got open, looked up, and there's the ball," Martin said. "I did the easy part."

On a third and 10 from Seattle's 29, Marino completed a 24-yard pass to Oronde Gadsden. "Dan just laid it in there perfectly," Gadsden said.

The Dolphins scored on a two-yard touchdown run and led for the first time all day. The drive delivered Marino's 36th fourth-quarter comeback. At the time that tied him with Johnny Unitas for most in NFL history. Johnson, who had spent the latter part of the regular season wanting to bench Marino in favor of Damon Huard, hugged Marino afterward. "Dan did a great job in the ballgame," Johnson said. "And I know he'd like to go back there and wing it a little more, but it's nice when we rush for over 100 yards, and he is patient, and the running game opens things up for the receivers a little more."

Marino had recently told quarterbacks coach Larry Seiple that he would like a greater say over the offensive plays. He said nice things about running first and winning while being conservative before letting his true feelings be known. "That drive was better than any I can remember in a long time," he said.

When Marino was finished talking to reporters, some lingered, and one made the point to him that Miami had run 37 times and passed 30 times, and the team was 6–0 in games that happened, but 4–7 in games they passed more. Marino looked at the guy as if he had a horn coming out of his forehead. "No comment," he said.

70 62–7

Dan Marino's first pass was intercepted. He ended the day with another interception. And two fumbles. And he was benched. The Miami Dolphins trailed 38–0 before he completed a pass.

The Jacksonville Jaguars ran 41 plays in the first half...and scored 41 points. Never one to take anything for granted, Jaguars coach Tom Coughlin inserted backup quarterback Jay Fiedler. He *knew* the game was already won. It was only the second quarter. Fred Taylor ran off the field at halftime blowing kisses to the crowd. Minutes earlier he had run through the Miami defense on a 90-yard touchdown.

Marino got only one series in the second half, and it looked too much like the first half. So he was replaced and spent the rest of the ugly game watching from the sideline. Marino's last pass was an incompletion intended for O.J. McDuffie. We can go on and on about how terrible January 15, 2000 was for the Dolphins. And it was. It was humiliating. It was historic to Dolphins Nation the way lost battles are historic to kingdoms of bygone eras—except the carnage here is counted in points on a scoreboard rather than blood on a field. This day in short was a clinic on how to fail in an NFL game.

But the reason this game goes down in franchise lore, and every knowledgeable Miami fan knows the painful details is because of what came next. What came next was more disastrous. This game at the turn of the new century marked a momentous change of direction and fortunes for the Dolphins. For decades the Dolphins had been about success. They boasted the second best winning percentage in all of professional sports. They boasted the winningest coach in NFL history. They boasted professional football's only Perfect Season.

But soon they were on their knees after this 62–7 gut punch.

Out of this playoff game's stench, Marino and coach Jimmy Johnson ended their careers. Playoff defeats eventually transitioned to a lack of playoff berths. And coaching changes. And the search for a quarterback. And rebuilding over and over and over. This game was the turning point in the franchise's fortunes. The Dolphins were an elite franchise the morning before this game was played. By late afternoon the franchise was on fire.

Johnson had won championships in the fourth year of his previous two stops—first at the University of Miami and then with the

Dallas Cowboys. But after replacing Don Shula in 1996, Johnson could not re-engineer similar results. All the talented first-round selections he found while coaching the Hurricanes were playing for someone else. The magic of the Herschel Walker trade that turned the thing around in Dallas was not repeated in Miami. Instead Johnson spent as much time bringing in Lawrence Phillips, Cecil Collins, and Dimitrius Underwood as he did finding great players like Zach Thomas and eventual Hall of Famer Jason Taylor. Johnson missed on as many first-round selections—such as Yatil Green and John Avery—as he connected on later picks such as Patrick Surtain and Sam Madison. He didn't draft Randy Moss. He drafted Larry Shannon, who Johnson infamously insisted was as good as Randy Moss.

And in that 1999 season, Johnson was often at odds with Marino. The coach of the franchise feuded with the face of the franchise. Johnson had chosen the Dolphins over the Tampa Bay Buccaneers in '96 because the Bucs lacked a quarterback, and Miami had Marino. But Johnson soon realized the Marino he inherited was aging, immobile, and diminished. So he wanted to throw the ball less. And Marino didn't. Johnson had a quarterback who had played in generally the same offense over the majority of two decades. That was a rarity after the advent of free agency. Rather than get his assistants to coach the new players better and get them up to speed, he dumbed down the system. Marino became a concert pianist playing chopsticks.

Johnson looked at his quarterbacks, Marino and backup Damon Huard, and often preferred Huard. Marino was no longer the player who once threw 48 touchdown passes. He didn't have the same ability to evade the pass rush. And when he passed, there wasn't Mark Duper or Mark Clayton to catch his passes either. So the Dolphins flew to Jacksonville overmatched. And overprepared, according to Johnson. "I take the blame for this," Johnson said. "I tried to prepare them too much when I should have pulled back after the long trip to Seattle. Our guys were dead-legged. They left their game on the practice field."

The Jaguars amassed 520 yards. They gained 257 rushing yards to Miami's 21. Fred Taylor, who rushed for 135 yards and caught a 39-yard touchdown pass, outgained Miami by 43 yards all by himself.

Jason Taylor, expecting a big game because Jacksonville starting left tackle Tony Boselli was out with an injury, managed only two tackles and no sacks. "All good things must come to an end," Jaguars safety Carnell Lake said afterward.

71 How It Ended for Dan Marino

He drew a deep breath and put his right hand over his heart to hold back a blitz of emotions. Dan Marino knew this final tribute would be emotional, but he wasn't prepared for love so strong that it hit like a defensive end. "From the bottom of my heart, I love you guys," Marino said on that humid August night in 2000, as he looked out over 52,000 adoring fans at Pro Player Stadium. "I love you, Dolphins fans. Thank you so much for making this a special night not only for me but my family, my kids, my wife. Having a chance to be here tonight to see this is very special. It's overwhelming."

The ceremony put on by then-Miami Dolphins owner Wayne Huizenga included a 16-minute fireworks display that would make any Fourth of July envious. It included a mini-concert from Hootie and the Blowfish. It included 1983's celebrated class of quarterbacks united for the first time.

Dan Marino's career had been an event for 17 seasons. He was DaVinci at the canvas or Mozart at the piano. He broke or tied 30 NFL records during his career, including the most significant ones for a passer—most yards, most touchdowns, most attempts, most completions.

And this elaborate production was an appropriate send-off. This was a celebration worthy of his amazing career that turned into a love affair with No. 13 for Dolphins fans. "One more year," the crowd implored.

"Sorry," Marino answered. "I want you to know I miss you. I would love to play one more year, but I can't."

This was the final chapter to a process that began late in the 1999 season when then-coach Jimmy Johnson had wanted to bench Marino but decided he couldn't. That process eventually included Johnson successor Dave Wannstedt not wanting Marino back for the 2000 season but also not wanting to force out the legend. So Wannstedt made it clear to Marino the offense he knew so well would be scrapped in 2000. The coach told Marino he'd have to compete for his job. And his salary would also be subject to renegotiation.

Marino understood his time with the Dolphins was over so he became a free agent. The next question was whether his career was over as well. Although multiple teams showed interest in Marino, and the Minnesota Vikings offered a chance to be their starter, Marino announced his retirement in March. "Most of all I'm going to miss Sunday afternoons," Marino said to the more than 200 who gathered at the Dolphins' training facility in Davie, Florida, to hear him make the announcement that March.

Wearing a blue wool suit and reading from an eight-minute statement, Marino acted as he did for 17 years in the Dolphins' huddle—cool—even while his wife, Claire, was sobbing only a few feet away. Marino's voice cracked only once, but otherwise one of the most outwardly emotional players in Dolphins history was able to keep his composure. "I was just trying to keep back the tears," Marino said. "If I had looked over at Claire, I would have been crying, too. I tried not to look at her because she was crying the whole time."

Marino walking away on his terms—while multiple chances to keep playing beckoned—was big news then because the choice meant he'd never claim a Super Bowl championship. "That was the only reason to continue to play," Marino said. "That has been a dream of mine my whole career, and I am not going to have that chance. But does it take away from what I have done personally? I don't think it does."

Marino's desire to get one last opportunity to win a Super Bowl caused him to contemplate Minnesota's offer most seriously. "He kept telling me it was a harder decision than getting married," said Marvin Demoff, Marino's agent. "A lot of people thought he was going to do the Vikings thing. I did, too. There was a time I thought he would."

Said Marino: "There were times I told Claire we were going, and two hours later, I said 'No, I don't think I can go.' It was the toughest thing that I had to deal with professionally in my life."

Those tough days paled in comparison with Marino's final season. Sure, he and Johnson had good times but also were often involved in tension-filled bouts that pitted their large egos and iron wills against each other. Those bouts wore on both men. Johnson's friends say the Marino issue was one reason the coach retired. And Marino's friends say the quarterback, though publicly silent about the feud, often went home and did what millions of Americans do around their loved ones. He complained about his boss. "I can't begin to tell you some of the things Dan told me about how bad things got last season," former Buffalo Bills quarterback and Marino confidant Jim Kelly said.

Marino made it clear to the Dolphins he preferred Johnson not attend his retirement announcement. The absence allowed Marino to speak his mind when the question everyone knew was coming finally arrived. Marino was asked if his time with Johnson was a difficult one. "Our relationship was up and down at times," Marino said. "And Coach Johnson, we had some great, great days together and some fun times, and sometimes I wasn't very happy here while he was coaching, and that's just being honest."

At the stadium celebration months later, Marino and former teammates and the quarterbacks from that '83 draft class ended the evening on stage with Hootie and Blowfish. They sang. They danced. Then they disappeared, leaving to a private reception Marino organized. The crowd simply headed for their cars as the stadium announcer put the event's purpose in perspective: "Thank you, Dan Marino fans," he said. "And thank you, Dan Marino."

Inside Jason Taylor's Hall of Fame Election

At precisely 6:00 am on the morning of February 4, 2017, I began to walk from my room at the Hilton Americas hotel in Houston to the George R. Brown Convention Center next door, where 48 Hall of Fame selectors, including me, would pick the Pro Football Hall of Fame class of 2017. My assignment that morning was to deliver a presentation convincing enough that those other 47 people in the room would select Jason Taylor as not only a Hall of Famer, but also a first-ballot Hall of Famer. This is how the presentation went down.

"Before I begin," I said. "I'd like to take a moment to remember my best friend and former selector Edwin Pope who passed away two weeks ago at the age of 88 years old. I talked to Edwin two days before he died, and knowing that I was to make this presentation today, I asked him for advice on what to say. And he said, 'Armando, tell them Jason Taylor is the best defensive player I saw in the last 20 years...and I saw them all.' So it's my privilege to deliver that message from Edwin Pope.

"A Pro Football Hall of Famer answers three basic questions in the affirmative. Did he dominate his era? Did he do anything to change games and more importantly to change *the* game? Do the greatest of his peers think he's a Hall of Famer? Ask these three questions about Jason Taylor, and the answers are an unambiguous yes, yes, and yes! Taylor finished with 139½ sacks in 15 seasons. He retired No. 6 in sacks all time and today he is No. 7 all time. No one eligible for induction into the Hall of Fame is ahead of him. Multiple players, who earned busts in Canton by pass rushing, had fewer sacks than Taylor—notably Richard Dent, John Randle, Derrick Thomas, Lawrence Taylor, and Charles Haley. Jason Taylor was named to the NFL's All-Decade Team for the 2000s. That's because from 2000 to 2009 Taylor collected 111 sacks—more than anyone during that time. The next closest was Joey Porter, who was 21 sacks behind.

"So if you're judging pass rushers...the first 10 seasons of this millennium belonged to Jason Taylor. His decade of dominance included six Pro Bowls. He led the NFL in sacks in 2002 and was top five five times. He was the NFL Defensive Player of the Year in 2006."

I then mentioned the opposing players he faced and included some quotes from them. "Without a doubt he's definitely a Hall of Famer," said first-ballot Hall of Famer Jonathan Ogden. "Even at your best, JT still got to your quarterback or he forced a fumble and was a threat to score. He was *that* guy."

"Taylor played six games against Ogden," I said. "And in those six games, Taylor had six sacks and two forced fumbles. Taylor played three games against Hall of Famer Orlando Pace in the 2000s. He had 1½ sacks. Taylor played four games against Hall of Famer

Walter Jones and had a sack and a fumble recovery. Tom Brady, on the 2000s All-Decade Team and in a certain game tomorrow, had been sacked more times by Taylor than anyone else when Taylor retired.

"Read Brady's endorsement letter on page two of your handout if you want to know how the QB feels about Taylor. I also ask you to read page three of the handout to answer whether the game's greats believe Taylor belongs in the Hall."

I then emphasized how Taylor impacted the game and left his mark on the sport. "Jason Taylor was nothing if not a *shock and awe* player," I said. "He had six fumble recoveries for touchdowns in his career. That is the *most by any player at any position* in NFL history. His nine touchdowns are the most in league history by a defensive lineman or linebacker. No front seven player ever scored more touchdowns than Jason Taylor. 'Jason was among my favorite players to watch because he had a great ability to rush the quarterback and was an underrated run stopper,' said Hall of Famer Michael Strahan. 'More than that, however, he was the king of the Big Play.'

"The strip sack's a big play. Taylor had 39 strip sacks. No one in the Hall of Fame has that many. I'm not going to tell you Taylor changed the sport. But he was a pioneer because he convinced personnel men that speed rushers are a prized asset. 'He's the forerunner to guys like Dwight Freeney and Robert Mathis,' said Hall of Famer Bill Polian. 'In my mind he set the mold. And he proved guys like him could be versatile.'

"Taylor finished his career with 29 opponent fumble recoveries. That's tied for the NFL record with Jim Marshall. No one in the Hall has more than 24. Taylor had 99 passes defensed. That's the third most of any non-defensive back in NFL history—behind only Ray Lewis and Hall of Famer Derrick Brooks."

Then I addressed the issue of whether to induct him on the first ballot. "In conclusion," I said, "let me address the elephant in the room so please look at handout page four. Bruce Smith and Reggie White are the only players among the top six pass rushers who went into the Hall on first ballots. And Taylor didn't equal their sacks. But he had four times as many interceptions as Bruce Smith. He had six times as many fumble recovery touchdowns as Smith. And three times as many passes defensed. He had three interception return touchdowns to Smith's zero. He had more safeties and more forced fumbles. Reggie White also had more sacks than Jason Taylor. But again Taylor had more interceptions, and interception return touchdowns, and passes defensed, and forced fumbles, and fumble recoveries, and more fumble recovery touchdowns, and more safeties.

"Michael Strahan had to wait until his second year to get in. He finished with two more sacks than Taylor. Having said that, Taylor had six more defensive touchdowns, and four more interceptions, and more interception return TDs, and 25 more forced fumbles, and 14 more fumble recoveries, and five more fumble recovery touchdowns, and more safeties. So if Strahan is the picture of a second-ballot Hall of Fame defensive lineman with 141½ sacks and the rest of his impressive resume, I respectfully submit Taylor is a *first-ballot* Hall of Famer with 139½ sacks and his inventory of impactful statistics and game-changing plays that, as Strahan himself reminds us, made Jason Taylor 'the king of the big play.'"

Following every presentation the floor is open for discussion. There was minimal discussion, and no one dissented. And Taylor then was elected to the Pro Football Hall of Fame on the first ballot.

73 Jay Fiedler: The Man Who Followed Dan Marino

When the Miami Dolphins signed Jay Fiedler to be Dan Marino's successor, he'd spent 1995 with the Philadelphia Eagles but didn't throw a pass. He'd been waived by the Eagles and Cincinnati Bengals in 1996. He'd juggled stints in the World League and as a Hofstra University assistant coach in 1997. That's where a Minnesota Vikings scout found him while eying a Hofstra player, and in 1998 Fiedler threw all of seven passes for the Vikings. He signed with the Jacksonville Jaguars in 1999 and threw his first NFL touchdown.

When he put his signature on a three-year Dolphins contract on February 16, 2000, Fiedler had two NFL touchdowns and three interceptions to his credit. *Now go replace Marino, son.*

Fiedler's career had traveled a road lined with modest results. But there was no amount of moderate success Fiedler was going to have that was going to make this a smooth transition. There was no amount of merely adequate talent Fiedler could bring to a football field that could make people forget Marino. "Jay had the toughest job because he was the guy that came immediately after Dan Marino," said Fiedler's agent and longtime friend Brian Levy. "He was never going to be the guy Miami embraced because people down there thought Jay supplanted Dan instead of just replaced him. But Jay did the best he could with the weapons they put around him."

Fiedler came to the task armed with traits that made his time with the Dolphins seem, well, tolerable. He was gritty and extremely competitive. That showed the second week of the 2001 season when the Dolphins trailed the Oakland Raiders by five points with 1:51 to play. Fiedler directed a 10-play, 80-yard drive. And with 10 seconds remaining, he dove the final few feet for the winning score. The

Dolphins won 18–15, and Fiedler appeared on the cover of *Sports Illustrated* when that was still a thing. "Today Jay was special. He had a little bit of Marino in him, a little bit of that, 'Here we come. We're going down the field. Just stay with me, and we'll be all right,'" offensive guard Mark Dixon said.

It's easy to forget Fiedler signed with the Dolphins a month before Marino retired, and he never escaped the legend's shadow. But he never complained. He never said anything but kind things about Marino either in public or private. In fact, on the day Fiedler joined the Dolphins roster, he effusively praised Marino. "He's one of the greatest quarterbacks ever," Fiedler said. "When I was growing up in high school, Dan Marino was the quarterback in the NFL. I'd love to go up to him and shake his hand. The bar has been set at the position extremely high to the level that is almost unattainable to anyone. Dan Marino's records aren't going to be broken anytime soon. What I want to do is help take this team to a high level, not just the quarterback position."

The man who replaced Marino was never embraced by Miami fans. He knew this. And he didn't let it define him. "I don't think I'm ever going to win over every fan," he said with a shrug.

The Dolphins piled one mistake atop another during Fiedler's five seasons in Miami. There were personnel mistakes. Coaching staff mistakes. Ownership mistakes. But the further everyone now gets from Fiedler's tenure—and his 36–23 record—the better Fiedler looks.

"You can't argue with going 11–5 with him at quarterback his first two years," said Rick Spielman, the Dolphins' senior vice president and then general manager at the time.

Fiedler never got the Dolphins as far as they needed to go. Neither did Marino, by the way. But Fiedler did win two playoff games with the Dolphins. He remains the last Dolphins quarterback to win a playoff game. That came on December 30, 2000 against Peyton Manning and the Indianapolis Colts. Yes, Lamar Smith

rushed for 209 yards that day. But Fiedler sent the game into overtime by throwing a nine-yard touchdown pass to Jed Weaver on
third and goal with 34 seconds to play.

Fiedler had other fine moments that showed his grit and toughness. He helped Miami beat the Denver Broncos in 2002 while
playing with a fractured thumb in his throwing hand.

The Dolphins thought of replacing Fiedler multiple times. They
considered Drew Brees in the 2001 draft and Troy Aikman before
the 2002 season. They signed Brian Griese in 2003. They traded
for A.J. Feeley and asked Fiedler to take a pay cut in 2004. Fiedler's
confidence never seemed shaken. He never lashed out at critics or
the team. "No, not at all," he said. "Nothing they could say would
hurt my ego. You guys know the type of confidence I have in my
ability. Rumors are going to fly around. I hear it all. You can't help
but be cognizant of what's being said; you can't be blind to it. But
that doesn't mean you have to react in a negative way. That doesn't
mean you lose your way."

74 When the Lights Went Out

Don Shula was sitting behind his lacquered mahogany desk with
much of his team's important business strewn before his eyes, but
he didn't see any of that. His focus instead was on an opportunity
missed, a chance at one final Super Bowl trip...lost. "We should
be getting ready for the Super Bowl now," said Shula after the San
Diego Chargers beat the Pittsburgh Steelers in the January 1995
AFC Championship Game. "We were better than San Diego and
should have beaten them. And I believe we would have beaten
Pittsburgh. That's what we've got to live with."

The Miami Dolphins lost to the Chargers 22–21 two weeks earlier, and it indeed was a blown opportunity, considering Shula's team led 21–6 at halftime. There were plenty of football reasons for that loss. Limited to 26 yards on eight carries, the Dolphins running game didn't make the trip west. Having allowed only two first-half field goals and delivered a goal-line stand on San Diego's first possession of the second half, the defense wilted the rest of the game. Then there was Pete Stoyanovich's missed 48-yard field goal with one second to play. A potential game-winner turned to a disappointment when it sailed wide right.

But those weren't the reasons that had the Dolphins privately fuming. The Dolphins felt they were mistreated and put at a competitive disadvantage multiple times by the Chargers. The day before the game, Shula clashed with San Diego general manager Bobby Beathard. The two had worked together in the 1970s when Beathard was Miami's director of player personnel, and they had remained friends.

But that Saturday, Shula took his players to Jack Murphy Stadium because he wanted them to work out on the same field they would play on the next day. It was a Shula routine. But the stadium entrances were padlocked, and the Dolphins were told they had to use the Chargers' adjacent field if they wanted to work. Shula ordered the locks cut and the tarpaulin on the field removed. Beathard arrived and argued with his former boss that he couldn't use the field, and the tarp had to stay because rain was expected and indeed materialized several hours later. Jerry Seeman, the NFL's senior director of officiating, was on hand as the arbiter and he compromised, allowing the Dolphins to work along the sidelines, which were quite wide in a facility that doubled as a baseball park. That incensed Beathard. "The guy [Shula] owns the league, so he gets whatever he wants," Beathard shouted at Seeman. "Anything he wants, he gets."

Beathard was still hot after the game even in victory. He was asked if he'd patched things up and offered his old friend Shula a consoling handshake. "Hell no," he replied. "I lost a lot of respect for Don for what he pulled yesterday."

Back in Miami days later, the Dolphins didn't feel a lot of respect for the Chargers. They were fuming that the lights in their locker room did not work during halftime. And while they didn't publicly accuse the Chargers of being responsible, they were dubious about it being payback for the tarp incident the day before. To make things worse in the Dolphins eyes, the lack of light—caused when a circuit breaker to their locker room was tripped (or thrown)—may have directly cost them points when they gave up the second-half safety.

While defensive coaches made their adjustments in the dark, offensive coaches scrambled to a lit cramped hallway and a small room adjacent to the Miami locker room. In that room that had no blackboard, offensive coordinator Gary Stevens discussed the possibility of running at San Diego's overshifted nose tackle, a departure from the team's gameplan. Miami plans called for players to read which way the defense was shifted on running plays and then run away from the overshift. "Because it was so dark and there was no blackboard and some players didn't even fit into the room, some players thought we had decided to make the change," Stevens said. "And others didn't know."

The offensive linemen thought the change had been made. Quarterback Dan Marino didn't think the change had been made. Some running backs thought the change was made, and others didn't know. Stevens, in fact, didn't make the change. That confusion would become important after the Miami defense stopped San Diego at the Miami 1-yard line to open the third quarter. Stevens sent the offense on the field and called for a handoff to running back Bernie Parmalee coming out of the end zone. The offensive linemen on the right side of the line were as surprised as anyone when Parmalee squeezed up behind them on the play. They believed he would be running left. Parmalee was tackled in the end zone for a safety in a game the Chargers would win by one point. "Don't even bring that up," Shula said after the Chargers beat the Steelers.

Ironically, the next week the same Chargers that made it tough on the Dolphins at their place used the Dolphins' facility while preparing for Super Bowl XXIX in Miami. Shula visited with Beathard that week, and the men agreed to put aside their differences a couple of days before the Chargers got blown out by the San Francisco 49ers.

75 The Meadowlands Meltdown

The stands at Giants Stadium in the Meadowlands began to empty after the third quarter as the *New Yowkas* retreated from this apparent New Jersey debacle. Everything was perfect for the Miami Dolphins during this fall *Monday Night Football* game as they looked up at the scoreboard and saw themselves with a 30–7 lead going into the final quarter. The Dolphins had crafted the 23-point lead and believed it was a hole too deep for the New York Jets to dig out of. What would happen next proved the hole wasn't a grave.

The Jets scored 30 points in the fourth quarter. They used 13:07 to tie the game *twice*. They scored four touchdowns against one of the NFL's top defenses. And by 1:22 AM when John Hall's 40-yard overtime field goal sailed true, they would own a 40–37 victory that stands in the history of two NFL franchises under two different names: the Meadowlands Miracle or the Meadowlands Meltdown.

The name you prefer defines your team allegiance. "That was a meltdown—no two ways about it," Dolphins president Eddie Jones confided days after the collapse. "I've never seen anything like it and I hope I never do again."

It was the biggest comeback in Jets history. It was the most points a Miami defense allowed in one quarter. Jets quarterback Vinny Testaverde threw four fourth-quarter touchdown passes. The last was a three-yard throw to offensive tackle Jumbo Elliot with 42 seconds left. "Hard to believe," Dolphins defensive end Trace Armstrong said.

Those four Jets touchdowns in the span of 13:07 in the fourth quarter were even more shocking because the Miami defense had allowed only three touchdowns the previous six games. And make no mistake: the unit was sturdy enough that even after the collapse it was third in the NFL in fewest points allowed.

So how could this happen?

Testaverde operated almost exclusively out of a no-huddle, hurry-up attack. He called most of the plays at the line of scrimmage. Testaverde called plays the Jets hadn't practiced in two months and the Dolphins were unprepared for. "Under that circumstance it's hard to call the plays from the sideline," Testaverde said. "So I said, 'Just let me do it.'"

The Jets used four and five-receiver formations. The Dolphins had to counter with reserve defensive backs, and their secondary appeared confused at times. Testaverde completed passes to seven different receivers and delivered an epic fourth quarter with 18 completions in 25 attempts for 236 yards. He threw four touchdowns in the fourth quarter after throwing three interceptions the first three quarters. One of those touchdowns was, well, lucky. Testaverde got the rally started with a 30-yard touchdown pass that went through cornerback Sam Madison's hands to rookie Laveranues Coles, making it 30–13 with 13:49 left. "Nine out of ten times, I intercept that ball," Madison said afterward.

The Jets tied the game at 30, and Miami's defense looked as if it was in a fog. But the Miami offense answered with a moment of clarity. Jay Fiedler connected with Leslie Shepherd for a 46-yard touchdown that gave Miami a 37–30 lead with 3:33 remaining. That was the only first down the Dolphins managed in the fourth quarter while the Jets had 20.

But Miami's answer didn't deflate the Jets' offense. And it didn't save Miami's defense. New York responded by driving to the Dolphins' 3-yard line. Then in the twilight of his career, Elliott entered the game and told the officials he would be lining up on the end of the line, making him an eligible receiver. On his second play after coming in, Elliott made a juggling grab of a Testaverde pass for a touchdown. This was the first pass Elliott ever caught. This was the only touchdown Elliott ever scored. This was the snapshot of the game.

The game bled into Tuesday and overtime, but the zaniness was not yet complete. The Dolphins won the coin toss, and then Fiedler, who had not thrown an interception during regulation, threw two interceptions to Marcus Coleman *on the same drive*. Coleman intercepted Fiedler's third pass of overtime, but Thurman Thomas stripped the ball on the return, and Oronde Gadsden recovered it, giving the Dolphins a reprieve. But five plays later, Fiedler threw another errant pass to Coleman at the Jets' 34.

After Hall connected on his game-winning 40-yard field goal early on Tuesday morning, Dolphins cornerback Patrick Surtain slung his helmet to the turf in disgust. Defensive end Jason Taylor simply laid on the ground, motionless, emotionless. "We came out like gangbusters, but that wasn't enough," Fiedler said. "I guess we thought we had it over before the game was done. This was a tough loss to swallow. It's hard to believe right now, that's for sure."

Five days later in a home game against the Green Bay Packers, the Dolphins fell behind 17–0. They scored 21 points in the third quarter and won the game 28–20.

76 The Bizarre 2017 Season

By the end of the 2017 season, Reshad Jones was familiar with recent Miami Dolphins history. The Pro Bowl safety had seen two head coaches fired, two interim head coaches discarded, a harassment scandal in 2013, and multiple weird moments and episodes no one could have predicted. So at the end of that fateful season, Jones was asked if he'd ever been through a year with so many twists and turns as the one just completed. "I've been here eight years," Jones said, "so yes, I have. I have for sure. But this one is right up there."

The 2017 season is on the Mount Rushmore of weird for the franchise. That year was a journey through the bizarre. And the uncomfortable. And the unexpected.

How else to put it when the starting quarterback goes down with a knee injury the second week of training camp? Then the regular-season opener was postponed because of hurricane. Then the team fled the storm by flying early to California for the next game—against the Los Angeles Chargers—and the evening before that game, linebacker Lawrence Timmons inexplicably went AWOL.

That was just the start. While Timmons was serving a suspension for freaking out and leaving the team, free agent Rey Maualuga was signed to provide depth. And within the six weeks, Maualuga went into a local bar, refused to pay the $40 tab, choked somebody, and was arrested. Yeah, he was cut that morning.

These Dolphins played their third game of the season in London. All the players stood for the British national anthem. And a handful led by receiver Kenny Stills and tight end Julius Thomas knelt during the Star-Spangled Banner. The team was shut out 20–0 by the New Orleans Saints. The following week the Dolphins beat the Tennessee Titans in the afternoon. That evening a video of offensive line coach Chris Foerster snorting cocaine in his Dolphins office dropped on the Internet. The video was posted by a Las Vegas "model," who had been having an affair with the assistant coach.

Foerster agreed to resign the next morning. "I was to the point where I was just praying to God. I want this stuff out," Foerster told NFL.com three months later. "I want this out of my life. I can't do this anymore. All this [expletive] I had going on outside of work, I don't want to do this anymore. I don't want to drink anymore. I don't want to use anymore. And sure enough, two weeks later the video came out. So you can say it's divine intervention. It wasn't the way I saw everything leaving my life like that. But I knew it was coming. At 55 years old, man, I just couldn't do this anymore."

Weird enough yet? This season featured second-round rookie linebacker Raekwon McMillan blowing out his knee on the first play of the preseason while playing special teams.

It featured Miami trading starting running back Jay Ajayi, who had gained 1,272 yards the previous season, after seven games. The 2017 season did not feature a bye week for the Dolphins. After Hurricane Irma blew away the opener, the NFL rescheduled the Dolphins and Tampa Bay Buccaneers for a game on a weekend both were supposed to have their bye. So both teams had to play 16 consecutive games. "I'll figure out a way to make our own bye," a scrappy Adam Gase said early on, suggesting he'd find ways to rest players.

Then after losing the season's final three games, Gase said, "Not having a bye hurt us."

These odd challenges threatened the Dolphins season. But ultimately it was one moment that defined Miami's troubles. That came the second week of training camp when quarterback Ryan Tannehill, who missed the end of the 2016 with a torn ACL and sprained MCL in his left knee, had the same knee buckle on an otherwise routine scramble. An MRI that day revealed Tannehill's

ACL was torn. Again. That crashed the season. Losing the starting quarterback—disastrous for any NFL team—doomed the Dolphins in 2017. The Dolphins ended up signing and starting Jay Cutler. The quarterback, who had played under Gase while he coached the Chicago Bears, was talked out of retirement after having signed a broadcast deal with FOX.

But in keeping with the strange theme of the season, Tannehill's circumstances were unorthodox. Tannehill had opted to rehabilitate and seek alternative treatments for his original knee injury in December 2016. Experts believed he should have opted for the traditional way of addressing a torn ACL—surgery. The injury or injuries eventually kept Tannehill out of the lineup from December of 2016 to September of 2018. "Back from the dead," Tannehill said when he first addressed reporters following his second knee injury.

The Dolphins traded him after the 2018 season.

The Lamar Smith Game

In a locker room buzzing from the 23–17 overtime playoff victory, coach Dave Wannstedt tried to talk above the din. He congratulated his team for beating the Indianapolis Colts and then called on Lamar Smith, who had melted into his locker stall, to stand up and get this game ball. Smith was spent. He didn't move. So two teammates helped him to his feet and walked him over to the coach. And then Wannstedt delivered the game ball and playfully jumped on Smith's back.

The moment was perfectly symbolic. Because on a day Smith delivered a record-breaking, 209-yard performance, Wannstedt was simply doing what the entire franchise had done for the nearly five

Running Backs with a Dark Past

Lamar Smith, who had the horrific drunken driving accident in 1994, wasn't the only Miami Dolphins running back with a troubled past. Over the years Miami backs have done some really outlandish things.

Cecil Collins went to jail for breaking parole after stalking a female neighbor, Sammie Smith did hard time for dealing drugs, Lawrence Phillips hit a woman at a local club to go along with his other out-of-state domestic violence assaults, and Irving Spikes pled guilty to drug and firearms charges.

Lamar Smith was different than those others in at least one notable way. He was extremely productive. He gained 1,139 yards in 2000 and, of course, had that epic playoff game.

quarters that took three hours and nine minutes to play. Ride Lamar Smith.

It was December 30, 2000. Humiliated out of the playoffs with a 62–7 loss a year earlier, the Miami Dolphins got to enjoy postseason success again. And hopefully they enjoyed it because the Dolphins wouldn't win another playoff game for 20 seasons—and counting.

Thank you, Lamar Smith. You brought this win to South Florida. You carried the football 40 times to gain those 209 yards. You scored from 17 yards out in overtime to send your teammates into a frenzy and 73,193 people at Pro Player Stadium home happy. If only he could've come to a postgame press conference to say a few words. "I stay pretty quiet," Smith said after declining to do a press conference. "It's just a matter of confidence. Nothing needs to be said. It's just confidence in the huddle. Everyone in the huddle knows I'm in a rhythm. We don't talk much. We just go out and get the job done. I will say this is the highlight of my career."

That was voluminous as Smith got. "I think I've heard him say 14 words since I've known him," defensive end Jason Taylor said. "But his actions spoke for him today."

The Miami media relations department spent much of the 2000 season shielding Smith, shooing unwanted questioners away from his locker stall. The Dolphins, you see, didn't want Smith thinking about and addressing the 1994 drunk driving accident that left Smith's then-Seattle Seahawks teammate Mike Frier paralyzed from the neck down. In 1996 Smith pled guilty to vehicular assault and was ordered to pay Frier a portion of his salary for seven years. But the tragedy obviously endured for Frier and didn't stop shadowing Smith. So it was still controversial when the Dolphins added him to the team four years later.

In the victory against the Colts, Smith rewrote the Miami record book, erasing the single-game rushing record of 197 yards set by Mercury Morris in 1973 and the postseason single-game record of 145 yards set by Larry Csonka in Super Bowl VIII against Minnesota. The performance was heroic. Afterward Csonka told *Miami Herald* sports editor Edwin Pope that he watched the game and wanted to meet Smith and shake his hand.

But the performance was costly. Smith had to go to the hospital after the game and spent hours hooked up to an IV. The game left Smith so battered he practiced only once that week and had to rock himself back and forth merely to get out of bed, and that process took about five minutes. "I was sore and stiff all over," he said. "I had problems trying to sleep. I didn't want to eat too much or try moving around too much. It took a toll."

The toll was obvious the following week in a playoff game loss at the Oakland Raiders. Smith only got eight carries and gained all of five yards. The Dolphins lost 27–0. It was a stark contrast to the week before. "Last week," tight end Hunter Goodwin says, "we felt like he [Smith] could have gone for 300 yards if we wanted."

78 The 2004 Disaster

The seeds to the Miami Dolphins' wasted 2004 season were sown in May when offensive coordinator Joel Collier, mentally exhausted by the pressures and rigors of replacing Norv Turner, was advised by doctors to step down. Head coach Dave Wannstedt then surveyed his staff and considered quarterbacks coach Marc Trestman and receiver coach Jerry Sullivan—both former NFL offensive coordinators—as replacements. Wannstedt told Trestman he'd been chosen for the spot and some sort of press conference or announcement would follow the next day. Except the next day when Trestman showed up for work, Wannstedt told him he wasn't Miami's offensive coordinator after all.

Offensive line coach Tony Wise, Wannstedt's close friend dating back to the mid-1970s, had heard of the head coach's choice and balked at the prospect of working under Trestman. Wise told Wannstedt if he kept Trestman, he'd quit on the spot and maybe even take a couple of other offensive coaches with him. So Wannstedt instead named the tight end coach Chris Foerster the team's second offensive coordinator in as many months. And that was the calm part of the 2004 offseason. Because in the previous couple of months, the Dolphins had demoted Wannstedt, stripping him of final say on personnel matters; hired Dan Marino as part of the front office and then announced three weeks later Marino had changed his mind; conducted a national search for a new general manager; and after interviewing half a dozen candidates, some of whom went on to win Super Bowls with other teams—including Ted Thompson—promoted Rick Spielman.

The Spielman promotion was awkward in that he'd been hired by Wannstedt and answered to the coach for four seasons. Then he had to tell Wannstedt what would happen on the personnel front, including a trade for quarterback A.J. Feeley while Wannstedt remained loyal to Jay Fiedler. "If you wrote a book about it, it would be a best seller," tight end Randy McMichael said of the season. "Anything that could go wrong has gone wrong."

Amazingly, the biggest problems were just ahead. Running back Ricky Williams tested positive for marijuana and faced a suspension. He had grown tired of being ridden like a mule in Wannstedt's offensive plans and saw the suspension as a way out. He announced his retirement days before training camp. Publicly, the Dolphins tried to spin their problems. "The season hasn't started," Spielman said jokingly. "So how can anyone be worried it's over already?"

Spielman traded a second-round draft pick for a backup running back named Lamar Gordon, who injured his shoulder in his first game and never played for the Dolphins again. After Gordon was injured, two other running backs went down. The Dolphins started some games in 2004 with their fifth-string running back.

The coaching staff wasn't the only part of the team at war with itself. In the locker room, defensive players grew frustrated with offensive players. That showed the second game of the season during a Sunday night game against the Cincinnati Bengals, when Feeley threw an interception, and cornerback Sam Madison went after the quarterback in full-throated frustration so intense he had to be restrained by safety Shawn Wooden.

The offense itself was immersed in a debate about who should play quarterback, a debate Wannstedt and Spielman engaged in earlier. Fiedler started the season opener but was benched at halftime. Then Feeley started the next two games and was benched. Then Fiedler started five games and was injured, tossing the reins back to Feeley. The Dolphins started the season 0–6. They were 1–8 the evening of November 7 when Wannstedt and owner Wayne Huizenga talked. The coach asked the owner what he was thinking.

Huizenga said he had no intention of firing Wannstedt in season but would probably make a change after the season.

Wannstedt resigned. The day Wannstedt resigned, the Dolphins had the worst record in the league, a total collapse for a franchise that had not had a losing season since 1988. As the Dolphins were imploding from within, they were also taking shots from outside the team—albeit from a familiar source. "Sometimes you can only do bad to people and make poor decisions for so long before it catches up to you," former cornerback Terrell Buckley told the *New York Post* that October. "They've got some good players down there, some good guys. Wayne Huizenga is a good owner, and Eddie Jones is a good president, but you have to look at the guys who make the football decisions down there—Dave and Rick. They've had a bunch of talent down there and a bunch of good guys and they don't get to the playoffs. We as players always get evaluated. I think you have to evaluate the people in charge of making the football decisions there."

Jim Bates took over as interim coach the final seven games. He authored a 3–4 record. including a 29–28 upset of the defending champion New England Patriots. This suggested the team's problem was the head coach as much as anything else. "People say we're a different team under him, and it's true," McMichael said of Bates. "I will play for that man anywhere any day of the week."

79 The Ongoing Search for Marino's Heir

Some franchises move seamlessly from quarterback great to quarterback great. The Green Bay Packers went from Brett Favre to Aaron Rodgers. The San Francisco 49ers went from Joe Montana to Steve Young. Some coaches do it, too. Don Shula went from

Johnny Unitas to Bob Griese and eventually to Dan Marino—three Hall of Famers.

But from January 2000, when Marino played his final game, to current day, the Miami Dolphins have endured a desert experience that has offered little hope and precious few playoff moments. So what happened? Why this drought at the game's most important position?

Blame a conspiracy of mistakes undertaken by different administrations. And the common thread among the group is failing to recognize their mistake quickly enough. Dave Wannstedt and Rick Spielman discussed drafting Drew Brees and even signing Troy Aikman but stuck for five seasons with Jay Fiedler. Nothing against Fiedler, but his success was mostly a result of great defense. Nick Saban picked Daunte Culpepper over Brees. Tony Sparano knew in 2010 that Chad Henne wasn't right, but he stuck with him and was fired after 2011. This says nothing of Joey Harrington, Cleo Lemon, A.J. Feeley, Trent Green, and Brian Griese, who all failed as veteran acquisitions. And Pat White and John Beck failed as draft picks.

In the 2012 NFL Draft, the Dolphins selected a quarterback in the first round for the first time since they selected Marino 27th overall in 1983. Ryan Tannehill, the eighth overall pick in 2012, struggled through injuries and inconsistency. During the 2019 offseason, Miami traded him to the Tennessee Titans, where he played the best football of his career and led them to the AFC Championship Game.

The Dolphins used to reach that plateau themselves. They won Super Bowls with Griese and fascinated a generation with Marino. The organization knows how important it is to have a great quarterback. "We will never be a great team again," owner Wayne Huizenga said in the 2004 offseason, "until we have a great quarterback again."

80 The Championship Defense That Never Was

The NFL's sack leader in 2002 was Jason Taylor, who had 18½ to lead the league. The NFL's tackle leader that same year was Zach Thomas, who collected 156, which was more than future Hall of Famers Ray Lewis, Derrick Brooks, or Brian Urlacher. Both Taylor and Thomas were selected to the Pro Bowl. So was defensive tackle Tim Bowens. So was cornerback Patrick Surtain. So was safety Brock Marion.

The 2002 Miami Dolphins' defense was third in total defense. It was fourth in points allowed. That was just behind the Tampa Bay Buccaneers and ahead of the Oakland Raiders in both categories, so the Miami defense was in the same company as the two Super Bowl defenses.

"This defense has the best talent maybe in the entire league," Thomas said in the spring of 2002. "If we don't have the best talent, we got just as much as anybody else. Just look around. That's a championship defense right there. But you can't really say it until you go out and win that championship. That's what we got to do: live up to all the talent we got."

Despite all the laudable defensive statistics and list of accomplished defensive stars, the Dolphins did not win a championship in 2002. They didn't even make the playoffs. And that was the galling thing about those late 1990s and early 2000s Dolphins teams: the defense was good enough to win big. The defense was arguably championship caliber. But the Dolphins never won big and obviously didn't win the championship.

We know the Dolphins haven't been to a Super Bowl since 1984 when Dan Marino and the fading Killer Bs made their fateful trip to Stanford Stadium to play the San Francisco 49ers. But the Dolphins had a unit worthy of such a run after that appearance and indeed after Marino's time: the 2000–03 defense.

That unit was largely put together by Jimmy Johnson. He drafted outstanding players such as Taylor, Thomas, Surtain, and Sam Madison. He developed or nurtured players Don Shula brought to Miami like Trace Armstrong and Tim Bowens. He added veterans such as Marion. And those pieces became the foundation of what was a well-respected unit at the time. "There's no doubt that defense is outstanding," said New England Patriots head coach Bill Belichick before being swept in the season series by the Dolphins in 2000.

But even as the Miami defense finished third in the NFL, allowing only 16.3 points per game in 2003, the Dolphins failed to make the playoffs—just as surely as they'd failed the previous season. With Taylor as a future Hall of Famer; with Thomas earning eight Pro Bowl trips and All-Pro honors five times; and with Pro Bowl players in Armstrong, Surtain, Madison, Marion, Bowens, and Adawale Ogunleye; the Dolphins missed the playoffs as often as they made it.

The Dolphins' 1972 defense allowed 12.2 points per game, and the 2000 Dolphins defense allowed 14.1 points per game. One was perfect, and one was bounced from the playoffs in the divisional round. "We have a lot of talented players," Taylor said after the Dolphins were eliminated from postseason contention in 2002. "But are we a good team? Obviously not. We came to New England in a must-win situation and let it get away from us. Good teams don't do that."

So what was the problem? How could the Dolphins waste so much excellence on defense? The obvious answer is the Miami offense was not the equal of the defense. That unit never found a proficient quarterback while the defense was in its heyday. Sure, Ricky Williams led the NFL in rushing in 2002, but that made the offense one-dimensional, something defensive coordinators love.

Despite similar struggles by their offenses, other defensive units of the time still carried their teams to championships. The Baltimore Ravens did. Tampa Bay did. The Miami D could not.

And that leads to the next possible reason that great Miami defense didn't win big. That unit was predictable. And that unit was often gassed late in seasons. Under Johnson and definitely under coach Dave Wannstedt, the Dolphins had a philosophy on defense that hadn't changed since their time with the Dallas Cowboys in the early 1990s or even at the University of Miami of the 1980s. Those defenses played sound. They played up the field. They attacked. And they did that practically every play over and over in the same way.

It worked for the Hurricanes and later the Cowboys because both were supremely talented. They simply had superior talent than opposing offenses. It also worked because teams didn't figure them out. But when Wannstedt tried the same formula in Miami, opponents adjusted. And so in 2001 and 2002, the Dolphins beat New England in the first meeting. And lost the second. In 2002 they beat the New York Jets in the first meeting. And lost the second.

Late-season losses became a topic of concern. Miami won the AFC East in 2000 but lost two of its final three games. Miami was 11–5 in 2001 but was only 2–2 its final four games. And the Dolphins lost their last two games of 2002 with the playoffs at stake. "Teams are figuring us out," Thomas said in 2003. "We're not making any big adjustments or throwing monkey wrenches at teams late in the season."

81 Watch *Ace Ventura: Pet Detective*

Harvey Greene spent much of his time as the Miami Dolphins media relations director keeping Dan Marino's public image pristine. The quarterback recognized that. That's the reason Marino asked Greene what he thought of him joining *In Living Color* comedian Jim Carrey in a movie about, well, a pet detective. "A what?" Greene recalled saying.

Greene advised Marino to be careful. He doubted Carrey was big enough to carry a movie. And Greene wasn't alone in warning Marino. Other friends had already told Marino the movie's script was "dumb," and he agreed. Marino was going to turn down the role but took a lunch (Hollywood lingo) anyway to meet Carrey. "And then Jim was late," Marino said, suggesting that cemented his decision to decline the role.

But when Carrey arrived, the actor stuck out his hand "and plopped his face right on the table!" Marino said. By the end of lunch, Marino thought the comedian was "a complete lunatic, but maybe doing the movie was not so bad an idea."

And so in May of 1993, *Ace Ventura: Pet Detective* began filming in and around South Florida. Marino was in the movie. Don Shula was in the movie. Multiple other Dolphins players were in the movie. And that script Marino thought was "dumb?" Well, it was. It was moronic.

Carrey, as Ventura, is an excellent but down-on-his-luck detective with an angry landlord and overdue office rent. He specializes in solving mysteries involving pets, so the Dolphins contacted him just prior to the Super Bowl.

The team, headed for a Super Bowl, was desperate because its mascot dolphin named Snowflake had been stolen and its quarterback, Marino, has been kidnapped. Coach Shula, it seems, had a team of superstitious players who needed Snowflake, not to mention Marino, at the Super Bowl. Plus, Snowflake was the star of the halftime show.

Ventura began his quest to solve the crime and during that time he did some *Star Trek* imitations, wore a tutu, caught a bullet in his mouth with his teeth, and struck up a little chemistry with Melissa, who worked for the Dolphins and was played by Courteney Cox.

Ventura eventually narrowed his field of suspects to Ray Finkle, the kicker booted from the team after missing a kick in the 1984 Super Bowl, which the Dolphins also played in. Finkle was one disturbed dude who blamed Marino for holding that fateful kick with the laces facing him. And Finkle had always told Marino, "Laces out, Dan!"

The pet detective visited Finkle's mom, who clearly was no fan of Marino. "Dan Marino should die of gonorrhea and rot in hell," the mom said. "Would you like a cookie, son?"

Gene Siskel hated the film. Audiences loved it. It was the leading box office draw for multiple weeks when it debuted in February 1994. It was one of the top money-making films of the year. Carey rocketed to stardom. "He was great to work with," Marino said, "But I made his career."

Marino said he still gets occasional residual checks, "like one for $24, and then a while later, maybe one for $34." Marino visited England in 2015 as an NFL ambassador for the league's International Series that featured the New York Jets playing the Dolphins at London's Wembley Stadium. He participated in a charity walk along with other celebrities, including Prince Harry. While taking a break from the walk, participants began throwing a football around. "Laces out, Dan!" Harry shouted.

82 Don Shula's Least Favorite Player

Don Shula was seated at breakfast. Over a plate of eggs, he talked about the players he's coached in his career. And there are great ones like Johnny Unitas and Dan Marino, and there are good ones, and then there's that guy Shula hates. "You want to know the guy I could not stand?" Shula said, leaning away from his food and closer to his guest. "I can tell you if you want to know."

At the time Shula has been an NFL coach for 30 years, had coached in six Super Bowls, pieced together a perfect team, and coached some 3,000 men on his rosters. And he's asking if I want to know who he couldn't stand the most? *Tell me, Coach!* "Tim McKyer," Shula said. "Not even close."

Wait, what? Most Miami Dolphins fans wouldn't know Tim McKyer from Tim McGraw—except one's a pretty good singer, and the other was once a pretty good cornerback for the Dolphins. But McKyer was in Miami for all of one season. And there's a reason his Dolphins days didn't extend past the 1990 season. McKyer, it seems, gave Shula fits. The coach nursed more headaches and called more private meetings because of McKyer than perhaps any other player. And it was all in the span of about 11 months.

From the time McKyer came to the Dolphins before that '90 season for a second-round pick to the time Shula told then-president Tim Robbie and general manager Eddie Jones he didn't want him back, the Tim McKyer experience was a something of pain for Shula.

What McKyer viewed as bravado, Shula viewed as arrogance. What McKyer viewed as truth, Shula viewed as stupidity. Like the time McKyer called the Kansas City Chiefs secondary "suspect." And said they were "soft." And also said the Dolphins were not as tight-knit as the San Francisco 49ers, the team he played on for four seasons before arriving in Miami. And also when he said Dolphins players, who try to be leaders, aren't always granted the respect they deserve.

He said these things throughout the season, and the Kansas City comments came days before the Dolphins met the Chiefs in the play-offs. "I feel like he's lost the respect among players maybe because of his comments, maybe because of his actions," linebacker E.J. Junior said of McKyer. "It can get on your nerves. There have been times he's done things that have irritated me."

It irritated Dan Marino, who told reporters he told McKyer to "shut up."

And it bothered Shula because Kansas City coach Marty Schottenheimer was a respected friend. And in his mind, the comments disrespected Schottenheimer's team. McKyer didn't care. After the Dolphins scratched out a 17–16 win against the Chiefs, McKyer kept talking. "Their so-called Pro Bowl cornerbacks—I guess they got some extra weeks to get ready for the Pro Bowl now," McKyer said, referring to Chiefs corners Albert Lewis and Kevin Ross. McKyer then called the Chiefs "punks." And sporting an ice pack on a bruised right arm, McKyer explained, "One of their chumps hit me."

Shula hated this. But it continued the following week when McKyer called out the Buffalo Bills before another playoff game. "Come after me," he implored Jim Kelly in the press.

After that 1990 season, Shula traded McKyer to the Atlanta Falcons for a third-round pick. And then the cornerback bounced around the league, moving on to the Detroit Lions, Pittsburgh Steelers, Carolina Panthers, back to the Falcons, and finally to the Denver Broncos in 1997. But his travels didn't immediately change McKyer's approach to the game or being an attention magnet. Before the Steelers played the San Diego Chargers in the AFC Championship Game in 1995, McKyer recognized me in the Steelers locker room. "What happened to the boys from Miami?" McKyer asked, referring to the Dolphins quick exit from the '95 playoffs. "Don Shula just about ran me out of the NFL and blackballed me, but here I am, still in the playoffs. Where are the Dolphins? Looks like they choked a little bit, doesn't it? Everywhere Tim McKyer seems to land, that first year the team does something special."

The Steelers lost that AFC Championship Game several days later. Chargers wide receiver Tony Martin caught the winning 43-yard touchdown pass with 5:13 to play. The cornerback covering him on the play? Shula's least favorite player.

83 Jason Taylor vs. the Super Bowl Bears

Jason Taylor was reading the newspaper, and every paragraph was a like bitter pill swallowed without water. Taylor was in his 10th NFL season and he understood the criticism. The Miami Dolphins were picked by *Sports Illustrated* to be in the Super Bowl before the 2006 season began. They had traded for Daunte Culpepper, and he was supposed to upgrade an offense that would be paired with a playoff-caliber defense.

But the Dolphins lost their season opener. Then they lost again. And there they sat with six losses in seven games, Culpepper benched, and the season in shambles. The criticism was coming from all sides, including via friendly fire. Taylor read that former Dolphins offensive lineman Bob Kuechenberg had criticized coach Nick Saban for replacing Gus Frerotte, the quarterback on the 2005 team that managed a 9–7 record. He s criticized the players, saying the team "does not have a soul." Kuechenberg looked at the schedule and had given the Dolphins no chance to win that week because Taylor's hapless team was facing the Chicago Bears, who had won all seven of their games.

So Taylor was seething. He was mad at Kuechenberg, mad at the way the season had gone, mad that anyone believed his team was hopelessly overmatched. "They bleed like us and they can be beaten just like we have been," Taylor told reporters in the days before the game. "It's as simple as that. We'll go up there and get after them. It's not going to take a miracle to beat this team. I'm sorry, I'll give the Bears their respect. They're a good football team with a lot of the top players at their positions. But we're not playing the '72 Dolphins or the All-Madden team on the video game. These guys can be beaten; it's as simple as that. I give them respect, but sorry, guys, that's about it. We're still going to go up there to do what we have to do."

But, but, J.T., what about your record? What about their record? What about Kuechenberg's comments? "It's another chapter in the grumpy Kuechenberg story," Taylor snapped. "It's Kuechenberg. He gets up every year and bitches about something. If it ain't one thing, it's another. He needs a hug and a hobby. It's ridiculous"

This is the portion of this chapter where there's a lesson from the media playbook. One guy says something controversial. Another guy responds. So what happens next? Go back, of course, to the first guy to get a response to the response. "Maybe if fewer Dolphins had hugs and hobbies, they would have more wins," Kuechenberg retorted. "If they beat the Bears, I'll give Taylor a hug and buy him a steak at Shula's Steak House. Jason is a great warrior."

Taylor's rant wasn't exactly Namath guaranteeing a Super Bowl win. But it was prophetic. The Dolphins that week got 157 rushing yards from Ronnie Brown. Wes Welker, Marty Booker, and Chris Chambers caught touchdown passes. And the Miami defense suffocated Chicago. Taylor collected a sack, a forced fumble, and an interception that he returned for a touchdown in a 31–13 victory. The season was a disappointment for the Dolphins, and the Bears went on to play in the Super Bowl. But for one afternoon, an entire team rallied behind its leader. "You have to carry a big stick because if you're walking around just talking all day, eventually you're going to lose your credibility, and no one is going to listen," Taylor said.

Kuechenberg, who played on the undefeated Dolphins team, was thrilled the Dolphins won even as he remained aware the team was underperforming. "That's what they need to do all the time," he said. "Not many people, including me, gave them much of a chance against the Bears. But they played the game with their chinstraps buckled. Zach Thomas and Jason Taylor always have their chinstraps buckled, but this game the entire team did."

And a man of his word, Kuechenberg offered to buy Taylor that meal at Shula's. Taylor declined. "Tell him to send me a check," he said, "and I'll get my own dinner."

84 Missing on Drew Brees Twice

John Butler spent the days before the 2001 NFL Draft pondering a strategy he believed could be a monumental decision for his San Diego Chargers. Butler, the team's new general manager at the time, had the draft's No. 1 overall pick. And Michael Vick was the consensus No. 1 player in the draft. Everyone pretty much acknowledged this except Butler had inherited a roster that managed only one win the previous season. So he knew he needed more than one great player to turn that team around. And Butler believed Vick was an exceptional prospect, but he thought he wasn't necessarily the best player in the draft.

Butler believed running back LaDainian Tomlinson was that draft's best player. And Butler believed Vick might not be the best quarterback in that draft. Butler believed Drew Brees might be every bit as dynamic with his arm as Vick might be both passing and running the football. So for the Chargers GM, the days before that fateful draft were fraught with sleepless nights and franchise-defining decisions. History tells us Butler traded out of that top pick in the draft, and the Atlanta Falcons selected Vick No. 1. But Butler had another issue: with the No. 5 pick he now held, would he choose Tomlinson or Brees? "My thinking was if I pick L.T. at No. 5, could I still find a way to get Brees later in the first round?" Butler said in the spring of 2002. "We looked at the board and thought if we pick L.T., Brees might still be there for us when we pick in the second round if the Miami Dolphins don't pick Brees at No. 26."

The Dolphins, one year into Jay Fiedler's tenure as the immediate successor to Dan Marino, considered Brees. They looked at him hard. "At least three people on our staff have seen every snap in his career," Dolphins personnel chief Rick Spielman told *Sports Illustrated* before the draft. "We will have a substantial feel on Brees before we interview him at the combine in Indianapolis."

But something happened between that NFL Combine visit in late February and the draft in April. The Dolphins came off Brees and picked Wisconsin cornerback Jamar Fletcher in the first round instead. Why? "We thought Drew would be an upgrade over Jay," Spielman said days after the draft. "But we don't think he is *that* much better. We feel good about Jay. Plus, we think we *really* upgraded our secondary with Jamar. He can play press. He can help on special teams. He's going to play sooner. He's going to help us more."

The Chargers pounced on Brees with the first selection of the second round. The Dolphins did eventually pick a quarterback that draft. They selected Oklahoma's Josh Heupel in the sixth round. But he was cut before the season began. Fletcher, meanwhile, started a total of six games in three seasons for Miami and was traded to San Diego in 2004.

Interestingly, Spielman kept a photo of himself and Fletcher on his office wall at Dolphins camp. At first he said it was because Fletcher was his first ever pick with the Dolphins and wanted to remember that milestone. Years later, Spielman claimed the pick was hoisted upon him by Dolphins coach Dave Wannstedt and he wanted to remember how *not* to make a selection.

That's how that sad, first shot at Brees came to a close. But the shocking, frustrating thing for Dolphins fans is this was only the first opportunity the Dolphins had to pick Brees and probably change the course of their history. And, amazingly, there would be one more. Miami's second failed chance at Brees has gotten more attention over the years because, well, Brees developed into a good player in San Diego after Miami didn't draft him. But he became a superstar with the New Orleans Saints after Miami failed to sign him as a free agent in the spring of 2006.

Brees has led the Saints to a Super Bowl championship, multiple playoff appearances, and has been a record-breaking passer. Brees has become a pillar of the New Orleans community and was a life preserver for an area that was literally under water in the aftermath of Hurricane Katrina in 2006. But here's the most galling part for Miami fans: the Dolphins screwed up the second attempt at Brees even as he was eager to play for the team.

Brees made no bones about the fact he preferred Miami over New Orleans that spring. That was clear when he visited with the Saints at the start of free agency, got a lucrative offer to sign, but left town anyway to visit with the Dolphins. So how'd this get screwed up a second time? How did the Dolphins falter on landing the NFL's all-time leader in completions, yards, and touchdowns?

The trouble was not in the making of a football decision. Dolphins coaches and football people, by all accounts, wanted Brees. But the decision didn't come down to football people. Then-coach Nick Saban and then-owner Wayne Huizenga both said the hang up came in the Dolphins medical exams. "Let me just say this,"

Saban said weeks into the 2006 season when it became obvious the Dolphins had botched the decision, "It was a medical decision. I don't think medicine, personnel, or any of that is an exact science. I think we have good, professional people in that area. I think they made the best judgment they could make at the time relative to the circumstances. No one could predict the future. It is what it is right now."

Huizenga said Dolphins doctors told the team they were uncomfortable saying Brees, following his recovery from surgery to repair a torn labrum and partially torn rotator cuff in his right (throwing) shoulder, would be able to play in 2006. And even if Brees did recover, the doctors reportedly said they could not guarantee he'd have the same arm strength as before.

Those doctors had subjected Brees to a six-hour physical that centered, of course, around his surgically-repaired shoulder. And then they recommended the Dolphins consult other doctors who didn't work for the team. The Dolphins were thoroughly spooked about Brees.

Meanwhile, the same doctors, however, examined Daunte Culpepper's surgically-repaired knee and deemed him on track to play in 2006. Culpepper had shredded the ACL, MCL, and PCL in a game against the Carolina Panthers the previous season, but the doctors were of the opinion he was a better bet of regaining his mobility than Brees was of recovering his arm strength. So the decision was made to trade for Culpepper instead of to sign Brees. And this wouldn't be an gargantuan issue if Culpepper had continued on the same Pro Bowl career arc he had been on with the Minnesota Vikings before the injury. The problem is Culpepper never really reached those heights again.

Culpepper struggled with mobility early that season with Miami. He was sacked 10 times in the first two games. It took two more weeks and 11 more sacks before coaches decided to bench Culpepper. He became the backup quarterback. And then he became the third stringer. And then he was inactive and finally required another knee surgery that ended his season.

It was October 2006. The Saints were on their way to a first-round playoff bye after Brees helped them bounce back from going 3–13 the previous season. Selected by *Sports Illustrated* to play in the Super Bowl, the Dolphins were on their way to a bitterly disappointing season. Three months later Saban quit the Dolphins. In July of 2007, Culpepper was cut. Brees would go on to break nearly every NFL passing record during his career.

85 Nick Saban Wanted Ngata

The Miami Dolphins strung together three long tables—the kind public schools use to serve kids lunches—in a row in the team's media room, and Nick Saban was sitting at the head of the row with reporters sitting along the sides. "The guy I really wanted was Haloti Ngata," Saban said, revealing the Dolphins' thought process during the first round of the 2006 draft. "That son of a bitch is as big as one of these tables."

This revelation came a couple of days after telling reporters he was "extremely, extremely pleased and happy" about selecting defensive back Jason Allen in the first round. This came after the Dolphins, picking at No. 16 overall, reached into Saban's knowledge of SEC players and personal knowledge of Allen, a defensive back out of Tennessee, to make their selection. "The price was too high to go up and get Ngata," Saban lamented. "We just couldn't get up there."

The Dolphins had the 16th overall selection in the first round of the 2006 draft. The Cleveland Browns, holding the No. 12 overall selection, wanted to trade down. And the Dolphins engaged the Browns to move up and pick Ngata. But the price for that move fluctuated anywhere from a second to a third-round pick in addition to Miami's No. 1. Saban decided the price was too steep. The Browns instead moved down one spot, getting a sixth-round pick from the Baltimore Ravens, who then took Ngata.

And here was the unseen fallout of the failed Drew Brees decision in the spring of 2006. The Dolphins decided not to sign Brees as a free agent because their doctors had concerns about his throwing shoulder. Yet Miami's doctors had no such concerns about Daunte Culpepper's surgically reconstructed knee. So instead of signing Brees, the team sent its 2006 second-round pick to the Minnesota Vikings for Culpepper. And aside from ultimately being the most boneheaded decision the Dolphins made during the Saban era, that trade also greatly increased Miami's internal value of its third-round pick because that pick effectively became the team's second pick of that '06 draft. So when the Browns asked for that pick, the Dolphins balked. That meant the team that could have added Brees and Ngata in the spring of 2006 instead got Culpepper, Allen, and that third-round pick. With that third-round selection, Miami took receiver Derek Hagan, who was gone within three years.

Saban and personnel chief Randy Mueller identified a dozen players they might select if available at No. 16 overall. All but one, Allen, were gone by the time Miami was on the clock. "We were hoping a front-seven player would be available—if you're going to put my feet to the fire," Saban said. "You always want big people."

The Dolphins added four free-agent defensive backs before that draft so Saban had no choice but to admit the secondary wasn't a "pressing priority." But he still liked Allen. Saban had recruited Allen when he was the coach at LSU. In fact, Saban was perhaps the only head coach who projected Allen as a defensive back while other schools recruited him as a running back. In adding him to the mix in Miami, Saban told Allen he might play some at cornerback, some at nickel, and also at safety. "That's the perfect scenario for me," said Allen, who started 14 games at cornerback and 12 at free safety during four seasons at Tennessee. "That's what I'm looking forward to doing, moving all over the secondary."

It didn't quite work out. Allen wasn't instinctive enough as a safety nor did he have the ball skills to succeed consistently at cornerback. That's not to say Saban gave up on Allen. Midway through the 2006 season when it was increasingly clear Allen wasn't going to immediately factor to any great degree, Saban pulled a reporter aside and started talking about how another young defensive back in the league had struggled his first season before finding himself. Saban told the reporter he thought Allen was every bit as good as that player named Troy Polamalu.

Allen never found a real home in Miami's secondary. He started only 19 games in five seasons there before being released in 2010. And that left this final semi-prophetic twist. Although he had attended some of Saban's summer camps as a standout high school player, Allen ultimately went to Tennessee because he was worried Saban wouldn't remain the LSU coach throughout his college career. Saban ended up leaving the Dolphins after Allen's rookie season.

86 Flirting with Troy Aikman

The Miami Dolphins didn't just miss on Drew Brees. They also inexplicably missed on Troy Aikman. And this wasn't a draft day mistake. This wasn't a poor free-agency decision.

This was actually something of a mystery. Before the 2002 season, Dolphins coach Dave Wannstedt was at something of a crossroads. His offensive coordinator, Chan Gailey, was leaving to become the head coach at Georgia Tech. So Wannstedt was discussing the job opening with Norv Turner, who he'd worked with and won Super Bowls with when both were with the Dallas Cowboys. That wasn't Wannstedt's only issue because quarterback Jay Fiedler was opting out of his contract after two seasons. So, again, it wasn't a leap for Wannstedt to reach into his Dallas past and see if he could find a solution to that problem with Aikman

The quarterback had played for the Cowboys when Wannstedt was that team's defensive coordinator and Turner the offensive coordinator and was a sure-fire, first-ballot Hall of Famer. Aikman had been away from the game for a year, having retired after the 2000 season, and the narrative at the time was that Aikman had left the game because he was forced to after multiple concussions and a back injury. But Wannstedt heard differently. He heard Aikman left the game because he had grown disenchanted with the direction the Cowboys took after coach Jimmy Johnson and owner Jerry Jones parted ways. Aikman, he heard, had grown weary of bearing the responsibility for the Dallas failures in the late 1990s after so much of the talent Johnson had acquired has already left or grown old.

And, amazingly, he was right. Aikman, who was 35 years old in the spring of 2002, was not just willing to consider a return. He was actually all for it. His back felt better after a year off, and he didn't think the concussions were a problem. He was excited about the prospect. "I was going to come out of retirement," Aikman said during a candid moment in the NFL Network documentary, *A Football Life*. "I got a call from Wannstedt, and he was a head coach. He was with the Dolphins when they made a run at me. He says, 'I'd like to get with you.' And Norv was the offensive coordinator. So I visited with him, he talked to me, and he says, 'You think you can come back and play?'"

Aikman didn't answer right away. He returned to Texas, thought about it, and discussed it with his family. Then he came to a decision. "I called up when I got back and I said, 'You know what?

I think I want to do it,'" Aikman said. "So he says, 'okay.' And I said, 'Well, I'm going to start training as if I'm coming back.'"

Except it never happened. The Dolphins had a playoff-caliber defense at the time. Indeed they had a very good roster with six Pro Bowl players in 2002. Future Hall of Famer Jason Taylor was hitting his prime. Ricky Williams rushed for team-record 1,853 yards and 16 touchdowns in 2002. Middle linebacker Zach Thomas, a Pro Bowl player, was the quarterback of the defense. But somehow—for reasons not entirely clear—the Dolphins decided against making Aikman the quarterback on offense.

After making the Turner hiring official, the team opted to extend Fiedler's contract.

And what happened after the Dolphins abandoned the idea of signing Aikman? Miami missed the playoffs in 2002. And in 2003. Owner Wayne Huizenga took final say over all football decisions away from Wannstedt, and Aikman never played again.

87 The Marino-Elway Rivalry

Dan Marino has just added another individual award for his mantel. This time it was the heavy bronze NFL Man of the Year trophy that celebrates excellence on the field and charity and volunteer work off of it. And Marino was all smiles and telegenic while the cameras were capturing shots of him with the award. But soon the cameras had gone, and the Miami Dolphins quarterback was bearing his soul.

This award ceremony was in South Florida in January of 1999. And days from then in the very stadium Marino had played in during two different decades, the Denver Broncos played the Atlanta

Falcons in Super Bowl XXXIII. And John Elway was about to win his second consecutive Super Bowl ring. And that left Marino, who was without a Super Bowl ring, feeling somewhat empty. "It's nothing against John. He's a good friend, and I have a lot of respect for him," Marino said. "But it is what is. I have a competitiveness in me and I want [a championship] for myself. I want that for my team. And not having experienced that bothers me a little bit."

Marino attended a function that week as the commissioner's guest. He fulfilled other Super Bowl week obligations. But going to that game in his stadium only 20 miles from his house was not happening. "No, I won't go to the game," Marino said somberly. "I'll watch it. But I went to the game a couple of years ago in New Orleans, and there was something about being in the stadium but not in the game that affected me the wrong way. I didn't feel comfortable. I just felt like I should be playing. It's tough from the standpoint that you think down deep that you have the chance to be in the game. And to have it right in your backyard and everybody coming into town and looking at it makes it tougher. In some ways I wish it was in another city."

Marino and Elway shared a rivalry. And make no mistake: the two were friends from that moment both were selected in the first round of the 1983 NFL Draft. But that draft—in which Elway was the first of five quarterbacks selected in round one and Marino was the fifth—put Elway and Marino in the same league, in the same sentence, and on the same course while battling for the same ultimate goal. "When Danny came in his rookie year and set the world on fire, he set the bar awful high for the rest of us in the class," Elway said. "From that point on, we were all chasing Danny. I know I was."

If the chase was for passing yards, touchdown passes, or fourth-quarter comebacks, no one really compared with Marino. Elway tried to stay close. Consider this from the NFL record book at the time Marino retired after the 1999 season, one year after Elway retired.

Most career passing yards: Marino with 61,361.
Next highest: Elway with 51,475
Most career completions: Marino with 4,967.
Next highest: Elway with 4,123.
Most career fourth-quarter comebacks: Marino and Johnny Unitas with 36.
Next highest: Elway with 35.

But if a quarterback's main job is to chase, the chase between Elway and Marino wasn't close: Elway 2. Marino 0. "The No. 1 way to judge a quarterback is on championships because it's such a position of leadership," former NFL quarterback Ron Jaworski told the *Miami Herald* when he was working as an analyst for ESPN. "If a team wins championships like with Elway, Montana, Bradshaw, and Aikman, that's a special group. But if you just look at the overall ability of a guy to play the quarterback position, there is nobody better than Dan Marino."

So, yes, in the unofficial rivalry between the two most accomplished quarterbacks of the '83 class (sorry, Jim Kelly), Marino got the individual nod. But, again, Elway always had the Super Bowl. Five of them, actually. The Denver Broncos lost—and indeed were blown out—in three Super Bowls before winning two consecutive championships in Elway's final two seasons in the league. For 12 of the 16 seasons Elway and Marino were in the NFL, they never played each other. But the Super Bowl comparison was a barometer both always checked. "Not winning it bothers him," Boomer Esiason, who worked with Marino for years on the CBS pregame show, said of the former Miami quarterback. "It bothers me, too. We're human."

88 Ted Ginn and Brady Quinn

About 150 of the zaniest and most ardent Miami Dolphins fans—the ones wearing plastic dorsal fins on their heads and aqua and orange paint on their faces—were growing angry while they waited for someone, anyone, representing the team to explain to them what the hell just happened. It was Draft Day 2007, and everyone in the audience already knew the Dolphins screwed up.

Well, they didn't *know*. But they thought they knew because general manager Randy Mueller and head coach Cam Cameron just drafted Ohio State wide receiver Ted Ginn Jr. in the first round. And many of them never heard of Ginn. And most of them wanted a quarterback. And not just any quarterback. They all wanted the Dolphins to draft Notre Dame quarterback Brady Quinn.

Whipped into a frenzy by these facts, some booze, and team color analyst Jim Mandich, who was leading a "Brady, Brady, Brady" cheer before the pick, this Dolphins draft party crowd wanted someone's head on a figurative draft day spike. Cameron would serve as the sacrificial victim because the team's marketing department—in multiple promotions for this draft party—said everyone attending would get to hear from the head coach right after the first-round pick was made.

So just after the Dolphins made this wildly unpopular pick, Cameron heard for the first time he had to go see the fans. "I barely knew Cam because this is April, and he was hired in January, but I go up to his office after the pick and tell him, 'Coach, you're going to get booed when you talk about this pick,'" said Harvey Greene, who served 25 years as Miami's media relations chief. "He says, 'Why the hell should I go in there? Why should I go in there and get booed in front of all these people? Send somebody else.'"

Greene explained the team promised the head coach would address the fans. And if he didn't, reporters would ask why he didn't and probably portray him as weak. Greene told Cameron his choice was to look bad in the press or get booed by some fans. After complaining some more, Cameron decided he could turn the crowd in his favor because he's Cam Freakin' Cameron!

It didn't turn out that way. The moment Cameron walked to the podium the club had set up on the indoor field, a fan in the front row gave him a thumbs down. "Hey, we need that thumb to go this direction," Cameron said, giving the fan a thumbs-up sign.

Those words to this day are used as a drop by some South Florida sports talk radio shows when they reach for innuendo on where to place one's fingers. "I just want to thank all of you for being here," Cameron said as the booing continued. "We really, we really—excuse me one second—we really appreciate your support," he said, struggling now. "And let me tell you about the young man we just drafted. He's a young man named Ted Ginn. Ted Ginn Jr. And we drafted the Ginn family. I've known this family for over 10 years. I've watched this young man for a long time. You're going to be thrilled every time you watch him as a punt returner. He's going to be a great returner for us."

The crowd was now roaring its displeasure upon learning the Dolphins just picked a punt returner with the No. 9 overall selection. And the good news that the player's family was also playing for Miami didn't appease them. Cameron responded by clapping and thanking them. A chant of "Brady, Brady, Brady," echoed inside that bubble now. "Let me tell you this," Cameron said above the din, "Ted Ginn is a Miami Dolphin."

"Booooooo!"

"Ted Ginn is someone you're going to be proud of," Cameron said. "Ted Ginn and his family will give us everything they have, I promise you that. Thank you very much."

"Booooooo!"

Mueller later offered more logical reasoning for picking Ginn. He'd seen the Dolphins play the previous year, and there was a troubling lack of big plays. And he'd seen Quinn's tape, and there was a troubling lack of accuracy. "We have to be able to get over the top of defenses," Mueller said. "We have to stop playing three-yards-and-a-cloud of dust football and we need speed to do that. This guy has electric speed. I know fans want the quarterback. But we'll take care of that."

The Dolphins drafted BYU quarterback John Beck in the second round. He was a bust. But it turns out Quinn, who was drafted later in the first round by the Cleveland Browns, also was a draft bust. Ginn, meanwhile, is still playing in 2020. He's a journeyman, but he's been valuable to multiple teams because his speed seriously threatens defenses. He was definitely drafted before he should have been, but he had a better career than Quinn.

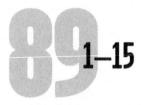 **1–15**

It was the first day of training camp in 2007, and Cam Cameron, whose team was about to endure the worst season in Miami Dolphins history, was already busy screwing things up. Before the first practice, the rookie Dolphins head coach had yelled at team leaders Zach Thomas and Jason Taylor because their family—Taylor was married to Thomas' sister at the time—was not sitting in the section assigned for family members. Later, he scolded Cleo Lemon because the quarterback was doing an interview while wearing earbuds. "Everything we did, he had to have a problem with," Taylor said years later. "That was his way of being the biggest voice in the room. If I talked or Zach talked in a team meeting or after practice, he would always need to have the last word. It was the weirdest thing. We'd all look at each other because he would repeat something one of the players already said. That dude lost me first day of training camp. Even at minicamp, I'm wondering, *what are we doing?*"

The answer to that question was easy. The Dolphins were preparing for a nightmare. The San Diego Chargers had plowed through the AFC in the 2006 season, posting an AFC-best 14–2 record and gaining the top seed in the playoffs. And in their lone playoff game, the Chargers led the New England Patriots 14–10 largely because future Hall of Fame running back LaDainian Tomlinson was plowing through Bill Belichick's defense. The Chargers ran more than they passed, and the Patriots couldn't stop them, allowing Tomlinson 5.6 yards per carry. So what did Offensive Coordinator Cameron do in the second half? Yeah, he flipped it. Although Tomlinson continued to average more than five yards per carry, he got the ball fewer times in the second half. Despite holding a lead, the Chargers passed more and lost the game at home. And out of that upset loss, Cameron got his head coaching job with the Dolphins in January 2007.

Cameron was amazing for his ability to believe the improbable. Quarterback Trent Green suffered a significant concussion in 2006 that forced him to miss two months of the season. But Cameron wanted Green as his quarterback because the two worked together with the Washington Redskins. So the Dolphins gave up a fifth-round pick for Green, and Cameron soon told reporters concussions would be no problem for the new quarterback. "It's not an issue," he said.

Green suffered a concussion in the fifth game of the season against the Houston Texans and did not play for Miami again.

Cameron predicted the Dolphins would be "top five" in scoring. They tied for 26th. Cameron said he wanted his players to "fail forward fast." "I want guys going out in this game not afraid to fail," Cameron said before a preseason game. "But if you fail, fail forward.

What does that mean? Well, if you're failing forward, that means you're failing, but you're learning. And you got to learn fast. Early in the first quarter, I want some guys to go out there and fail. Fail in the first half. We've got to be failing at a fast rate and we got to be failing forward. And that's kind of the theme I'll give them tonight. You hit them with that one. In the locker room, they haven't heard that one yet."

Taylor and Thomas would meet for a meal during every training camp, and 2007 was no different. They also would discuss what kind of team they thought the Dolphins would have that year. "It would be lunch or dinner and it would always naturally flow into, 'All right, whaddya got? Whaddya think?'" Taylor said. "It was after few days in pads when you'd start to see the pajama warriors disappear a little bit. So we'd be eating and eventually we'd make a prediction on the season. Most years we're going to be 10–6 or 8–8 or whatever. We both sat down in that lunch room in 2007, and it went to that conversation. And this is a week into camp, and we started talking about it, and Zach says, 'Dude, you know we're [expletive].' I'm sitting there and I think about it and say, 'Yeah, bro, it's going to be a long season.' Oh, my God. It was before we lost a game. That's a bad feeling when you're going to work, and you realize we don't stack up. We need a miracle to win some of these games."

Cameron decided to use the fourth preseason game as a dry run for his assistants because he wanted them to get the feel for running the team in case he was ever absent. Except defensive coordinator Dom Capers and tight end coach Mike Mularkey had previously been head coaches. And Cameron had never been an NFL head coach.

Then the season began, and things got worse. Players disliked Cameron so much that they openly talked about it among themselves and even to reporters. Joey Porter challenged Cameron to a fight on a team charter home. Owner Wayne Huizenga started thinking of a coaching change by the time the team got to London for the first ever regular-season game abroad. The Dolphins lost to the New York Giants and dropped to 0–8.

The only glimmer of daylight in the franchise's darkest season came on December 16 when the 0–13 Dolphins upset the Baltimore Ravens 22–16. Greg Camarillo caught a 64-yard pass from Lemon to give the Dolphins the walk-off win. "The next day, Wayne called me and told me the price of the team had just gone up," said Stephen Ross, who at the time was negotiating to make the purchase. "I said, 'okay.' It didn't really change anything. But that game cost me a lot of money."

The Dolphins would not win another one that season and finished 1–15.

90 The Bill Parcells Era

In spring of 2015, Stephen Ross was about to do something he has often done as owner of the Miami Dolphins. He was about to spend money. A lot of it. More than $100 million. Ross was excited because his football people presented him a plan to add the best free agent on the market—a player they said could transform Miami's defense in general and the pass rush and run defense in particular. The Dolphins were about to embark on a chase of Ndamukong Suh.

And Ross was telling Hall of Famer Bill Parcells about it. Ross was telling Parcells how Suh was a good man. He recounted his conversation with Warren Buffett and how the fellow billionaire thought it was a great idea. Eventually, Ross got around to asking what Parcells thought of the idea. "Don't do it," Parcells told Ross. "You can't fix your defense by adding one guy. He's *not* going to get you 15 sacks. He *is* going to get double-teamed every game so he's not going to fix all your problems. He's a very good player, but it's not wise to pay him like he's a quarterback."

Ross ignored the advice. And the two men, who shared a cordial relationship long after their years together with the Dolphins, soon grew apart. It's hard to pinpoint exactly when Bill Parcells' influence over the Dolphins ended. It could be said his time lasted from December 2007 to October 2010, the month he cleared out his office at the team's training facility. But that doesn't account for the players he hit on. Or his monumental misses. It doesn't account for the general manager and the coach he hired. Or their successes and massive failures. None of this accounts for the legacy Parcells left the Dolphins.

It's easy to say now—nearly a decade after he walked out of Miami's training facility the last time—that Parcells failed with the Dolphins. He even says it himself. "It didn't work the way I hoped," Parcells said. "I don't think that's a secret or breaking news."

The further out from the Parcells era the Dolphins get, the more defined the battle lines between Parcells' friends and foes becomes. The foes will coldly tell you Parcells picked Chad Henne. And Pat White. They'll tell you he signed a four-year deal worth $16 million and collected the entire amount despite quitting after 32 months. The foes will blame Parcells for the Jeff Ireland and Tony Sparano tenure because he hired both in 2008. And, depending on his mood, Parcells sometimes puffs out his chest and freely allows some of those arrows aimed at him to hit their target because he did indeed have final say over the entire organization at the time.

Picking White in the second round of the 2009 draft was disastrous. White was coming off a great college career, an MVP performance in a bowl game, another MVP performance in the Senior Bowl, and that made the Dolphins overlook the fact he looked like a high school quarterback. "He just wasn't a prototypical quarterback pick," Parcells said. "He was a great college player, and we let that color our judgment. We violated our principles."

Picking Henne in the second round of the 2008 when the Dolphins could have selected Matt Ryan or Joe Flacco in the first round was also a failure. Parcells sent Sparano, Ireland, and offensive coordinator Dan Henning on the road in the spring of 2008 to meet, interview, and work out Henne, Ryan, and Flacco. The consensus Miami's traveling decision-makers came back with was that the three quarterbacks were comparable. Except the three haven't had comparable careers. Two have taken teams to the Super Bowl. Henne, a career backup once he left Miami, is the other one.

But no one mentions that Ryan threw 19 interceptions his final year at Boston College. And the people, who now rip Parcells for passing on Ryan, never raised that criticism in 2008 when the Dolphins picked left tackle Jake Long. They certainly didn't say anything when Long went to the Pro Bowl his first four seasons. Those critiques come in hindsight. And everyone benefits from hindsight, including Parcells. So would he have picked Ryan over Long if he knew the quarterback would become a fine player? "Maybe," he said before pausing. "We should have."

The failures Sparano and Ireland suffered—many of them *after* Parcells left—are pinned on Parcells. Yes, the three came to Miami together. But it wasn't Parcells that kept Ireland as general manager for two more years after Sparano was fired. That was done by Ross in 2011. And Parcells wasn't even speaking to Ireland anymore at that time.

Parcells believes he handed over control of the organization to Ireland too soon. And he admits he should have handled his interaction with Sparano differently. "We had a young coach, and I didn't want to overshadow him too much," Parcells said. "I acted with the best intentions. The problem is I would see things happening during the week that I knew were going to come up later. Then gameday would come, and that problem would rear its head. Looking back, I should have stepped in more."

Despite all of this, the truth about the Parcells era cannot be written without including a complete picture of what the Dolphins were on his watch. And before his watch. Because the Dolphins were on fire when Parcells was hired in December 2007. The franchise, indeed, was something of a late-night show punch line after a 1–15 season in 2007. And in the span of one offseason, Parcells turned that smoldering heap into a team that won the AFC East in 2008.

It should be noted that Chad Pennington, who was released by the New York Jets when they signed Brett Favre, picked the Dolphins because of Parcells. He received MVP votes in 2008. Cameron Wake was a CFL player when the Dolphins signed him in 2009 under Parcells. Soon he was a perennial Pro Bowl pass rusher. Parcells traded Jason Taylor to the Washington Redskins for a second and sixth-round pick in '08 and then got him back as a free agent in '09.

Ricky Williams negotiated directly with Parcells when he signed an extension in 2008 and stayed with Miami through 2010.

Miami's 25–23 record in the three years Parcells was with the team is hardly a reason to boast. But it was the eighth best record in the 16-team AFC during that stretch. Yes, it was middle of the pack. But it was a status to which the Dolphins *rose* after being at or near bottom in 2006 and 2007.

91 Jason Taylor Dances with the Stars and Parcells

Gary Wichard was a no-nonsense NFL agent. He was both a tough negotiator and something of a tough guy. His upbringing among Irish and Italian immigrants in Glen Cove, New York, had hardened his demeanor and speech. Tough as nails and smart to boot, Wichard, though, had a soft spot for Jason Taylor. "He's like a son to me," said the agent who represented Terrell Suggs, Brian Bosworth, and Mark Gastineau, among others.

And in the spring of 2008, Wichard was feeling like Bill Parcells was messing with his son. And Wichard wasn't about to allow that. "That son of a bitch has bitten off more than he can chew this time," Wichard growled over the phone from his California home. "I'll get on a flight to Miami tonight if I have to and punch that weasel in the nose tomorrow morning. You write that if you want so he knows I'm coming."

Parcells and Wichard, you see, were embroiled in what the diplomatic Taylor would call a difference of opinion, which was nonetheless playing out like a feud in the media. In early December of 2007, Wichard had closed a deal for the prolific defensive end to be on *Dancing with the Stars*. The idea was for Taylor to do the show even as the Miami Dolphins were finalizing a rebuilding program that general manager Randy Mueller and coach Cam Cameron had begun a year before.

But nine days later, Parcells was hired, and Mueller and Cameron were fired within two weeks. So the Dolphins changed course again. The Dolphins began rebuilding again. And Taylor, 33 at the time, wanted no part of it. He realized his career was too close to an expiration date to suffer through another rebuild. So Taylor wanted to be traded, preferably to a contending team.

Wichard called the Dolphins in January to deliver the message. He talked to club president Bryan Wiedmeier, general manager Jeff Ireland, and, most importantly, Parcells. The talks yielded neither agreements nor promises from the Dolphins, but the Taylor camp was hopeful the Dolphins would see the logic of a trade. They didn't—at least not right away. Parcells wanted his team to be as good as possible as quickly as possible, and one way was to have Taylor on board. Plus, no team was going to give them via trade the value the Dolphins put on Taylor. "The only way Jason Taylor doesn't play for the Dolphins in 2008 is if he retires," Parcells said March 3. "The team is not going to trade him."

Although Parcells was obviously posturing and fully aware the situation was fluid, the words incensed Wichard. He now demanded Taylor be traded. And the Dolphins talked to a couple of teams, but nothing came of it. "We took some calls earlier in the week," general manager Jeff Ireland said in April. "But nothing's changed on that. Nothing's changed. We want the guy back."

Wichard's simmer was now close to a full boil. So he told the Dolphins that Taylor would not participate in the offseason conditioning program. Or minicamp. Or training camp. "I know that Jason is not going to be at any organized team activities," head coach Tony Sparano said. "I know that Jason is not going to be at any minicamps. And I know that right now Jason is not going to be at training camp. That's what we know. Jason is a player under contract with the Miami Dolphins. He knows that. Both parties are well aware of the information. That's all I'm going to say about it."

Taylor, who had become a South Florida fixture and intended to live in the community after retirement, didn't want to be portrayed as wanting to abandon the team. So he took a break from his dancing gig and visited the Dolphins. He visited with teammates in the locker room and after a warm reception decided to call on Parcells. Taylor walked into a room, where Parcells was watching tape, and Parcells ignored him. He looked at Taylor and went back to his work without saying a word. That incensed Taylor and, of course, made Wichard furious. But the defensive end still tried to paint a picture of civility in public. "This thing was never supposed to be a confrontation," Taylor said. "This is not about me versus Bill Parcells. It has digressed to be a confrontational situation. I'm here to tell you that's not the way I wanted it to be."

Taylor admitted he had "requested" a trade and pointed out there was a distinction between that and saying he "demanded" a trade. He was right. The difference was Wichard, who demanded one. With training camp starting up in a month, Taylor and Parcells met again. Parcells made it clear to Taylor that he did not hold his offseason participation on *Dancing with the Stars* against him. And he said that moment, which upset Taylor weeks earlier, was a misunderstanding. Faulty hearing aids, Parcells said, were the reason he didn't hear or answer Taylor that day. It was nothing personal. Parcells, of course, soon made a business decision.

He traded Taylor to the Washington Redskins for a 2009 second-round pick and 2010 sixth-round pick. The move satisfied everyone, including Wichard. Taylor dealt with injuries in 2008 while in Washington while the Dolphins won the AFC East. Taylor returned to the Dolphins in 2009. Then he left again, joining the New York Jets as a free agent in 2010. And he returned to Miami again in August 2011. Wichard never saw Taylor's final return to Miami. He died in March 2011.

92 Wayne Huizenga

He downed his fourth Scotch during this cross-country flight in his custom 737 and now Wayne Huizenga was feeling no pain as he talked about some agonizing moments as the Miami Dolphins owner. "My decisions in business were great," Huizenga said. "My decisions in sports? "Ehhhh," he added, waggling his hand, the universal sign for so-so.

When longtime Dolphins owner Joe Robbie died in 1990, he left his children a $50 million estate tax bill. They sold the team and what is now Hard Rock Stadium to Huizenga, who paid less than $200 million for everything when he took ownership in 1994.

Huizenga was the only entrepreneur ever to launch three *Fortune 500* companies: Waste Management, Blockbuster Entertainment, and AutoNation. He also was the was the original owner of both the Miami Marlins and Florida Panthers, bringing Major League Baseball and the National Hockey League to South Florida. But all those companies and other sports teams were a business to Huizenga. The Dolphins? "That's my passion," Huizenga said. "That's my love."

It was the spring of 2007, and Huizenga was returning to Fort Lauderdale from an NFL meeting in Phoenix. He was aboard the private jet the FAA calls "737 Whiskey Hotel" (for Wayne Huizenga). He was 37,000 feet in the air, but Huizenga had his feet on the ground about his career as a professional sports owner. "I know there have been mistakes," Huizenga began. "I don't need people to tell me that. I see it on the scoreboard. I see it in the won/loss column. I hear what has been said. What I need is people that will fix the mistakes, stop the bleeding. I hope we have that now. I hope I've found that now because I sure didn't find it before."

Huizenga's history as Dolphins owner is a mixed bag. Judge him for his ownership decisions, and the verdict is he ultimately failed his team. Judge him as a person, and there is no conclusion other than Huizenga was a great man. "As wonderful as he was as an owner, he was even better as a person," said Don Shula upon hearing of Huizenga's death in March 2018. "He was truly a great friend, who showed compassion and caring for everyone he knew and many he didn't, as evidenced by his wonderful work in the community. We lost a great family man, businessman, sportsman, philanthropist, and friend, but most of all, a great person."

Interesting, right? Shula, you'll recall, was escorted out of his job as Dolphins coach in January 1996 by Huizenga. It wasn't a push, but it was a very compelling nudge. The coach made it seem walking away from football was his idea, but it wasn't—as his flirtations with joining the Cleveland Browns or even returning to the Dolphins after Johnson later showed.

"I mean, I can't second-guess myself about hiring Jimmy," Huizenga said. "I can't second-guess myself about hiring Nick [Saban]."

Actually, neither of those decisions worked out. Huizenga both times landed the hottest, most sought-after coach that was available—Johnson in 1996 and Saban almost a decade later. The work should have made Huizenga a hero among Dolphins fans. But the hirings backfired both times. And both failed for basically the same reason: neither coach had his heart fully in coaching the Dolphins.

Johnson came to Miami promising a Super Bowl championship within three years but instead quit after his third year in 1998. Huizenga, amazingly, talked Johnson into returning and in so doing even offered Johnson the chance to ease up and coach only home games if he wanted. Johnson wisely declined that offer and returned but quit again after the following season.

Saban was the coach at LSU in 2005 when Huizenga's big plane landed in Baton Rouge, Louisiana. Saban had turned down a handful of other NFL offers, including the New York Giants, and didn't exactly jump at the chance to coach the Dolphins either. "He told me he wasn't ready to give me a decision because he had given his players his word that they would be the first to know if he was leaving or not," Huizenga said. "He said, 'I gave them my word,' and I said, 'That's cool. I understand.' I respected the fact he was sticking to his word."

Huizenga smiled and abandoned the subject there, recognizing the lingering irony of Saban's departure from Miami to coach Alabama after he said he wouldn't. The Dolphins made the playoffs in 10 of the 19 seasons Huizenga owned at least part of the team. And there were times he displayed amazing largesse. When assistant coach Bill Lewis' son, Gregg, died in a military training accident in September of 1998, the coach was scrambling to gather his family from different parts of the country and make necessary arrangements. Huizenga basically gave Lewis his private plane for five days to relieve the task during a terrible time for the family.

But Huizenga's time as owner also had some moments of serious ineptitude. Shula coached the Dolphins 26 seasons and won two Super Bowls but got no say on his successor. Johnson coached four years, won no titles, and basically named Dave Wannstedt his successor. And Huizenga went along with it. After Saban left abruptly in January 2007, Huizenga pleaded with fans and media for ideas on what to do next. Huizenga had been quoted as saying, "If you believe in something, you go do it." But at that moment seemed to have nothing to believe in.

Huizenga hired Cam Cameron after Saban. The Dolphins went 1–15 in 2007, and the owner turned the team over to Bill Parcells that December. Parcells and Huizenga had spoken initially, and the billionaire admitted he planned on selling the Dolphins. That sent Parcells looking for work with the Atlanta Falcons. Huizenga heard his target was headed elsewhere and tried to salvage the hiring by telling Parcells he wouldn't sell the Dolphins after all. Parcells then backed out of the Atlanta job. "Prior to the information becoming public, we reached an agreement in principle with Bill," Atlanta Falcons owner Arthur Blank said. "We met to complete the contract. At that time we were made aware that he is considering a revised offer from the Miami Dolphins. He later informed us he would not be signing a contract with us."

Within months of landing Parcells, Huizenga sold 49 percent of the Dolphins to Stephen Ross and he completed the sale of all but 5 percent of the team—for $1.1 billion—by the spring of 2009. "I know I'll have regrets and I know I will miss it," Huizenga said, discussing his decision to sell the team. "But I felt after 19 years—you know there's an old song out there, 'You gotta know when to hold 'em and know when to fold 'em.'"

93 The Joe Philbin Error

The tall, middle-aged guy was wearing a white tuxedo and top hat and fronting a makeshift band that got together maybe 10 minutes prior. He was reading lyrics from a script (we'd soon learn he does that a lot) that he tried to turn into a rap song. *When the Dolphins come to town…we ain't gonna mess around.*

This was Miami Dolphins coach Joe Philbin before the 2015 season. Wait, we're not done. He got out this white cane that matched the tux and hat. And he started using the cane as an air guitar as he jumped around, as if dancing. Dolphins players sitting as a captive audience thought it was funny. Some thought it was a good team-bonding exercise, which portrayed the uptight coach most didn't trust, as a cool guy. But the moment didn't hold up well over time. "Looking back on it today, he looked like a clown," one player on that long ago team texted. "I can't believe I fell for it and thought it made sense. That whole time made no sense."

The Joe Philbin era (error?) lasted from 2012 to 2015. The coach never had a winning season in posting a 24–28 record. He was fired in October of 2015 after a 1–3 start. And it would be awesome to remember this time in team history as a failure merely because of its stagnant mediocrity and missed opportunities. But the truth is this era rivals that disastrous year Cam Cameron had in 2007 when he did and said foolish things and won only one of 16 games.

How is that possible? How could this be that putrid? Consider that the first training camp Philbin had as coach was captured on tape in all its behind-the-scenes glory on *Hard Knocks*. And that show portrayed Philbin as an obsessive-compulsive guy who wanted things so tidy he picked up wads of paper off the practice field. It showed him struggling to connect with players. It showed him complaining that Vontae Davis used the bathroom too much during a practice. And it showed him allowing veterans to haze young players by, among other things, shaving their heads so that it seemed they had a penis on their heads.

The Bullygate Scandal

All of Joe Philbin's miscues paled in comparison to the harassment scandal that rocked the Dolphins in 2013. The NFL investigated the bullying of offensive tackle Jonathan Martin by Richie Incognito. The national media took the lurid details of a black player being harassed by a white one and turned the Dolphins into an object of scorn and mocking. None of it was graceful. None of it had a positive side. The Dolphins were getting punked daily, and Philbin, always deflecting during press conferences, seemed AWOL from it all.

The ensuing Wells Report released by the NFL cleared Philbin of any wrongdoing when it said he was unaware of any activities that directly or indirectly led to the trading of Martin, the firing of offensive line coach Jim Turner and head trainer Kevin O'Neill, and the sanctions against Incognito. But if Philbin emerged technically unblemished because he didn't approve or know about any wrongdoing, the report's 144 pages soiled the coach in excruciating detail for his obliviousness. Philbin was painted as unaware of things going on under his watch—if not under his very nose.

How else to say it when, for example, players were simulating sex acts they told Martin was with his sister or mom during practice, and the coach apparently didn't see it? "As I examined some of the things that as the head coach of the Dolphins I can do better, I think the visibility factor can be a difference," Philbin said. "Sometimes it's better use of a head coach's time to walk through the training room, walk through the locker room, walk through the hallways. It's not that I've never done that stuff, but it's fair to say I'm going to do it more. I frankly have to be a little more vigilant in my enforcement of policies and procedures that I want to have in the locker room and the program. That falls on me. There has to be better communication both ways: from them to me and me to them, players to me, me to players. That's something I felt, as you have a little bit of time to reflect on things, certainly needs to improve."

Then things got bad.

Philbin tried to get his team to mirror his personality traits of steadiness and stability. The problem is the Dolphins were neither stable nor consistent. So they didn't adopt those traits, but they did lack fire and swagger because they saw very little of those from their coach. In both 2013 and 2014, the Dolphins needed to rally the final month of the season to make the playoffs. They lost their final two games of '13 to division rivals with losing records and whom they had previously beaten. They lost three of the final four the next season, and in the finale, wide receiver Mike Wallace simply quit playing and went and sat on the bench.

Philbin is remembered for calling an inexplicable timeout against the his former team, the Green Bay Packers, when his defense had an advantage because he said, "the thought of Aaron Rodgers making a play makes you queasy." He stopped talking to general manager Jeff Ireland in 2013. He stopped talking to general manager Dennis Hickey in 2015. He did often consult with executive vice president of football administration Dawn Aponte. Philbin huddled with Aponte before every press conference to get possible talking points. She would also straighten his tie before his coach's show interviews and meticulously edit videos of Philbin's postgame locker room speeches that he read off index cards.

He had a strange love/hate relationship with quarterback Ryan Tannehill. The coach was on board with drafting Tannehill in 2012 and even named the rookie quarterback the starter that season. But by the spring of 2014, Philbin wanted Tannehill out. He approached Hickey mere days before the draft and asked him to draft Derek Carr. "You want me to do what?" Hickey answered.

Dan Marino, the most decorated player in franchise history, was negotiating with the team about a job as an advisor in 2014. One day Marino visited the team's practice facility and watched from the sidelines. "He's here to observe and chat," Philbin said. "It was great to have him here. I told him he's always welcome any time." Minutes later Philbin was on the phone with team president Tom Garfinkel, making the point he didn't want Marino overshadowing the coaching staff's work.

94 The Love of the Harbaughs

Think of the NFL as a small town where neighbors know each other's business. Everyone in town knows the family down the street—in this case the Miami Dolphins. And everyone is aware that family is plodding through a dysfunctional marriage. That marriage is between owner Stephen Ross and his head coach. Things may look rosy and well-pieced together in public in that relationship. There's lots of apparent love there with Ross saying the right things, the contract saying the right things, and the coach saying the right things. But everyone knows that marriage is tenuous because Ross changes his mind about his head coaches. A lot.

And Ross has somebody he loves more. Someone named Harbaugh, even though no Harbaugh has ever coached a Dolphins team. And yet we know about the Harbaughs because they have been at the forefront of Dolphins coaching searches, coaching flirtations, and coaching intrigue for nearly a decade. The latest was the 2019 coaching search that landed Brian Flores as Miami's 13th head coach and fifth under Ross.

The Dolphins never interviewed Jim Harbaugh during that search. They never interviewed John Harbaugh during that search. But Ross associates talked to both coaches or their agents to gauge whether they were fits in Miami. Jim Harbaugh and Ross spoke personally, and the Michigan coach made it clear he didn't want to leave the school. This was fine with Ross, a Michigan alumnus and major donor. So Ross announced Harbaugh would not be Miami's coach even as Miami's search was starting.

Rumors also swirled around John Harbaugh's status with the Baltimore Ravens in the fall of 2018. Even as the Super Bowl winning coach's remained on solid footing as the Ravens made the playoffs, Ross remained interested. And so on at least one occasion, a Ross associate unofficially checked in on John Harbaugh's ongoing contract extension talks to see if there was any daylight between the Ravens and their coach. Ultimately, neither Harbaugh ended up with the Dolphins. But do not be surprised if the last chapter of this ongoing flirtation has yet to be written because Ross truly admires the Harbaughs.

That admiration reportedly began in January 2011 when Harbaugh was still the head coach at Stanford University. The Cardinal played in the Orange Bowl that winter, and Ross, as the host of a game played in the stadium he owns, met Harbaugh for the first time. That lit a fire that nearly burned the Dolphins franchise to the ground. Within days of that meeting, Ross got on a plane, flew across the country, and met then-general manager Jeff Ireland in California, where the two tried to hire Harbaugh as the Dolphins coach. There was nothing wrong with that—except Tony Sparano was still sitting in the club's head coaching chair back at the team's training facility in Davie, Florida.

Sparano and Ireland were hired by the Dolphins in 2008. They came to the Dolphins as friends. But Ireland didn't tell Sparano of the owner's trip to see Harbaugh. He also didn't tell him of his part in the trip. Sparano found out about the whole trip from a reporter. "You are not serious," the head coach said.

Sparano never had a strong relationship Ross. He didn't call the owner, and it was rare when the owner called him. When they did talk, Sparano was often curt. So even if the coach wouldn't excuse

Ross going behind his back, he kind of understood it. *But Ireland? His friend?*

That, Sparano believed, was a betrayal. "He could never put it behind him," Ross said.

Ross saw that cross-country trip as an opportunity to do something bold, something dramatic, something "out of the box," as he said then. "Not until after I read the newspapers did I realize the anguish I'd put Tony through," Ross said at the time. "I'm not familiar with going through this process, but I never thought it would be national news. I was a little naive. Looking back, I can tell you I shouldn't be talking to any coaches seeking a replacement until I've decided that I needed to make a change."

Ross was unable to hire Harbaugh on that trip. It remains unclear why because Harbaugh was definitely available and became head coach of the San Francisco 49ers days later. And although Ross gave Sparano a contract extension and forced him and Ireland to sit together during a press conference to announce everything was all right, the relationship between coach and general manager was far from all right. "There's no doubt in my mind the lines of communication should be handled differently," Ireland admitted. "I was in a tough spot and I know we put Tony in a very difficult spot as well."

The Dolphins started 0–7 in 2011 before rallying to 4–8. But when the team laid an egg against the Philadelphia Eagles during the first week of December, Ross had seen enough and fired Sparano. "I didn't think he was the right head coach for the Miami Dolphins, but I couldn't change that when I took over because he had won the year before," Ross said.

Ross eventually replaced Sparano with Joe Philbin, who he fired and replaced with Adam Gase, who he fired and replaced with Brian Flores.

95 Dealing with Drew Rosenhaus

After the 1994 season, it was clear the Miami Dolphins defense needed help. The No. 1-ranked offense had been largely responsible for getting the team to the AFC divisional round of the playoffs, but the 19th-ranked defense urgently needed a pass rusher and probably help in the secondary to make the Dolphins more complete. And with Bryce Paup available in free agency and future Hall of Famer Ronnie Lott sending signals he wanted to finish his career playing for Don Shula, the Dolphins somehow decided their signature free agent signing would be Eric Green, a tight end. And the next most important addition to the team would be Randal Hill, a wide receiver. How could this happen? How did the Dolphins come up with these seemingly misguided ideas? Look no further than agent Drew Rosenhaus.

Rosenhaus was born in New Jersey but grew up in North Miami, where he and his brother Jason became big Dolphins fans. He attended the University of Miami and later graduated Duke University School of Law. In 1989 Rosenhaus became a certified sports agent and by 1991 he had his first major Dolphins client in Hill, who was the team's first-round pick in the April draft. Today Rosenhaus Sports Representation boasts more NFL clients than any other agency. But in the early '90s, Rosenhaus was mostly a very confident, very unproven, very ambitious guy who wanted to make his mark in the business. And he saw the Dolphins as one way to do that. "I'm confident I'm going to continue to pick up more Dolphins. I can guarantee it," Rosenhaus said after landing Hill. "Next year I'm going to represent a bunch of high draft choices. I'm going to try and get most of the blue-chippers from the University of Miami and be very aggressive with a number of Dolphins. Ideally,

I'd like to represent in excess of 10, 11, or 12 Dolphins, and that's going to happen in the near future. I'm not going to go away."

By 1996 Rosenhaus was representing 15 Dolphins or nearly 30 percent of the roster. Sometimes to the frustration of other agents—whose clients Rosenhaus often poached—and often to both the benefit and detriment of the team, Rosenhaus became a force to be reckoned with. The guy seemed to be everywhere. And in everything.

Hill held out after he was drafted in 1991. Rosenhaus did that. Mark Clayton needed his reputation rehabilitated with the team in 1992 after his statistics floundered, and his relationship with Shula soured. Rosenhaus attended to that. Yatil Green needed a shoulder to cry on when he tore the ACL in the same knee two consecutive years, effectively ending his NFL career before it began. Rosenhaus lent his client that shoulder. Zach Thomas, closing in on the end of his rookie contract, wanted to remain with the Dolphins, the team that took a chance on him in the fifth-round of the 1996 draft. Rosenhaus did that extension. Adewale Ogunleye held out in August 2004. You guessed it; Rosenhaus did that. And Ogunleye was eventually traded to the Chicago Bears, but that was contingent on him agreeing to a new contract, which went through a rigorous Rosenhaus negotiation that moved the Bears from offering a $4 million signing bonus to $10 million and another $5 million in guaranteed roster bonuses.

His ability to convince Dolphins players that a local agent only a 20-minute drive away could best serve their needs turned Rosenhaus into a cottage industry around South Florida's professional football team. And some within the team liked and appreciated Rosenhaus. And some didn't. But they all had little choice in having to deal with him. "I like Drew a lot as a person," former team president and general manager Eddie Jones said. "But I find that during negotiations, my feelings about him ebb and flow because I know he's not necessarily trying to help me very much. I know he lives here, and he's a fan of the team, but his agenda is always his players, and in a negotiation, my agenda is always getting the best deal for the team."

That brings us to the Eric Green deal in the spring of 1995, the one the Dolphins didn't need and probably never should have made. When Green got a check from the Dolphins for $2,465,455.66 to become the highest-paid tight end in NFL history at the time, it culminated a year's worth of ambitious scheming, posturing, and, yes, outright lying by Rosenhaus. A year earlier, after signing a deal with the Pittsburgh Steelers, an angry Green had called Rosenhaus and yelled, "Get me out of here!" He was so loud that Rosenhaus held the phone away from his ear.

So in free agency, Rosenhaus lined up the Dolphins, Washington Redskins, Green Bay Packers, and Oakland Raiders in a derby where the goal was to drive up the price of his client. And, yes, Rosenhaus admitted to stretching truth throughout the process. "It's not lying. It's negotiating," Rosenhaus said. "Everybody lies when they negotiate. It's like playing poker. It's no different from keeping a straight face when you know you're going to lose. I was just doing what I could do to put my client in the best position possible. I bluffed. I was never the type of guy who said check out our offer. I was never specific. I worked in generalities. Everything I said, I was doing for my client's best interest. Did I lie to the media? At that time maybe I did. It depends on what you consider a lie. Really, I was manipulating for the sake of my client."

While negotiating by phone, Rosenhaus' other lines would often ring, and he would tell the first party the new call came from a competing team. Sometimes it was indeed another team, but sometimes it was a relative or a salesman merely pitching insurance.

After Green was signed, it became clear the Dolphins had bid against themselves in the negotiation's final stages, costing the team an extra $200,000 per season. "This is not a situation where the Dolphins got ripped off," Rosenhaus said. "But I was a little bit embarrassed and felt a little bad afterward when I told them what the other offers were. Yes, I juggled and finagled. But the Dolphins didn't get used."

96 The International Dolphins

Dan Marino and John Elway were trading stories and shots of tequila at the bar of this Hard Rock cafe. The crowd and the noise was thick, and these two NFL legends were understandably the center of attention because everyone in the United States more or less knew about Marino and his 48 touchdown passes and Elway and his drives against the Cleveland Browns.

Except this wasn't in the United States. This was Mexico City in August of 1997. And days later the Miami Dolphins and Denver Broncos would play a preseason game in front of 104,629 people in Azteca Stadium. The game meant nothing in the standings, but it meant a lot to the NFL and its designs on stretching football's reach beyond America's borders.

The Dolphins have played a key role in this plot to, you know, take over the world. The league sent them to London to play the San Francisco 49ers in 1988, to Tokyo to play the Los Angeles Raiders in 1991, to Berlin to play the Broncos in 1992, and then to Mexico in '97. All of these games are part of the NFL's American Bowl series, which extended through 2003. All these games were preseason games and all came with memories.

Dolphins guard Keith Sims stood next to a sumo champion after one Dolphins practice in '91. The 305-pound offensive lineman was dwarfed by the 420-pound wrestler. Dolphins backup quarterback Scott Mitchell trekked over to the Brandenburg Gate in '92 to do some shopping among the sidewalk merchants that sprung up after the fall of the Berlin Wall. Mitchell didn't throw a pass as a rookie the previous season, but he completed 5-of-8 throws with touchdowns to James Saxon and Tony Martin at Berlin's Olympic Stadium, the same stadium where Jesse Owens won four gold medals to show up Adolf Hitler in 1936. Mitchell, by the way, also passed on a chance to purchase an East German army helmet, which some eastern bloc soldier abandoned when communist East Germany fell.

The Dolphins also played meaningful regular-season games abroad. They've played in four of them so far. It made sense that when the NFL picked teams to stage its first regular-season game outside North America that it selected the Dolphins. They played the New York Giants in October 2007 in London's Wembley Stadium. It was a trying time for Miami. The team was winless. Owner Wayne Huizenga spent one of the afternoons the week of that game meeting with reporters—over tea, of course—to tell them an internal study was about to begin on how to improve the team as quickly as possible. "We know it's bad right now," Huizenga said, "but we're going to take a good look at everything and figure out how to fix it."

The Dolphins lost to New England before heading to England that year. It was a 49–28 blowout loss to the Patriots, in which the score was something of a mirage because the game wasn't that close. The Patriots led 42–7 at halftime, having conducted surgery without anesthesia on the Miami defense. New England rested starters in the second half. The Dolphins were 0–7 when they boarded their flight to Gatwick Airport. "We can't win in America," Dolphins defensive end Jason Taylor deadpanned. "Maybe we can win overseas."

Nope. Miami lost a thrilling (not really) 13–10 decision to the Giants.

Miami's games abroad are often signs of things to come. After that failure against the Giants, Cam Cameron was fired after that season. Days after Miami lost 27–14 to the New York Jets in London in 2015, Joe Philbin was fired. The Dolphins lost again at Wembley

Stadium in 2017. That time it was a 20–0 at the hands of the New Orleans Saints. That season was a failure, and within 18 months, coach Adam Gase and longtime quarterback Ryan Tannehill were gone.

The Dolphins won the NFL's first ever game played in Canada, a 16–3 decision against the Buffalo Bills at Toronto's Rogers Centre in 2008. The Dolphins also won the AFC East in 2008.

The Dolphins traveled 7,450 miles to Tokyo. They traveled more than 2,100 miles to Mexico City. They covered 4,420 miles to London multiple times. And each time—amid winning or losing seasons—they draw many fans, often more fans than the opponent. "We're everywhere," Marino exclaimed during a toast at that Mexico City Hard Rock.

97 Jay Ajayi Goes for 200 Yards

The Miami Dolphins spent the months leading to the 2016 season looking for a running back because coach Adam Gase wasn't sure he had a starter in unproven second-year player Jay Ajayi. The club tried to sign C.J. Anderson because he played for Gase once, but that didn't work out. They tried to sign Chris Johnson because he was really fast once, but that didn't work out either. Then Miami added a 30-year-old and oft injured Arian Foster. That seemed fine through training camp, and Gase expected to go into the season with a running back-by-committee situation featuring Foster, Ajayi, and perhaps rookie Kenyan Drake. But the coach still needed Ajayi to take some snaps in the preseason finale because, well, "somebody has to play in that game," he said.

With all of 49 NFL carries as a rookie, Ajayi didn't like the idea of playing in that final meaningless game. And he hinted as much on Miami's first play when he fumbled the ball. And then his disdain was obvious when he didn't run hard on his other couple of carries before being pulled. The following week, when the Dolphins traveled across the continent to Seattle for the regular-season opener against the Seahawks, Gase ordered Ajayi to stay behind and "get his mind right" if he wanted to be part of the 2016 Dolphins.

Out of that inauspicious start, Ajayi burst onto the scene that season. Soon fans were calling Ajayi the "J-Train," and he was living up to the name because he was their ride into the playoffs. So how did Ajayi go from dud to stud? He obviously deserves credit because he needed a course correction after that preseason game and he made it. "I needed to improve some things and address some areas personally," Ajayi said. "And I'm working very hard in practice and in meetings to get that done."

The Dolphins wanted Ajayi to know his role and do his job without complaint. But even after he did that the next three weeks, Ajayi was still mired behind Foster and others on the depth chart. Then a door opened. Foster had been in Gase's office crying (literally) after the season's second week because he was injured (again) and didn't think he could continue. Gase convinced him to keep playing, but the running back's workload was diminished as the Dolphins lost two of the next three games

Gase looked to fill the void. Ajayi, Drake, and Damien Williams got carries in a loss to the Tennessee Titans without much fanfare, but within that failure, Gase saw hope. "I know you think the world is ending, and we suck, but I'm starting to see something out of Jay," Gase said in a private moment the following week. "He's showing us something. You'll see."

The next week against the Pittsburgh Steelers, Ajayi got the call and delivered runs of 12, 13, 14, 33, 35, and 62 yards among his 25 carries. Six of Miami's longest plays that day were Ajayi runs. He finished with 204 rushing yards. The Dolphins won 31–15. The season was about to be saved. "Man, no need to sugarcoat that," Pittsburgh coach Mike Tomlin said. "We got beat soundly today."

The idea that Ajayi had burst onto the scene was a thing the next week. But so was the possibility he simply surprised the Steelers and would not surprise the next opponent, the Buffalo Bills. Well, he may have not surprised them, but he certainly ran through them.

Ajayi's one-cut style battered Rex Ryan's defense for 214 yards. The Dolphins used their outside zone runs to gash the Bills over and over. And that put Ajayi on the short list of humans who'd run for 200 yards in consecutive NFL games. That list is O.J. Simpson, Earl Campbell, Ricky Williams, and Ajayi.

Foster retired the morning after the Buffalo game. Not many people in South Florida noticed. They were busy riding the J-Train. "I had my adversity and challenges early, but I'm grateful for the opportunities and just taking advantage of it and being able to showcase to the world what I can do," Ajayi said. "For me it's all good, but I believe I'm only getting started in the NFL and I'm grateful to my o-line and my whole team for just helping me have a productive year."

The production reached a climax on Christmas Eve in the rematch at Buffalo. "We think we'll be much more effective this game," Ryan told writers that week. "Were we tired? Yeah, it was about 100 degrees out there, but that won't be the case this week. That was at their place. Now I'm excited to have them in our building. I truly believe we're going to play a great game."

Ajayi realized repeating his 200-yard feat would be difficult. "Defenses definitely respect our running game now," he said. "They've been doing a lot of things to try and make us a little bit more one-dimensional: stacking the box, giving us different looks and schemes."

Yeah, whatever. Ajayi rushed for 206 yards in that Buffalo rematch. And he saved his best for the game's most important moment. His runs accounted for 75 of the 77 yards the Dolphins gained to set up the winning field goal in overtime. "Adam gets a rash from calling too many run plays," offensive coordinator Clyde Christensen said with a smile. "But he loves to win, so he keeps calling them."

Ajayi joined Tiki Barber, Campbell, and Simpson as the only NFL players to rush for 200 yards three times in a season. "When I step out on the field, I don't really have any worries about if someone else thinks I'm not good enough or if I'm a fluke or whatever," Ajayi said. "I know what I'm capable of. And I think I'm proving I can be one of the best running backs in this league."

Ajayi was a comet seemingly out of nowhere that season. But the comet faded as quickly as it appeared. Gase grew tired of Ajayi, who even sulked after a win, complaining about his number of carries. Ajayi was traded in October 2017 to the Philadelphia Eagles and won a Super Bowl with them that season.

98 Dion Jordan: The Biggest Bust

The evening before the 2013 NFL Draft, Miami Dolphins owner Stephen Ross invited the club's brass and their spouses to dine at his Palm Beach, Florida, estate. Head coach Joe Philbin was there as were general manager Jeff Ireland, club president Mike Dee, and executive vice president Dawn Aponte. After dinner the group sat around the table, and Ross asked who they believed the Dolphins should select the following day and why.

Aponte said she would like West Virginia wide receiver Tavon Austin. Dee said he would take Austin. Philbin then chimed in, saying he had watched hours of Dion Jordan tape and believed he was the best player in the draft. So he'd take Jordan. And Ireland, who would later have great disagreements with Philbin, this time agreed with Philbin that Jordan was the draft's most impressive player, and that was who he would take if he had a chance. Ross, by the way, shared that he, too, was a big fan of Austin and would make him the pick.

The next evening, the Dolphins, holding the 12th overall selection and looking to move up, found a trade partner in the Oakland Raiders. And after Ireland and Oakland general manager Reggie McKenzie hammered out the trade, Ireland considered it a gift that he could climb nine slots to No. 3 overall by merely giving up a second-round pick. So with their general manager and coach in full agreement, the Dolphins made the trade and then immediately selected the club's next great pass rusher: Dion Jordan.

Jordan looked the part. He was 6'6", weighed 248 pounds, and had run the 40-yard dash in 4.54 seconds in the weeks prior to the draft. Basically, he was like an NFL linebacker except taller and he could run with wide receivers. Oh yeah, and he had collected 12½ sacks at Oregon his previous two seasons. So, the Dolphins thought he was a proven college pass rusher who would develop into a star. Except Jordan was never great for the Dolphins. He was an epic disappointment. He came to embody a shameful waste of draft resources and time invested.

And that makes Jordan the biggest bust in Miami Dolphins draft history.

That's not a designation casually bestowed. The Dolphins have had other draft busts. Everyone has. But being considered the biggest bust of all time when a franchise has more than 50 years of history is truly a feat. Or a defeat. And Jordan merits that draft scarlet letter of sorts.

Consider that Jordan was with the Dolphins from April 2013 to March of 2017. In those four years, Jordan played 26 games, starting only one. In those four years, he played a complete season only once. In those four years, he collected as many NFL suspensions as sacks.

Jordan didn't exactly burst out of the career starting blocks his rookie year, rehabbing a shoulder surgery the team knew about. He missed all the offseason and the start of training camp. When he finally got healthy enough to compete in the preseason, he promptly injured the same shoulder in his first game. "It's hard," Jordan said. "Man, you get out there and see all the guys working and doing all the drills and stuff and you want to get out there because it doesn't feel right for me to sit back and watch. It's really tough. But I understand what's more important right now, and that's my body. That's my longevity."

Jordan didn't start any games for the pass-rush needy Dolphins in 2013, but he did contribute two sacks. And that is as good as it would get. The next year Jordan was suspended four games for violating the NFL's performance enhancing drug policy. A week before that suspension was scheduled to expire, the NFL suspended Jordan two more games for violating the league's street drug policy. When he returned Jordon scoffed when a reporter asked if he had a problem. "No," he said before turning away, ignoring the fact that part of his suspension came after testing positive for ecstasy and marijuana. He was suspended the next spring for the entire 2015 season when he violated the performance-enhancing drug policy a third time.

Jordan came to the Dolphins a svelte linebacker in 2013 but showed up in 2016 as a 275-pound defensive end. He was out of shape. His knees were bad. Jordan had been conditionally reinstated, but he didn't play a down for the Dolphins that season. No wonder coach Adam Gase didn't think very highly of him. "Everybody tells me he can be great on special teams," Gase said. "Are you kidding? Special teams? He sucks right now."

The Dolphins determined by the end of the season that Jordan was no longer in their plans and eventually cut him on March 31,

2017. Jordan had signed a four-year contract worth $20.5 million after he was drafted. Eventually, he cost the Dolphins $14 million of that, the third overall selection, and that second-round pick they used to trade up. Miami's significant investment on Jordan netted the team three sacks in return.

But the lack of production and unmet potential is not what makes Jordan the franchise's biggest bust. Other high draft picks have failed to perform. Other high draft picks had careers derailed by injury. Jordan was different. He was a disaster because he was a rare combination of failures with injuries, off-field missteps, and limited production all conspiring to form one big disappointment. The total package. And the problem is the chronic drug issues and injuries that caused Jordan's time in Miami to suffer fits and starts affected his chances of actually developing his athletic abilities.

Philbin was disappointed early on. He heard of the 2014 suspension and knew immediately Jordan probably wouldn't be a factor. "Let's be honest," Philbin said, "missing a month isn't going to be good for Dion Jordan's development."

The Seattle Seahawks signed Jordan after he was cut by Miami. It went well at first. Oh, he still had injuries, including knee injuries and a stress fracture to his leg, but Jordan collected four sacks in five games in 2017. He added another one-and-a-half sacks in 12 games the following season. But then the script reverted to his Miami days. Jordan was suspended the first 10 games of the 2019 season for testing positive for Adderall. "I made a mistake," Jordan told the NFL Network.

So did the Dolphins in the first round of the 2013 draft. An epic mistake.

99 The Miami Miracle

It looked like something drawn up in the dirt moments before. It looked like chaos. But mostly the 69-yard play, which was officially designated as the NFL's Play of the Year for 2019, was a miracle. More specifically, it was "The Miami Miracle."

On December 9, 2018, the Miami Dolphins' thin hopes of sneaking into the playoffs seemed dead as they trailed the Super Bowl-bound New England Patriots 33–28 with only seven seconds to play. So it was over, right? Except coach Adam Gase told quarterback Ryan Tannehill to run *Boise*—a hook-and-ladder play taken directly from Boise State's 2007 Fiesta Bowl upset of Oklahoma—as a last gasp hope.

Gase had his team practice *Boise* usually once every week. They practiced it days before the New England game, and as usual running back Kenyan Drake got the ball last and culminated his sprint into the end zone against air by showing off his best dance moves. "It just gives you a chance to get the ball into the hands of a dynamic guy in space and has the opportunity to try to hit one," Gase said. "Throw a Hail Mary, you've got a guy trying to tip it, and then hopefully it falls into somebody's hands. It's a long throw you're trying to get off before you get sacked, and a lot of bad things can happen. And you're, what, 70 yards away from the end zone? He's really got to put a lot into that one. I don't know if he could have gotten it there. At least [*Boise*] gives you a chance. It gives you a chance almost like a kickoff return."

On the miracle play, Tannehill threw a 14-yard in-cut to Kenny Stills, who pivoted to the sideline and flipped the ball to DeVante Parker. The wide receiver was supposed to surge upfield for 10 or 15 yards, but after about five yards, Parker lateraled to Drake instead. "I saw Kenyan there. I said to DeVante Parker, 'Pitch it! Pitch it!' He pitches it. Kenyan came back inside," Tannehill said. "Then I saw him and Rob Gronkowski—about 10 yards away."

Patriots coach Bill Belichick inexplicably put his 6'6", 268-pound tight end in the game as a deep safety to guard against a jump ball of some sort, perhaps not realizing a 70-yard Hall Mary was improbable. Former Patriots safety Rodney Harrison questioned the strategy on NBC's *Sunday Night Football*. He was astonished that Devin McCourty—the fastest player on the New England defense—was replaced by Gronkowski.

As a result, on the last leg of the miracle, Drake, an accomplished kick returner with 4.39 speed, weaved in and out of traffic for the next 52 yards through the befuddled Patriots defense. The crowning moment was when Drake simply outran the lumbering and overmatched Gronkowski into the end zone. "Honestly, I'm sitting before you all and I still don't believe it," Drake said during interviews after the improbable conclusion sent New England to its fifth loss in the last six visits to South Florida. "I just saw it was Gronk in front of me and I was just like, 'Look, sorry, I've got somewhere to be.' So I had to get in the end zone."

Drake heaved the ball into the stands where it was caught by a Patriots fan. That play caused more than a $1 million swing in Las Vegas sportsbooks. There was no champagne in the Dolphins locker room so players celebrated by dousing each other with water from plastic bottles. A Pittsburgh-area media company recreated the Miami Miracle by using Nintendo's classic Tecmo Bowl video game.

During the annual NFL Honors event the night before the Super Bowl, the Miami Miracle was awarded the Play of the Year, and Drake recounted the play. "It's definitely a part of NFL history," Drake said. "Seven seconds left, you can never count anybody out. For the fans that stayed, thank you, because it was history and amazing to be a part of it. For the fans that left, it still was an amazing play, and you got to see it on TV."

The ball, which was sold in the stands, was then resold at auction for $18,678. It is now displayed at Hard Rock Stadium, where the play endures forever.

100 Tua

In 1966 when the Miami Dolphins drafted quarterback Eddie Wilson with their No. 1 pick in the expansion draft, the expectation was not for Wilson to go to the Hall of Fame. In 1967 when the Dolphins drafted Bob Griese in the first round, no one asked the Purdue quarterback to save the franchise from irrelevance. That day in the spring of 1983 when Dan Marino unexpectedly, and luckily, dropped to the Dolphins late in the first round, no one anywhere set the goal for Marino to take the team to a Super Bowl championship or three.

And when Ryan Tannehill was selected in the first round of the 2012 draft, the move was a hopeful one for a franchise suffering from a great quarterback drought. But no one demanded Tannehill rain championship rings on South Florida.

It's different for Tua Tagovailoa.

He's unlike any of those other players because he isn't on the team to practice and develop, and we'll see how it goes the next few years.

Born March 2, 1998, in Honolulu, Hawaii, Tuanigamanuolepola Tagovailoa is the fifth quarterback selected by the Dolphins in the first round of any draft and he needs to be no less than great. Hall of Fame worthy. Championship-winning. Tagovailoa knows that's what Miami fans want. "I'm very grateful and I'm honored that the fans think so [highly] of me," Miami's newest quarterback said the night he was drafted. "It's a different ballgame. What I did in college can't translate to the NFL. It's a clean slate. What I've got to do is: I've got to go out there and earn my respect and earn the trust from my teammates. It's how you go about doing things."

Tagovialoa, in other words, has to fulfill the prophecy his grandfather Seu Tagovailoa spoke of him two decades ago. "My father saw in Tua something the world is just starting to see now," his aunt Sai Amosa told *Sports Illustrated* in 2018, "that's he's playing for God and playing for the universe—an audience of one and an audience of all.

Tagovailoa was brought into this world to be special. His family believed that decades ago. Dolphins fans now hope it's true. The Dolphins, you see, need a savior. And they don't need just any savior because the team has had good coaches, good running backs, good defensive ends, and good cornerbacks for years and still Miami is under .500 this century.

The Dolphins need a quarterback to rescue them. They need somebody to finally pick up that mantle of greatness Marino laid down after his final season in 1999. This team rescue thing isn't necessarily new for Tagovailoa because he comes with a history of many tall tales and high praise. When he was being recruited out of St. Louis School in Honolulu, then-Alabama offensive coordinator Lane Kiffin texted Alabama coach Nick Saban that the left-handed Tagovailoa was like Steve Young. Tua was 17. And Young was already in the Pro Football Hall of Fame. Greg McElroy, Alabama's quarterback during the 2009 national championship season, said Tagovailoa is the greatest Alabama quarterback in recent memory. And Pat Dye, the former head coach at rival Auburn (of all places), said on Paul Finebaum's radio show that Tagovailoa is the best quarterback in Southeastern Conference history. So Tagovailoa should be used to the high expectations and living up to them. But this is bound to be different than his assignment at Alabama.

The Dolphins were able to select Tagovailoa with the No. 5 overall selection in March 2020 because they were a 5–11 team the year before. It was that level of terrible that put the franchise in position to make such a pick. Compare that to Alabama. When Tagovailoa accepted Saban's scholarship offer over schools he grew up loving, such as USC, the Crimson Tide was already a powerhouse. Under Saban the Crimson Tide had won national titles in 2009, 2011, 2012, and 2015 before Tagovailoa stepped on campus.

When he ultimately committed to Alabama, Tagovailoa was the country's top-rated high school quarterback and he was fearless. He said he wasn't concerned about competing with Jalen Hurts, who was merely the SEC Player of the Year in 2016 as a freshman. But Tagovailoa needed time to reach his heights. During his freshman year, he began to question his decision to enroll at Alabama when Hurts held on to the starting job, and his only playing time came late in games that were essentially already decided. "I wanted to leave the school," Tagovailoa said in the spring of 2018, speaking to children in his native Hawaii. "So I told myself if I didn't play in the last game, which was the national championship game, I would transfer out."

Before that national title game, Tagovailoa hadn't appeared in four of the previous five games. But the Crimson Tide offense had staggered during the playoffs leading up to the title game. Saban decided before that championship game against Georgia that if Hurts didn't put a charge into the offense, he'd turn the game over to Tagovailoa. That's exactly what he did.

And he immediately regretted it.

Tagovailoa was inserted into the game to start the second half with the idea he might help Alabama overcome a 13–0 deficit. And on Alabama's first possession with Tagovailoa in the game, the Crimson Tide went three and out.

Eventually fortunes turned. Tagovailoa led four scoring drives in regulation, including two drives culminated by touchdown passes to Henry Ruggs III and Calvin Ridley. The crowning moment came in overtime: on a second-and-26 play, Tagovailoa threw a 41-yard touchdown pass to DeVonta Smith. Alabama was the national champion. Tagovailoa had saved the game with a walk-off touchdown pass. And he'd become an instant Heisman Trophy candidate for 2018. "Not going to say he was our savior," Ridley said, "There's only one of those. But Tua did save the day. Give him that."

Now he's expected to do the same for the Dolphins.

Acknowledgments

How could this possibly happen? You know I wasn't born in this country, right? You know English is not my native tongue, and football is not my birth country's national sport. The freedom to write books—other than those approved and complimentary of the government—is not allowed where I was born.

But look at this. I wrote a book.

About the Miami Dolphins.

In English.

While living in a free country.

So this is all quite improbable. It never would have happened without the wonderful people that brought me into this world and came into my life. Things would be so different, so terrible without them.

I need to thank my parents, Armando Salguero Sr. and Hilda Salguero. My father and mother didn't just make me and love me. They gave up everything and risked everything for me.

I was born in Cuba under a communist government that to this day has its boot on the throat of a great people. But my parents decided not long after I was born that I must have a better life than scrounging for food scraps, or cutting sugar cane, or fighting and dying in Angola for the communist cause. So they pushed all their chips to the center of the table and endeavored to bring me to the United States.

This involved becoming an enemy of the communist state. It involved years of unemployment. It even involved a dramatic airport departure, in which a Fidel Castro guerrilla pointed an AK-47 at my father's head, telling him he couldn't board the plane that would carry me and my mother to the United States.

We were separated for three years. And during that time, my mother worked two jobs to make ends meet.

And by the time my father landed in New York that summer of 1970, his son spoke fluent English and loved football. So, yeah, thank you, Papi. Thank you, Mami.

My parents saved my life. Then Joan stole my heart. And helped save my soul.

I met her in 1983. And by 1990 she was asking if I was ever going to marry her. And being the fool I was, I didn't jump at the opportunity. So she went off to Bible College and served in 31 countries around the world as a missionary.

But her greatest mission field was me. She dragged me to church. She introduced me to Jesus Christ.

We didn't talk for 15 years, and though I thought of her, I never thought I'd see her again. But God had other plans. We reconnected in 2005 by sheer happenstance. And we married in 2006. And I thank her for being my love, my counselor, my greatest gift.

I want to thank the Miami Dolphins. All the players I've known, all the coaches and general managers I've covered. You've been a great subject as I've painted your portrait for 30 years.

I must thank Edwin Pope, who passed away in 2017. You were my road trip buddy for 20 years. You were my mentor, my friend, my best man. And I know you're looking down from heaven, still rooting for Miami's teams.

I must thank Jeff Fedotin, my editor at Triumph Books, for his guidance and insightful suggestions.

I must thank my teammates at the *Miami Herald*, many of whom have climbed to higher plateaus after lifting me on their shoulders for a time.

And I must thank Dolphins fans. From the north, the south, the east, and the west, both nationally and abroad, you've been kind and loyal to me—even when you disagreed with what I wrote or how I wrote it.

It is my great honor to present you with this book. Even if it's written in my second language.

Sources

All material was independently cultivated except for materials provided from the following sources:

Miami Herald
The Palm Beach Post
The Miami News
Hollywood Sun-Tattler
The Associated Press
Sports Illustrated
NFL Network
NFL Films
ESPN.com
ABC Sports
ESPN
FOX Sports